Sex...
According to
God

BOOKS BY KAY ARTHUR

Lord, Give Me a Heart for You

Lord, Heal My Hurts

Lord, I Want to Know You

Lord, Is It Warfare? Teach Me to Stand

Lord, Where Are You When Bad Things Happen?

Lord, Only You Can Change Me

Lord, I Need Grace to Make It Today

Lord, I'm Torn Between Two Masters

Lord, Teach Me to Pray in 28 Days

God, Are You There? Do You Care? Do You Know About Me?

How to Study Your Bible Precept upon Precept

The International Inductive Study Series

Beloved: From God's Heart to Yours

His Imprint, My Expression

The Peace and Power of Knowing God's Name

As Silver Refined

Our Covenant God

Search My Heart, O God

A Sanctuary for Your Soul

My Savior, My Friend

A Moment with God

With an Everlasting Love

Marriage Without Regrets

Discover 4 Yourself Inductive Bible Studies for Kids

Sex...
According to
God

How to Walk with Purity in a World of Temptation

KAY ARTHUR

WATERBROOK
PRESS

SEX...ACCORDING TO GOD
PUBLISHED BY WATERBROOK PRESS
2375 Telstar Drive, Suite 160
Colorado Springs, Colorado 80920
A division of Random House, Inc.

All Scripture quotations, unless otherwise indicated, are taken from the *New American Standard Bible®* (NASB), © Copyright The Lockman Foundation 1960, 1962, 1963, 1968, 1971, 1972, 1973, 1975, 1977, 1995. Used by permission (www.Lockman.org). Scripture quotations marked (NIV) are taken from the *Holy Bible, New International Version®*. NIV®. Copyright © 1973, 1978, 1984 by International Bible Society. Used by permission of Zondervan Publishing House. All rights reserved. Scripture quotations marked (KJV) are taken from the *King James Version.*

Italics in Scripture quotations reflect the author's added emphasis.

ISBN 1-57856-843-9

Library of Congress Cataloging-in-Publication Data
Arthur, Kay, 1933–
    Sex—according to God : the Creator's plan for his beloved / by Kay Arthur.—1st ed.
       p. cm.
Includes bibliographical references (p. 247).
    ISBN 1-57856-639-8
    1. Sex—Religious aspects—Christianity. I. Title.
    BT708 A78 2002
    241'.66—dc21   2002006401

Printed in the United States of America
2003

10 9 8 7 6 5 4 3 2

Contents

Sex Is Like a Can of Drano

I got up from the table, carried the dishes to the sink, and as I looked down all I could think was, *Good grief! A clogged sink. I don't have time for this!*

I was scheduled to drive to a nearby town to speak to a group of teenagers about sex, and here was a mess of soggy garbage floating in a sink that was probably as old as our farmhouse!

I couldn't just walk out and leave the mess. Dropping to my knees, I began rummaging under the sink through cans of scouring powders, cleaning solutions, and dishwashing soap, looking for the Drano. Finally, way at the back, I spotted its red-white-and-blue can. I couldn't remember when I had last used it.

"I probably should have been using you regularly and this wouldn't have happened," I mumbled to the unhearing can as I looked for the directions. The skull and crossbones on the front and the word *POISON* in all caps reminded me why I had buried it at the back of the cabinet.

Following the directions carefully, which the manufacturer of Drano had convinced me was important, I cautiously popped the red top, did exactly what I was told, then stood at my gurgling sink—mesmerized, relieved, and delighted as I watched the product work its magic.

In minutes the sink was clean and shiny.

Great! I thought. *I'm out of here!*

Minutes later as I turned onto Interstate 75, heading toward Dalton, Georgia, I eased back into the driver's seat and began to review my message on sex, but my mind quickly went from sex to sinks. I was still amazed at what an incredibly quick job Drano did on my sink. *What a great product!* I thought. *Read the directions, do what it tells you, and it works! And nothing dire happened because I followed the directions.*

Then it hit me: *Lord, sex is like a can of Drano! It's a wonderful "product," does a great job, but you have to use it according to the Manufacturer's directions.* What a great opener for my message on sex!

Drano will do just what the manufacturer says, but if you don't use it properly, it could do one of three things: burn you, poison you, or erupt violently! The same is true of sex. That's why so many are traumatized by sex instead of delighting in it as God intended.

Maybe this is your experience, my friend. You've been burned and you bear the scars, whether others see them or not. Maybe the poison still seeps through your mind or body. Maybe you've acquired a sexually transmitted disease—even AIDS. Maybe sex exploded, with results you never anticipated. You had an abortion, or you paid for her to get one. Or your infidelity was discovered, and your life and your plans were ruined. You never dreamed it would turn out this way.

You hadn't carefully read God's warnings, written in black on the white pages of His book, the Bible. If you had, you would have found the dangers of misuse clearly identified, much like the cautions listed on the can of Drano.

MANUFACTURER'S WARNINGS

"Read Back Label Carefully." Therein lies our problem today. Those who bear the title *Christian* haven't read the label carefully to learn what the Manufacturer says about sex. That's why I'm so excited that you're reading this book, even if you've done everything right when it comes to sex. If you're one of those rare people who clearly recognize the sexual seduction so prevalent and pervasive in our world today, if you have your passions reined in and under control, you still need this book. It's a thorough guide to all that God says about sex—the good, the bad, and the beautiful. Although the word *sex* won't be found in a Bible concordance—except for two places in the *New International Version*—the Word of God, through a variety of terms, deals thoroughly with all God intends for us to know about the subject. Wherever you are, whatever your past experience, you and I and those who join you in studying this topic are going to discover for ourselves exactly what the Manufacturer has to say about His product. We're going to look at what sex is and why God created it in the first place. You're going to see and know for yourself what God says about the where, the when, and the how of it—and what happens when you don't follow God's directions. And of course, since it's so necessary, we'll also explore what to do if you've experienced the harmful side of sex because you didn't know, didn't listen, or were victimized.

It grieves me to say that many have been and are being victimized either in counseling situations or by people they trust, who supposedly know and serve God. Anyone who knows what God says about sex will always be able to discern the validity of any counsel or advances they receive with respect to sexual activities. If it doesn't line up with the Word of God, without exception it is not from God—no matter who says it, no matter how godly that person seems or how much it looks as if God is using him or her. God's Word is there to free you from deception and protect you from deceivers.

As you study the Bible, you're going to learn truths that will enable you to grasp all God intended you to experience in the incredible miracle of becoming one flesh with your husband or wife, and you're going to know how to conduct yourself until you get married or if you never marry. You are going to learn so much, my friend, that you'll find God using you in a significant way to help others in these critical, difficult days. You could be used of God to start a new sexual revolution. How awesome that would be!

What other warnings does the Manufacturer offer?

"Poison: Keep Out of the Reach of Children." That was what I wanted the teens to understand that night in Dalton, Georgia! Sex is not for children—or for anyone else who doesn't know the rules and how to handle it in a responsible way. If we engage in sex without understanding and without following the Manufacturer's instructions, it will poison us. Sex is not for children, yet many in our society believe differently and are doing everything they can to legalize sex with children. Think of the children who have been abused for the pleasure of some adult. Think of the children exploited for child pornography. When you look in their eyes, it's as if the light of life has been turned off and their precious bodies have been vacated. All is dark, hopeless. They have been forced into an adult world they cannot handle.

No matter what anyone says, sex is not for children, and woe to those who use children for their sexual gratification or the gratification of others. According to Jesus their judgment will be great.

"Causes Severe Burns on Contact." This crystal drain cleaner, the back label informed me, would not "harm pipes, septic tanks, or cesspools"—but it could burn skin! Not only that, but the contents could *"violently erupt or boil out"!* That evening as I talked to the teens about the similarities between sex and Drano, I used a little body language to illustrate this fact that both could explode. Arching my back and sticking out my tummy, I ran my hand over my abdomen as if I were pregnant. From the response of the group, I knew my point was made.

Tragically, in the two decades since I talked to those teens, sex has erupted more and more frequently in other ways—STDs (sexually transmitted diseases), AIDS, abortions, and even hysterectomies because of too many sex partners or botched abortions. I know far too many who have been burned by sex or who watched in disbelief as it exploded into horrific consequences! Sex is powerful and grievously destructive when used by those who don't know what they are doing.

Let me ask you a question: As you read this, do you wish with all your heart that someone trustworthy had sat you down long ago and made sure you knew the truth about sex? That your parents had put restraints on you, or that your convictions had been strong enough for you to say NO! because you respected God and knew what He said about sex—and therefore you were convinced you did the right thing?

I just viewed a promotional tape for a video series called *Sex and Young America: The Real Deal,*[1] which features teens discussing the issues they're facing and the choices they're making about sex. These were the words of those being interviewed:

"Sex is out of control."

"Sex is everywhere."

"Temptation is everywhere."

"Don't shelter us. Help us deal with it."

"I need my parents to hold me, tell me it's wrong, but we can make it all right."

They all wished their parents had sat down with them and talked about the subject, even if they acted as if they didn't want to hear it!

Well, my friend, that's what this book is all about—the truth about sex. What sex is according to the One who created it. Truth is always liberating; it lets you know exactly where you are, what is right, what is wrong, whether it can be fixed and how. And I want you to know—no matter where you are—it *can* be fixed. We'll see how.

When you read the bottom of the back label of a Drano can, you'll find these words not only written in red but also outlined in red:

Poison

May Be Fatal or Cause Permanent Damage if Swallowed.
Causes Severe Burns to Eyes and Skin.

The label goes on to say the product *"may cause blindness."* Can you see how that correlates with our society today? The blindness that comes from misunderstanding and misusing sex, from not knowing what the Manufacturer says?

I recently received this e-mail from someone who "accidentally," in the sovereignty of God, caught my television program.

> For the first time last night I watched your program. You discussed the purpose of marriage and read scriptures from the Bible that very much identify with the situation I am in. I have lived with a guy for 4.5 years now, and for some reason both of us are afraid to commit for various different reasons. We know we want to be together, but [we] just think if it's working okay for right now, why bother with getting married. Now I know why we should get married. I have never been much into reading the Bible. I have tried several times but find it hard to comprehend. You put meaning and explanation behind the scriptures that people in everyday life can relate to. I want to thank you. I am glad I was channel surfing...

This book, this study of God's Word, is vital and crucial in its timing, because our postmodern culture denies all absolutes, cries for tolerance toward everyone except Christians, and encourages people to do what is right in their own eyes. In such a world, many, even in the church, are ignorant about the consequences of sex outside God's parameters. Tragic consequences follow when sex is pursued without rules or restraints, and God doesn't want you to be blind or blindsided on this subject. Therefore our goal in this book is to discover His instructions so your vision is not clouded by the misuses of sex.

But let's continue our look at the Drano label. What if you don't follow the instructions on the can of Drano and you get burned or poisoned, or there's a violent eruption? What does the manufacturer advise? *"Immediately Give First Aid."*

As you've been reading, have you been holding your breath, shaking your head, wondering if there's any help, any hope for you or others you know? Oh, how I wish I could say this to you in person: There is *still* hope no matter how far you've deviated either unintentionally or willfully from what is right. There *is* hope no matter what has been done to you sexually. You can recover; your loved ones can recover. Our society could recover!

I know that may seem impossible, given the appalling state of our morals—but the situation *can* be reversed. It happened in England in the late 1700s, when the tide of social principles was turned for the better under the leadership of William Wilberforce. This godly man sought to reform the morals of his nation as he in 1787 conceived of a society that would work "for the encouragement of piety and virtue; and for the preventing of vice, profaneness, and immorality."[2] Biographer John Pollock wrote that "Wilberforce...made goodness fashionable."[3]

Can you imagine how such a movement might transform our country, our world today? There *is* a way to recover, because God is God, and He is all about the business of redemption, reclaiming what was lost and transforming it into something of value. Who knows how God could use you to liberate this generation with these truths in your heart and in your hand!

Just remember: Because God is God, no one—absolutely no one—is outside the reach of His healing, restorative power.

If you will listen and go forward from here, I guarantee it will be "well with your soul"—and by *soul* I mean the "inner man," the deepest part of self where we face a sinful nature we all have to live with and can never shake in this life, no matter how hard we try!

THE ROAD BEST LEFT UNTRAVELED

I know what it is to battle that "inner man" in the area of sex, because I have been there. I know the pain, the regret that comes when sex takes place in a way that isn't according to God's plan. I didn't read the directions in full, and the one command I did know, "Thou shall not commit adultery," I flagrantly broke mentally while I was married and numerous times physically after my husband and I divorced.

Why did I do those things? I wanted to be happy, to be loved. I wanted to be sexy—irresistibly, delightfully appealing—because I thought that was where I'd find happiness!

It was the 1950s, the days of the sweater girl, pinups, and the emergence of Hugh Hefner's Playboy bunnies. The girl next door was viewed in a new light, which would lead to moral darkness. Religion was routine, the Bible was boring, and so much preaching had more to do with questioning the veracity of God's Word than with living in the fear of God, in holiness.

I saw morality in my parents but had no biblical basis for it in my own understanding. Consequently, I really messed up my life and the lives of others. I sinned. I broke God's commandments. That's what sin is—living independently of God. It's *you* acting like God, *you* deciding what is right and wrong instead of listening to what God has already said in His book. Sin is choosing not to believe God. It is knowing to do good but not doing it.

I sinned, and it took me farther than I ever wanted to go and cost me more than I ever intended to pay. How I wish someone had helped me see the warning signs, the dangerous curves ahead, and had put me on another road, God's straight and narrow road that leads to life.

I didn't consider my future; I simply lived for the moment, a moment I believed might give me the future I thought I wanted. But it didn't. It was a downward spiral until, at the age of twenty-nine, I fell on my knees and told God He could do anything with me that He wanted. Oh, if only I had known before what He wanted, I would have been on my knees in full surrender much earlier.

When I finally listened and decided to live God's way, the recovery began. I look back now and cannot help but grin and shake my head. Never! Never did I dream what God had in store. It's awesome. Only God could do it! Yet with all my being I wish I had never taken that other road. I wish I had known what God said and had used sex accordingly.

Well, my friend, let's begin this adventure of learning about sex according to God. I have to warn you, however, that we're going to see more negative warnings about sex than positive instructions, although the positive *is* there. It has to be; God invented sex, and He is a God of good and perfect gifts. But sex is high, holy—so sacred, so finely tuned in its creative power that this is where our sinful nature is most likely to cause us to self-destruct. Thankfully, because God's business is creation and redemption rather than death and destruction, He's given you absolutely everything you need to keep from self-destructing.

So let's see what He has to say—positive and negative and redemptive.

In the Beginning

Why Did God Create Sex?

There's great confusion in our society today about sex. We live in a culture where we almost breathe sex! Grab the television remote for a few minutes of channel surfing, and it's there, discussed, debated, demonstrated, and used to sell anything and everything from cars to shampoo, from coffee to toothpaste. The message is loud and clear: We have to be desirable. One way or another we have to attract the opposite sex if we ever want love. It's no longer love that makes the world go round; it's sex!

Go on the Internet, type in an innocuous word, and without warning you're offered titillating sights and experiences you never knew existed—or you wish you never knew. Your curiosity tempts you to investigate further. Your mind tries to rationalize how you can go where you know you shouldn't. You find yourself battling a desire—a longing so unexpectedly awakened.

You get out of the house, walk down the street, and it steps right in front of you—parading long, luscious legs and a short, tight skirt that rides every movement of her hips. You look up to distract yourself from the thoughts invading your mind, and you see a billboard that only entices you to carry the thoughts further.

You walk into a corner store to grab something to eat or drink, and the magazines catch your eye. The pictures and headlines promise answers to your questions, ways to get or keep a lover excited and interested, and ways you can test your sexual IQ.

You get together with your friends, and eventually the subject turns to the opposite sex—conquests are shared, frustrations are expressed, advice is given, or you're laughed at because you haven't had it! You're told you just don't know what true excitement is.

That night you go to a movie; it's rated PG, but the upcoming attractions are not. Most of them sell sex, and you're sitting with your arm around someone whose skin is warm and soft, her perfume sweetening the aura of her femininity—or you're snuggling closer to a guy who exudes strength and tenderness. Your mind is going where it shouldn't go, your flesh is longing for what it shouldn't have; she's not your wife…he's not your husband.

You go home with your date and what do you do? Should you really go in, even for just a few minutes? If you do, will you engage in intercourse—or everything short of it? And whether or not you "go all the way," will you experience sex the way God intended it to be when He created sex?

THE ORIGINAL DESIGN

Let's go back to the very beginning, to Genesis, the first book in the Bible. I want you to see for yourself what God says about sex, about our gender differences, and why He made us this way. As you read Genesis 1, a portion of which is printed out for you below, I suggest that you mark the text as you read it. When you do this and then write out your observations, it helps you not only grasp for yourself exactly what God says and means, it also helps you remember what you discovered. Now then, color or underline every reference to *man,* including every pronoun (every *him,* every *them*).

GENESIS 1:25-28

²⁵ God made the beasts of the earth after their kind, and the cattle after

their kind, and everything that creeps on the ground after its kind; and God

saw that it was good.

²⁶ Then God said, "Let Us make man in Our image, according to Our like-

ness; and let them rule over the fish of the sea and over the birds of the sky and over the cattle and over all the earth, and over every creeping thing that creeps on the earth."

²⁷ God created man in His own image, in the image of God He created him; male and female He created them.

²⁸ God blessed them; and God said to them, "Be fruitful and multiply, and fill the earth, and subdue it; and rule over the fish of the sea and over the birds of the sky and over every living thing that moves on the earth."

What did *you* learn from marking the references to *man*? Did you notice the word *you* in that question is italicized? That's because this book is about you. Our study together is not an issue of your agreeing or disagreeing with what I write; rather it's about seeing with *your own* eyes exactly what God has to say about sex. Then you can make an informed, intelligent, rational decision about what you're going to do with what you've learned. And when you come to the final page of this book, you'll never have occasion to say with regret, "Well, if only I had known!" You will *know.* You'll know it all, because we'll cover it all.

Now let's get back into our study, starting with listing your insights. Observing the text in this careful way helps you see exactly what God is saying, and it keeps you from straying into "I think," "I heard," or "I just feel" as you strive to grasp God's truth. These comments are not bad; you just need to get the facts first and go from there. So in the space provided, record the facts you learned about *man* from reading Genesis 1.

Before we discuss what we observed in Genesis 1, let's look at Genesis 2. What God does in this next passage is tighten the focus on the telescope and take you in for a closer look, enabling you to see the details of the creation of man and woman.

As you read the text, mark every reference to the *man* like this ♂ and every reference to the *woman* like this: ♀. Also mark pronouns the same way.

GENESIS 2:7-8,15-25

7 Then the LORD God formed man of dust from the ground, and breathed into his nostrils the breath of life; and man became a living being.

8 The LORD God planted a garden toward the east, in Eden; and there He placed the man whom He had formed....

15 Then the LORD God took the man and put him into the garden of Eden to cultivate it and keep it.

16 The LORD God commanded the man, saying, "From any tree of the garden you may eat freely;

17 but from the tree of the knowledge of good and evil you shall not eat, for in the day that you eat from it you will surely die."

18 Then the LORD God said, "It is not good for the man to be alone; I will make him a helper suitable for him."

19 Out of the ground the LORD God formed every beast of the field and every bird of the sky, and brought them to the man to see what he would call them; and whatever the man called a living creature, that was its name.

20 The man gave names to all the cattle, and to the birds of the sky, and to every beast of the field, but for Adam there was not found a helper suitable for him.

²¹ So the LORD God caused a deep sleep to fall upon the man, and he slept; then He took one of his ribs and closed up the flesh at that place.

²² The LORD God fashioned into a woman the rib which He had taken from the man, and brought her to the man.

²³ The man said, "This is now bone of my bones, and flesh of my flesh; she shall be called Woman, because she was taken out of Man."

²⁴ For this reason a man shall leave his father and his mother, and be joined to his wife; and they shall become one flesh.

²⁵ And the man and his wife were both naked and were not ashamed.

Now list below what you learned in this passage from marking *man* and *woman*.

MAN   WOMAN

Genesis 1 tells us that both man and woman were created on the sixth day, yet Genesis 2 shows us there was an order to their creation. Adam was created first from the dust of the earth, while the woman was created from a rib taken from the side of the man. God makes sure we know His purpose in creating the woman: She is to be a helper to the man, because among the beasts of the field no suitable companion for him was found. The Hebrew words in this passage translated as *helper suitable* (*help meet* in the *King James Version*) are *ezer neged*. *Ezer* means "an aide," while *neged* means "a counterpart, a mate."

If it wasn't good for Adam to be alone, why didn't God just create another man to be Adam's companion? Is there a difference between the sexes? You need to know what the Bible teaches, because an opposing view has long been promoted—and many have bought into its lie.

I've saved a page of notes given to me by a college student who wrote them down while sitting in a class on child development in 1979. As you read verbatim what my friend wrote, please know these are not the ravings of a lone liberal. I wish they were. Rather these notes reflect the cleverly wrought lies that had to be presented—and believed—to make way for the perversions that would follow in the name of "scientific" research. I will share only the first three; they're enough.

1. We are born asexual, neither homosexual nor heterosexual.
2. Children's sex is determined by labels parents place before two years of age.
3. All our sexual behavior is learned. Sex drive is learned, influenced by our environment.

Although these statements were supposedly based on the latest scientific research in the study of human sexuality, are they true? Do they concur with the Word of God?

What did you see in Genesis 1 and 2? Were we created asexual?

And were we designed to reproduce asexual offspring? Genesis 4 answers that quickly: When Eve gave birth to their first child, she said, "I have gotten a manchild with the help of the LORD" (verse 1). Eve could tell the baby was not female like she was. A human, yes; a woman, no. His anatomy was different and the difference was evident from birth. So it was then, and so it has always been.

God determines the sex of the child, and the sex, except in very rare situations, is evident from birth. But the difference is not one of mere anatomy. You can put a little boy in a feminine environment, but it won't remove the Y chromosome that makes him male. It won't diminish his levels of testosterone, a hormone that shoots up six to seven weeks after the sperm meets the egg and far exceeds the testosterone levels in females.

When children reach the age of puberty, it won't matter what environment they've been raised in, what clothes they were dressed in, what gender they were labeled with. A girl's estrogen level will be eight to ten times higher than a boy's, and his testosterone level will exceed hers by a factor of fifteen.[1] Our environment can greatly impact how we view ourselves, what we think of as normal, and some of our preferences—but it cannot change our gender. If it could, people wouldn't be seeking sex-change operations.

If you want truth without distortion, you'll find it in the Bible. God's Book tells us we were created distinctively male and female. Eve was designed to be a suitable helper, a companion for Adam. Both were also designed for the purpose of procreation. Two men, no matter how they were raised, cannot have sex and produce a child. Neither can two women. It takes a sperm and an egg to make a child—and for those elements you need a man and a woman.

As I said, God didn't create another man to be Adam's companion; He created Eve, a woman. It was Adam and Eve who were to be fruitful and multiply by producing male and female babies, who in turn would grow up and produce more male and female babies.

And how would this happen? Did you notice that Genesis 2:24 says, "and they shall become one flesh"? What does that mean?

God explains it very clearly in 1 Corinthians 6:15-18. As you read this passage printed out for you, remember that the apostle Paul is writing these words to Christians. A genuine Christian has the Holy Spirit dwelling inside him or her. Christianity is Christ in us; therefore, our bodies become His temple.

Also as you read, mark the following three things each in a distinctive way: every reference to *you* and *your,* every occurrence of *prostitute,* and every mention of *immorality.* In marking words, I find it most helpful to use different colors, so they're easily recognized. (As you continue in this book, you may want to keep on hand a half-dozen colored pencils—or at least a three-colored ballpoint pen.) If marking these words in different colors isn't practical, you can underline *you* and put a downward arrow over *prostitute* like this ↓ and a big **I** over *immorality.*

1 CORINTHIANS 6:15-18

[15] Do you not know that your bodies are members of Christ? Shall I then take away the members of Christ and make them members of a prostitute? May it never be!

¹⁶ Or do you not know that the one who joins himself to a prostitute is one body with her? For He says, "THE TWO SHALL BECOME ONE FLESH."

¹⁷ But the one who joins himself to the Lord is one spirit with Him.

¹⁸ Flee immorality. Every other sin that a man commits is outside the body, but the immoral man sins against his own body.

What did you learn from marking *you* and *your*?

According to what you read in this passage and in Genesis 2, how would you explain the phrase, "the two shall become one flesh"?

What is the "immorality" to which Paul refers in these verses?

It's so incredible, so awesome: Sex, by God's design, is *becoming one flesh.* When God made Adam and Eve distinctively male and female, He designed them anatomically so they could physically become one flesh in the act of sexual intercourse.

God formed us to know no greater ecstasy than when a man and a woman literally merge into one flesh. Hormones, nerves, sensory receptors, and other specific physical characteristics are all part of His divine design for our pleasure in the physical oneness of marriage.

An ecstasy beyond exquisite.

A oneness washing over you, a wave of passion carrying you weightless to a sea of delight.

Passion that loses consciousness of anything else.

Exhaustion that leaves you spent, drained of tension, and filled with satisfaction, total satisfaction.

Sex has a beauty all its own and—wonder of wonders!—God invented it.

You do realize, don't you, that God didn't have to make sex so pleasurable! He could have designed it to be very mechanical, much like the instructions on the Drano can: To make a baby, first do this, then that, and follow with this. Be careful of such and such. Nine months later you should produce a child; if not, repeat entire process again until successful.

No feelings, no passion, no exhilaration—just mechanics.

Never! That's so far from what God intended in creating sex. Sex is not meant to be mechanical; it's meant to be passionate. Sex, in its perfect form, brings the intimacy of not only truly belonging to another but longing for the presence of our beloved. In its hallowed purity, the union of a husband and wife becomes a holy metaphor of the wife God seeks for His Son, of the oneness He longs to have with His chosen people Israel.

THE ULTIMATE LOVE STORY

From beginning to end, the Bible is about a divine romance. It opens with the account of a man and woman becoming one flesh. It ends with the Spirit and the Bride inviting others to join God's forever family. The Old Testament shows us the joy of fidelity and the heart-wrenching pain of adultery. We watch as God takes the canvas of the Old Testament and paints the picture of His love affair with Israel.

In Ezekiel 16, He sketches the picture of Israel's birth, her abandonment, and His compassion when He found her in the field, her cord uncut, her body bloody and unwashed. Our hearts are touched as we observe His care in raising her until the time of love had come. In Jeremiah 2 we watch as He pauses for a moment, a smile crossing His face as He remembers the devotion of her youth, the love of their betrothal, the way she followed Him through the wilderness. Then the day came when Israel became His wife: "'I passed by you and saw you, and behold, you were at the time for love; so I spread My skirt over you and covered your nakedness. I also swore to you and entered into a covenant with you so that you became Mine,' declares the Lord GOD" (Ezekiel 16:8).

A covenant is a solemn, binding agreement between two parties—one lesser and one greater, or both of equal status—who commit themselves to each other under certain conditions. A covenant once made is never to be broken. In a covenant relationship, two become one; they no longer live independently. They are now bound to protect and defend one another, share everything in common, be there for the other until death. So solemn is this arrangement that God becomes the sovereign administrator of every covenant, watching to make certain its conditions are fulfilled and, if they are not, to come to the defense of the violated one and to deal out retribution against the violator of the covenant. In the book of Malachi, God calls marriage a covenant and expresses how He hates divorce, a man putting away the wife of his youth.[2]

God's love for His covenant nation is so evident in the Bible, in the telling of their love story. Nothing is too good for her. He adorned her with ornaments, putting bracelets on her hand, a necklace around her neck, a beautiful crown upon her head. Her dresses were of fine linen, silk, and embroidered cloth. She ate the choicest of food. Exceedingly beautiful, she advanced to royalty. He bestowed His splendor on her, and her fame spread.

Then it happened.

She trusted in her beauty and began to play the harlot, pouring out her favors on every passerby. She sacrificed their children on the altars of fame and fortune.[3] What once was beauty became lewdness. Her nakedness was experienced by many…and His heart broke.

Eventually, to get her attention, He wrote her a bill of divorcement and sent her away—but she was never far from His heart.

She descended down and down into greater degradation until she ended up for sale in a slave market—and God went to redeem her, Israel, His beloved. (We're given the picture in the book of Hosea, in the story the prophet tells of himself and Gomer.)

Israel's redemption would come through their own son, Jesus, whose very name means "God is our salvation," for it was He who would save their people from their sins. When Jesus came of age, God sought a bride for their son. This half-breed—Jew and Gentile in one body—was offered for redemption in a slave market at a terrible price, but the Father and Son did not hesitate to pay. They counseled together to redeem her with the blood of her betrothed, God's only begotten Son.

The covenant of marriage has been cut at Calvary, but it has not yet been consummated. Jesus is at home preparing a place for His bride, the church, in His father's house. The Father's servants are watching over her, urging her to stay pure so that she might be presented as a chaste virgin when the trumpet sounds and He at last comes, with shouts of joy, to take her home. Longing and looking for that day, she is preparing her bridal gown, white and clean, and sending out the invitation to come to the marriage supper of the Lamb.

The Book of books, the Bible, opens with a wedding and a home in a garden, then it closes with a wedding and the new Jerusalem coming down out of heaven, made ready as a bride adorned for her husband.

And what do we find in the middle of this Book of books? We find the greatest of all the love songs ever written: the Song of Solomon. A song that from beginning to end extols the beauty of sex according to God. A story of unquenchable, priceless love, a love that so satisfies our deepest longings that we turn to no other, for we know, "I am my beloved's and my beloved is mine,…and his desire is for me" (6:3; 7:10). A book that does not mention God—and doesn't need to, for it is the very expression of all God intended when He made us male and female and brought woman to man. A book that cautions us not to arouse or awaken love until it pleases, lest we mar its intended beauty and unique intimacy.

2

Portrait of a Virgin

What's the Big Deal About Saving Sex for Marriage?

A young woman wrote to me,

> I am lucky to have a loving, moral family whose members are the top
> priority. My parents are now in their thirty-fourth year of marriage
> and have remained faithful and true to each other through it all…a
> rarity today.
>
> Unfortunately for me, however, those high moral standards meant
> I was all alone when it came to dealing with life issues and sexuality.
> My parents thought good moral people don't talk or think about sexu-
> ality and sexual matters. I lived a good life because I never had to con-
> front temptations. I figured that people who run around with a wild
> crowd and party all the time are the only ones who have to deal with
> temptation and sexuality.
>
> Being born with limited sight and being oversheltered, I was
> always anything but popular and included at school, and likewise at
> college. Because of my legal blindness I couldn't drive, so I withdrew
> into my family. I didn't seem to mature. While my peers and classmates
> were learning the ropes of life with friends and beginning to date and
> eventually becoming seriously involved and even marrying their sweet-
> hearts, I went on living as a little girl in the comfort of the family.
>
> Then somewhere I began to rebel. I couldn't take all the teasing
> for being immature and not knowing how to have fun. I tried so hard

to be included, but when they saw how naive I was, they turned elsewhere, leaving me all alone. I literally had no social life. I went home from college every weekend and buried myself in my studies and writing projects—novelettes I never completed.

Then came my senior year of college. I saw my required internship at a local radio station as my first shot at 'becoming normal' by becoming involved with a thirty-four-year-old man (we'll call him Don). This was where my real rebellion against my parents began. I was almost twenty-one and had never dated or even liked anyone, but upon first meeting him, I decided that if he's single, he would be the man for me. He was thirty-four and divorced, with a thirteen-year-old son.

I did all I could to pursue him, including things totally against our family values, like how I dressed. Suddenly my life became one massive deception. With my family I conveniently avoided the subject of Don. In many ways I knew he wasn't my type, and much I learned about him really bothered me, but I was finally free—and I didn't care!

Finally my plan worked and he asked me out. My parents were real supportive and let me go. It was really fun—miniature golf, hours of just talking at his apartment, and my first kiss. As we dated we started experimenting more sexually. On our third date Don showed me my first X-rated movie after an afternoon at the mall and dinner at a restaurant.

Eventually, in the weeks to come, I hesitatingly conformed to his sexual expectations, upon Don's insistence that all normal girls do it and love it. It was all so gross, so perverted that I ended up in psychological counseling. With the help of my therapist I tried to return to a decent life, but the nightmares kept haunting me.

Finally I got involved at a local Christian television station, and it was like beginning anew, although the scars remained. Then I was saved.... But I was real confused as I sought out the truth. Then I found your teaching ministry on TV, and all of a sudden I knew. You taught me much in an area I never really dealt with, my sexuality. And the lingering brokenness finally left.

I feel like a virgin again.

THE GIFT OF A LIFETIME

If marriage is a metaphor of God's union with Israel, and He calls Israel a harlot because of her unfaithfulness…and if it's a metaphor of the church as Christ's bride, and God calls her an adulteress because of her friendship with the world…then what value does God place on our virginity as women or men? This is what we want to explore next. However, if you are single but not a virgin, please don't stop reading. Don't think that, because you lost your virginity or it was taken from you by force, you cannot bear the pain of reading on. Running away from the issue won't help; the past will always plague your thoughts. Rather, you need to be healed, to reclaim the beauty God intended for you, as did my friend who wrote the letter I quoted from earlier. So keep reading, beloved of God, and learn what God says.

We'll begin with Deuteronomy, one of the first five books of the Bible. Collectively these five books are called the Book of the Law, the Torah, or the Pentateuch.

Read Deuteronomy 22:13-21 for yourself. This passage explains what is to be done if a husband claims his wife was not a virgin when he married her. As you read it, color every occurrence of the word *virgin* (and *virginity*) or put a big **V** over it. (I suggest using various colors for the key repeated words that are important to the text, because colors are much easier to distinguish than a bunch of symbols all in the same color.)

DEUTERONOMY 22:13-21

13 If any man takes a wife and goes in to her and then turns against her,

14 and charges her with shameful deeds and publicly defames her, and says, "I took this woman, but when I came near her, I did not find her a virgin,"

15 then the girl's father and her mother shall take and bring out the evidence of the girl's virginity to the elders of the city at the gate.

16 The girl's father shall say to the elders, "I gave my daughter to this man for a wife, but he turned against her;

17 and behold, he has charged her with shameful deeds, saying, 'I did not find your daughter a virgin.' But this is the evidence of my daughter's virginity." And they shall spread the garment before the elders of the city.

18 So the elders of that city shall take the man and chastise him,

19 and they shall fine him a hundred shekels of silver and give it to the girl's father, because he publicly defamed a virgin of Israel. And she shall remain his wife; he cannot divorce her all his days.

20 But if this charge is true, that the girl was not found a virgin,

21 then they shall bring out the girl to the doorway of her father's house, and the men of her city shall stone her to death because she has committed an act of folly in Israel, by playing the harlot in her father's house; thus you shall purge the evil from among you.

Who are the various characters in this scenario? List them below.

Now, what did you learn from marking the word *virgin*? Record everything you learned from the text—and *only* from the text, because you and I want to know what *God* says about sex. List your insights below.

A virgin is a woman who has never had sexual intercourse with a man, and God has a wonderful way of marking this distinction for her. When God created woman, He gave her a vagina, where she receives the man in the beautiful act of sexual intercourse. Within her vagina is a hymen, a mucous membrane that partially seals the entrance into the vagina, leaving only adequate space for the woman's menstrual discharge. It's as if God sealed a woman's virginity in such a way that she might present it to her husband as a gift for him to unwrap on the sacred night in which they become one flesh.

Reading about this may be embarrassing for you. (If so, I think it's wonderful that you can still blush!) Please know I wouldn't even bring it up if you didn't need to understand how it can be proven that a woman is or isn't a virgin. And while this may be embarrassing, it's not repulsive if you understand this is the way God made us. When God finished creating man and woman, He Himself saw "it was very good."

So what is the proof of a woman's virginity, to any who would question her in those times or in that culture, or to a husband who tired of her and wanted to divorce her? It is the bridal garment or cloth from their wedding night.

From all that we can piece together from various scriptures, in the days spoken of in Deuteronomy there wasn't a ceremony or the exchanging of vows in a marriage ceremony, as we observe in our Western culture today. Rather, a covenant agreement would be made that pledged a woman to a man in marriage. Although this contract could be made long before the actual marriage took place, it was a binding agreement and was not to be broken unless it could be proven that the woman was not a virgin.[1]

When the time of the actual wedding came, the bride's family would spend the day decorating the house, preparing food, and getting the bride ready for her bridegroom, dressing her in her bridal garments. When all was ready, the bridegroom would send his friends to get his bride. Torches aflame, the joyous procession lit up the black velvet of night as they went to snatch the bride and bring her to the bridegroom's house. All those invited to the wedding feast—the virgins with their oil lamps, the men with their torches— would turn out dressed in their wedding garments. It was a boisterous and exciting occasion, awakening the whole town as neighbors scurried to their flat roofs to catch a glimpse of the bride.

As the bride neared the home of her bridegroom, all would hear the shout, "Behold the bridegroom comes," as he went out to meet his wife of the covenant.

Later the bride and groom would slip away to the bridal tent, or to the bridal chamber in the bridegroom's home, to consummate their pledge. The bridegroom was "to go in to his bride," it was said. Over the bridal bed would be a canopy, a *chuppah,* while under the bride would be her bridal garment or cloth. The blood on the garment or cloth would attest to her virginity, as the covenant of blood was cut "by passing through pieces of flesh." The two became one flesh; the marriage was consummated. Her bridal garment, stained with the blood of the covenant, would be wrapped up and put away. It was evidence of her virginity, the gift she saved for her husband. A gift that could be given only one time, to one person.

As we consider this, it seems clear that, at one time, a woman's virginity was a priceless treasure to be protected at all costs. The man who won her heart would win her body. He would be the first and the last to ever "know" her in this way while both lived. Their covenant relationship, confirmed by the proof of her purity, offered her security and protected them both from "the little foxes" that would rob the vine of its pure and delightful fruit, as the Song of Solomon expresses it (2:15).

Today so many people see virginity as something to scoff at, almost a reproach, because apparently the person is so undesirable that no one wants to sleep with him or her. Virginity is considered outdated, because morality is almost extinct in this age in which we live.

People of my generation recall the renowned *Ozzie and Harriet* of the beginning days of television, a couple who were married with children. The program was about a wholesome all-American family—mom, dad, kids all living in the same home. The show illustrated morality and character and handling the issues of life with integrity. We enjoyed the program, related to its story lines, and benefited from the picture it offered of what marriage was all about: family.

Yes, the adults knew there was a *Peyton Place.* They realized that not everyone lived moral lives, but at least those who didn't were embarrassed enough to hide their immorality. It wasn't condoned, even on television. Why?

Years earlier, the motion picture industry had paraded rampant sex, violence, and all sorts of immorality across the screen because it meant big box office returns. In 1933 Hedy Lamarr played a brief nude scene in the film *Ecstasy.* That same year, the story line of the Barbara Stanwyck film *Baby Face* included a father who prostituted his daughter to pay his gambling debts. America was enraged! Concerned citizens determined that Hollywood would not corrupt our morals. The Roman Catholic Church, along with others, began pursuing legal action. To avoid government censorship, the movie industry began in 1934 to enforce the Motion Picture Production Code, which was supported by a strong contingent of Americans—Catholics, Protestants, and Jews—who wanted to protect America's culture.

While they agreed that we all cherish the First Amendment (which does not protect obscenity), supporters of the code understood the importance of identifying and restraining forms of "entertainment" that harm individuals and society. "Among the general principles of the code was the requirement that 'no picture shall be produced which will lower the standards of those who see it. Hence the sympathy of the audience should never be thrown to the side of crime, wrongdoing, evil or sin.' "[2] Also included in this code was the declaration that "the sanctity of the institution of marriage and the home shall be upheld. Pictures shall not infer that low forms of sex relationship are the acceptable or common thing." It stated, "Many scenes cannot be presented without arousing dangerous emotions on the part of the immature, the young or the criminal classes. Even without the limits of pure love, certain facts have been universally regarded by lawmakers as outside the limits of safe presentation."[3]

The television industry didn't want to expose itself to the same level of controversy the movie industry had faced. Consequently, anytime the camera took the television audience into the bedrooms of Ozzie and Harriet Nelson, June and Ward Cleaver of *Leave It to Beaver*, or Lucy and Ricky Ricardo on the *I Love Lucy Show*, we were shown twin beds. The censors of those times were careful to make sure no man and woman were ever seen in the same bed, nor would they even imply it.

Even I as a young girl noticed the separate beds. In fact my comment to anyone who wanted to listen was, "When I get married, we're not going to sleep in twin beds." It seemed to me that you wouldn't want to be on the opposite side of the room from your spouse!

Marriage was my heart's desire. I loved watching my mother and father. I never thought of them in bed together, having sex. It never entered my mind. I just knew they loved one another. Daddy would pat Mother on the fanny when she walked by. If some good tune came on the radio, Mother would come out of the kitchen, wiping her hands on her apron, and walk into Daddy's waiting arms. They loved to dance...and so did I.

I guess we all enjoyed *Ozzie and Harriet* and *Father Knows Best* because they portrayed families just like ours. Daddy went to work; Mother kept house. We ate dinner together every night. My brother Jack and I did our homework and squabbled over whose turn it was to wash the pots and pans. I primped and fussed in front of the mirror and was terribly attracted to boys. I couldn't wait to mature—to fall in love, get married, have a family. Our home was open, friends would stop in and visit, my parents knew my friends and always knew where I was. Home was the center of my world. We didn't have a lot of material things, and money was tight, but our home was filled with affection. We hugged and kissed and told each other we loved them. Mother and Daddy modeled that for us; they were always saying they loved each other. I was secure. I was protected.

A FRAGILE BEAUTY

One night I was sitting at the table in our little two-bedroom home, doing my homework and listening to the radio. It was a science program about the Rh factor of blood, explaining a situation that could cause problems in giving birth if the father and mother's blood were not compatible. I listened with fascination because someday I wanted to be a nurse.

Puzzled, I put my pencil down and turned around toward the kitchen. "Mother, what does the father's blood have to do with the baby anyway?"

All I remember was Mother's first words, "Oh, Kay, it's so beautiful." That was my first lesson on sex!

How different that is from what we see on television and in the movies today! The sexual revolution brought with it new sitcoms and soap operas. In 1968 the Motion Picture Production Code was abolished; in its place was a voluntary rating system for movies promoted by the MPAA (Motion Picture Association of America). Then a 1978 Supreme Court decision further weakened censorship by allowing portrayals on television of certain forms of content inappropriate for children—except during specific times of the day when children were most likely to be watching. By the 1990s *NYPD Blue* was broadcasting partial nudity and gross profanity without censorship. And what happened to the salt and light? Where were the Christians who should have been vocally fighting such blatant disregard for family values? It seems a great majority of them were enjoying the show!

Today, there are no twin beds in the daytime soaps or on sitcoms aired during the hours that used to be considered family time. The characters on

Friends hop in and out of bed, and the big question at one point was, "Who is the father of Rachel's baby?" What is the message the family takes in night after night? What is portrayed as normal? Virginity is passé. Sex is expected to be just a common part of life, the norm—whether you're a teen, a swinging single, a single parent, or one of the over-the-hill gang. Nearly every conversation is rife with sexual innuendo.

We see on television and in other forms of "entertainment" the excitement, the desire, the passion, the pleasure of sex, but we rarely see it in the context where it belongs, within the confines of marriage for the sake of a healthy and wholesome family. Unfortunately we see how ugly, dirty, disgusting, demoralizing, and destructive sex can be—without the corresponding truth of its beauty when experienced as God planned.

What does God intend? Mother said, "Sex is beautiful." But is it? And if so, what makes it beautiful and keeps it beautiful? I believe the beauty comes when we approach God and ask, "For whom is sex intended?"

This question needs to be answered with every generation. Although God's "moral production code" never changes, our culture does—as you have seen. So each generation needs to hear what God says. Let's look again at Genesis 2:22-25:

²² The LORD God fashioned into a woman the rib which He had taken from the man, and brought her to the man.

²³ The man said, "This is now bone of my bones, and flesh of my flesh; she shall be called Woman, because she was taken out of Man."

²⁴ For this reason a man shall leave his father and his mother, and be joined to his wife; and they shall become one flesh.

²⁵ And the man and his wife were both naked and were not ashamed.

For whom is sex intended? A man who had a woman brought to him by God, a woman for whom he would take full responsibility, a woman he would care for and cherish. Bone of his bones, flesh of his flesh. A woman for whom he would forsake even his father and mother. A woman to whom he would cleave for the rest of his life. This is the woman he would become one flesh with! The commitment would come *before* the sex.

But is sex only for people who are married? Let's look at another powerful verse, one that was written many centuries later:

> Marriage is to be held in honor among all, and the marriage bed is to be undefiled; for fornicators and adulterers God will judge. (Hebrews 13:4)

According to this verse, who is sex for?

How did you come to that conclusion from this verse?

I know we're living in much different times than when I was a girl. With all the emphasis on sex today—as the main thing, the common thing, the everybody-does-it thing—it's hard to believe any mother could get away with saying, "You just have to endure it," when she explained sex to her daughter sometime before the young woman went on her honeymoon. Though that was the common statement years ago, these days a passionate relationship with the opposite sex seems to be foremost on the minds of those between their teens and their forties—or those going through a so-called midlife crisis. Sex is seen as the door to love. But in God's Book, love is the door to sex.

As you read this you may be among those who wish with all your being that you had waited until marriage. Your heart may be filled with regret because you so foolishly, unthinkingly gave away the one gift that can be given only once. Maybe you gave it to someone you didn't even know or care about. Maybe no one taught you differently—or maybe you knew better but gave in to the drive of your desire. Maybe the gift was taken away without your knowing it because you were drunk or on drugs, or maybe someone assaulted you, stole your virginity—and now bitterness fills your soul.

Did you carefully read the letter I shared at the beginning of this chapter? Like that dear young woman, you will never regain your physical virginity. All the sorrow, all the tears, all the "if onlys" will never bring it back, but you can, dear one, like my friend, "feel like a virgin again." God can bring that about as He restores a purity to your life, as He cleanses you with the water of His Word that He might present you to Himself as a chaste virgin, a bride without blemish, without spot or wrinkle, as He teaches us in Ephesians 5:25-27.

THE WAYS OF A MAN

Let's turn to the men for a moment. People have thought for generations that the woman is to remain a virgin until marriage, but not the man. Is that true? *After all,* you may be thinking, *he's a man! And men—well, because they're men, they have to have sex! Those young studs with all that testosterone can't wait until marriage! God Himself knows how strong that male sex drive is, how easily it is triggered by what a man sees, hears, and thinks. God ought to know; He's the One who made man like he is, with sex on the brain. Nah, God doesn't expect a man to wait!*

Of course, a man is usually the one offering this rationale. He knows how he can be turned on so easily simply by what he sees! He's all too aware of the battles he faces night and day once those hormones kick in.

But what does God say? That's what we need to know, isn't it? Does God not expect a man to be a virgin, since He deals only with the woman's virginity in the passage we studied in Deuteronomy? As a matter of fact, in the Bible the term *virgin* is never used for a man. So does this mean that a man's virginity doesn't count with God, that God doesn't expect that of him?

If you can find the answer to these questions, you will know how important your virginity is supposed to be in your own eyes and in the eyes of society. Let's look at two passages of Scripture and see what you think after you read them.

Proverbs 5 opens with, "My son, give attention to my wisdom." Let's look at some of the verses that follow this admonition, and as you do, underline or color every reference to the *son.*

[15] Drink water from your own cistern and fresh water from your own well.

[16] Should your springs be dispersed abroad, streams of water in the streets?

[17] Let them be yours alone and not for strangers with you.

[18] Let your fountain be blessed, and rejoice in the wife of your youth.

[19] As a loving hind and a graceful doe, let her breasts satisfy you at all times; be exhilarated always with her love.

[20] For why should you, my son, be exhilarated with an adulteress and embrace the bosom of a foreigner?

[21] For the ways of a man are before the eyes of the LORD, and He watches all his paths.

[22] His own iniquities will capture the wicked, and he will be held with the cords of his sin.

[23] He will die for lack of instruction, and in the greatness of his folly he will go astray.

Now read through the verses again and answer this question: In light of the context (the subject matter) of this passage, what do you think the father means when he uses the imagery of water and cistern and then the term *your springs*?

What, if anything, do you see here that would tell you where a man is to get his sexual satisfaction?

What is God saying in Proverbs 5? He's telling a man that he's to satisfy his sexual desires at home. The breasts of his wife are to be his satisfaction, not the breasts of some stranger, some prostitute, or some immoral woman. He's to drink water from his own well, his own wife, when he thirsts for sexual satisfaction. His springs—his semen and sperm—are not to be dispersed all over town, up and down the streets, given to one woman after another! His life, his DNA, his genes are in his sperm.

It is the man's sperm that determines the sexuality of a child. He makes sons! He makes daughters! This is sacred. The man is in partnership with the Creator of all life, the One who knew us before He formed us in our mother's womb. The One who numbers our days when as yet there was none of them![4] A man's sperm is to be his, raised in his family, bearing his name, inheriting his legacy. A man's sperm is a man's future. If you want to be blessed by God, sow your seed the only place it should be sown—with the wife of your youth.

A man is to know his children, to raise his children. Let me ask you a question: Don't you want to know who your father is? Or do you just want to be known as someone's illegitimate child? Why would you do this to a child just to satisfy your own desires?

Have you ever stopped to think about it? It's sobering, isn't it?

Now, let's look at 1 Corinthians 7, which was written to a church that was birthed through the work of the apostle Paul, a church that was located in a city steeped in immorality. In fact, these people were such fornicators and adulterers, indulging in all sorts of sexual sin, that a term was coined in their name: To *corinthianize* meant "to be involved in sexual debauchery."

In 1 Corinthians 7, Paul is addressing some questions the church had posed to him. The time was the first century A.D. This church was comprised of people who had "corinthianized" in the past and were now being Christianized. No wonder they had questions.

In Paul's response to these questions, we find the answer about men remaining virgins, not having sex until marriage or staying pure if they don't get married.

Let's look at four verses out of this chapter. As you read, mark two words: *immoralities* and *self-control.* Obviously you will have to mark them differently because they are opposites in meaning. Also underline anything that relates to *marriage*.

1 CORINTHIANS 7:1-2,8-9

¹ Now concerning the things about which you wrote, it is good for a man not to touch a woman.

² But because of immoralities, each man is to have his own wife, and each woman is to have her own husband....

⁸ But I say to the unmarried and to widows that it is good for them if they remain even as I. *[Paul was not married when he wrote this.]*

⁹ But if they do not have self-control, let them marry; for it is better to marry than to burn with passion.

Let me give you a side note before we go on. The word *touch* in verse 1 means "to take hold of a woman"; specifically, it implies touching her sexually. In classical Greek, the word meant "to light a fire."

Now then, what did you see? Why don't you write the answers to the following questions.

In verses 1 and 2, what is God saying a man is to do and why?

What is God saying is good for the unmarried?

And what if the unmarried cannot stay single? What are they to do and why?

Now, let me put it another way so you don't miss the point. According to verse 9, why are they to marry?

Think with me: Does God forbid sexual immorality?

Then according to these verses, what is the solution for taking care of one's sex drive?

If a man is burning with sexual desire, the answer is not to have sex outside of marriage, but to get married. It's as simple as that! You have seen it in God's Word for yourself. You have your answer: There is to be no sex outside of marriage for the male as well as the female. Marriage is God's means for satisfying our sex drive, and sex is to be experienced only within the confines of marriage. According to God—and regardless of what society says or portrays—a man, just like a woman, is to remain a virgin until marriage.

Years ago I traveled to Daytona Beach, Florida, to an ocean home someone had loaned me. Jan Silvious, a dear friend of mine who's now an author and speaker, accompanied me. I was going to write a new Precept course that the Lord had laid on my heart: *A Marriage Without Regrets.* Jan would assist, reading and doing the study and giving me her feedback. We enjoyed wonderful days of studying, writing, and talking it through during long walks on the beach. The only bad thing was our timing, which coincided with spring break. The beaches were soon swarming with students out to enjoy themselves to the fullest.

As we walked the beach one afternoon, I looked from the ocean back to the houses on the right. My attention was caught by the shouts and cajoling of a group of young men diving off a roof into a swimming pool. "They're crazy. They could break their necks," I said to Jan.

"That's boys for you." Jan's response brought the conversation to a close; we both had sons, and I knew exactly what she meant.

The next day, when it was time again for our afternoon walk, I wondered if the guys were still jumping off the roof into the pool. Instead of boys on the roof, we saw a huge sheet with enormous lettering: "GET LAID HERE!" I was outraged. Not only were college and high-school kids on the beach, but families were there with their little children! They shouldn't have to see that, and parents shouldn't have to explain it—or dodge the question.

"Someone should talk to them. That sheet has to come down." I walked about five feet farther, and it was as if God said, "*You* talk to them."

I stopped in the sand, looked at Jan, and said, "I've got to go talk with them. Someone has to tell them, and I think God wants me to."

Jan said she'd wait and pray.

We were both in our bathing suits, obviously not college girls but certainly not over the hill either! As I walked past the sand dunes, the sea oats waving in the gentle breeze, I noticed a rush for the house. Two young men saw me coming and ran for cover. Was it a guilty conscience, or did they think I was answering their ad? Who knows. At the time I didn't even stop to think about it. I watched as they peeped like little kids from behind the curtains.

I continued walking toward the door while I beckoned them with my finger to come out of the house. The door opened and we stood face to face. We had an interesting conversation, to say the least. I told them how I felt about the bed sheet and its message and why. They stammered, stuttered, and sputtered, trying to say they didn't mean anything by it. What was wrong with it anyway? It was just a joke.

Then I said, "Let me ask you a question. Would you want someone to lay your sister? And what about your mother? Would you want someone laying your mother? And when you get married and have a daughter, do you want some young guy like yourself to lay your daughter?"

Of course the response to each question was a shake of the head accompanied by a barely audible "no."

"Then, guys, why are you offering to lay a girl? Every girl is someone's daughter, many are someone's sister, and in all probability most will be someone's mother someday."

Let me ask, dear reader, have you considered your behavior in that light? In your lust, have you defrauded a woman, taken her virginity simply to satisfy your desire? What foolish, far-reaching things we do when we don't stop to consider God—and consider the future!

Please hear and embrace the truth of God's Word on this. Don't be a thief and rob a woman—and her future husband—of her virginity. And don't lose your virginity. Your wife has just as much right to marry a virgin as you do. God never has a double standard. Don't sacrifice the purity and sanctity of sex on the altar of your lust.

3

Caution: Sex Can Be Dangerous

What Are the Consequences of Sex Outside of Marriage?

A s I told the teens in Dalton, Georgia, that night, "When I read the directions on the can of Drano, I could have brushed them off, thinking, *Who are you to tell me what to do? This is my body; if I want to risk getting burned, I will. It probably wouldn't happen to me anyway because I can handle it! Don't put your restrictions on me. I don't need your advice!*

But you know what? These thoughts never entered my mind when I read the warnings on the can. I trusted the manufacturer. He made it; he knew his product.

Believe me, it's the same way with God. He *knows* His product.

You know what *you* think about sex, what your parents told you, what your friends say on the subject, what society says about it, and what our culture finds acceptable—or at least what it will condone. But what about the Manufacturer? Do you know what *the* Authority says about the subject?

We have seen that our sexuality is an unbelievably awesome gift from God, a gift to be enjoyed to the fullest measure within the confines of marriage. We'll explore with greater depth the dimensions of its beauty in the final chapter of this book. However, as I told you earlier, God says more about the negative side of sex than about the positive side. Why? Simply because He's a gracious and loving God, and He doesn't want you to be

burned, bruised, broken, disillusioned, and scarred for life because you listened to the philosophy of men. Our loving Father is brokenhearted that so
many have dived headfirst into the shimmering sea of sex, become caught in
the undercurrent of the culture, and now find themselves gasping for air as
they go down for the second time. He offers in His Word the lifeline, the rescue from certain death.

Thus we have to raise the following questions and seek out the answers—
God's answers rather than man's.

What about those who aren't married but have sex?

What about sex as…

the outcome of the heat of passion?

the expected climax to dinner and a date?

a means of hopefully luring another into a permanent
relationship?

a desperate cry for someone to care?

What about sex…

with someone who's already married?

with someone for hire to fulfill your fantasies?

that involves sharing a bed, living together…but not being
married?

with someone of the same sex?

What about it?

God tells us in Deuteronomy 22. Read the text, and every time you come
to the word *virgin* color it or put a big **V** over it. Also mark *lies* in another color,
such as brown, or circle it. By the way, I'd strongly suggest you read the text
aloud. It will help you get the point and be able to remember it better.

DEUTERONOMY 22:22-29

22 If a man is found lying with a married woman, then both of them shall

die, the man who lay with the woman, and the woman; thus you shall purge

the evil from Israel.

23 If there is a girl who is a virgin engaged to a man, and another man finds

her in the city and lies with her,

24 then you shall bring them both out to the gate of that city and you shall stone them to death; the girl, because she did not cry out in the city, and the man, because he has violated his neighbor's wife. Thus you shall purge the evil from among you.

25 But if in the field the man finds the girl who is engaged, and the man forces her and lies with her, then only the man who lies with her shall die.

26 But you shall do nothing to the girl; there is no sin in the girl worthy of death, for just as a man rises against his neighbor and murders him, so is this case.

27 When he found her in the field, the engaged girl cried out, but there was no one to save her.

28 If a man finds a girl who is a virgin, who is not engaged, and seizes her and lies with her and they are discovered,

29 then the man who lay with her shall give to the girl's father fifty shekels of silver, and she shall become his wife because he has violated her; he cannot divorce her all his days.

Remember, Deuteronomy is a book of the Law. The nation of Israel was to be governed by God, by His laws, statutes, precepts. This particular portion of the Law deals with situations that pertain to sexual crimes and immorality, providing specific instructions so that Israel would know exactly how to handle any circumstances that might arise. As you examine these verses from Deuteronomy 22 more closely, you'll gain an understanding of sex according to God. Therefore, to be sure you don't miss anything God has to say, state the situation described in each of the following verses and write out what is to be done and why.

verse 22

verses 23-24

verses 25-27

verses 28-29

Did you notice how many times the words *death* and *die* came up? Read back through these verses and put a tombstone like this ⌂ over every reference to *death* or *dying*.

Death seems like a rather extreme punishment for the people in the first three incidents, doesn't it? What is God's reason for putting them to death? The answer is there; it's given twice. Discover it for yourself, and each time you see it in the text, put a cloud around it like this ☁.

Now stop and think about this phrase: "Purge the evil from among you." According to God—note that I said, "according to *God*"—what is the evil? What is to be purged, gotten rid of? The answer is obvious, isn't it? It's sex outside of marriage.

What's the big deal? you may wonder. *Why does God call this evil?*

If you study history, you'll see that immorality is a chief contributor to the demise of a nation. British historian Arnold Toynbee said, "All civilizations which have been destroyed have destroyed themselves. They perished not from conquest from without, but from decay within.... Overemphasis on sex precedes the fall of a civilization."

Look at Rome and Greece. What moral standards were followed in the days preceding the downfalls of these once-great cultures? We'll examine these more closely later. For now let's consider a more current situation, right on our doorstep.

"The global statistics on HIV/AIDS are chilling," writes U.S. Senator Bill Frist, a godly man and an experienced surgeon. "Every thirteen minutes, seventy-two people die of AIDS somewhere in the world. That's three million people a year."[1]

It's obvious that sexual immorality not only demoralizes a culture, it destroys people. And because God is a God of life, not death, He prescribes extreme measures to stop it "dead" in its tracks!

GOD'S RIGHTEOUS JUDGMENT FOR SEXUAL SIN

Now let's go back to Deuteronomy 22 and take a closer look at the various scenarios God presents in this passage. The first deals with adultery: A man lies with a married woman. What's God's judgment? Death for both.

Stop for a moment and think about this. Do you realize how implementing this judgment would affect the population of many existing nations, including the United States of America? Think about the high incidence of adultery in this country, which has more churches and ministries, more Christian seminars and conferences, more Christian radio and television programs, more versions of the Bible, and more Christian books than any other nation in the world. According to the Barna Research Group, as we entered the third millennium, "born-again Christians are more likely to go through a marital split than are non-Christians."[2] What percentage of those "splits" involve adultery, do you suppose? Sobering, isn't it?

Now look at verse 23. In this second scenario, again both individuals are to be put to death. Why? Because their sexual act took place in the city, where the girl could have cried out and received help. Of course in those days it was safe to assume someone in the city would hear and come to her rescue.

When this passage speaks of the virgin being "engaged," it means she was promised by a covenant agreement in marriage to another man, as we talked about in the previous chapter. Although she had not yet consummated the marriage by their sexual union, a covenant had been violated that promised the woman to another. They had sex outside of marriage, and therefore both were to be stoned. This tells us two things: First, the man and the woman are held equally accountable for immorality; there is no partiality. And second, one cannot casually break a covenant and get away with it.

Doesn't such extreme punishment support what you read earlier in Hebrews 13:4—that "marriage is to be held in honor among all, and the marriage bed is to be undefiled; for fornicators and adulterers God will judge"? This is a New Testament verse, but God's precepts, His standards about sex and marriage don't change from Old Testament times to New Testament times—or even in our times. Sex outside of marriage will be judged. God said it, and when He says it He means it. What a difference it would make in our lives if we really understood that judgment always follows the flagrant disobedience of God's commands, even for those who live under grace.

In Old Testament times, Israel began as a nation under a theocracy, which means God determined how the nation was to be governed. He established the laws. He meted out the punishment. He ordained judges. And the people were to order their lives accordingly, carrying out all that He put in place. When God declared that the man and the woman were to be put to death, this was accepted as the decision of a righteous, omniscient God.

Times changed, however, even though God's Law and the precepts behind it did not. From New Testament times on, God's people, Jews and Gentiles alike, have been scattered across the world, citizens subject to a multiplicity of governments. Stoning a person because they break God's Law doesn't work anymore, because few governments recognize or honor the God of the Bible. Does this mean that fornicators and adulterers will escape God's judgment? No. God has other ways of judging immorality, as we will see later. His standards of righteousness are never altered by the culture, and His just judgment will be meted out in His way and in His time. He is God. He never abdicates His throne.

In the third situation we looked at in Deuteronomy 22, because the virgin is taken sexually in the country where no one could hear her cries for help, only the man is put to death. Why? He violated a betrothed woman, one promised to another. Notice that once again the man is not excused from accountability. Compare this with the current view, so prevalent since the sexual revolution, that all men are sexually driven animals and therefore cannot be held accountable for acting on their hormonal surges. As you think about this, consider also how the enforcement of God's prescribed punishment would protect so many women from rape. Rapists would be put to death—and those who were tempted would be greatly deterred if they thought conviction might mean losing their life rather than receiving only a short prison sentence.

Now let's see what God says is to be done in scenario number four. Read Deuteronomy 22:28-29 again. Did you notice there's no death sentence? Why? Because the virgin is not engaged.

So what is the man to do? Write out your answer.

What does this tell you about the importance of virginity, about God's view of sex outside of marriage?

According to Deuteronomy 22:29, two single persons who engage in illicit sex are to marry and *never* divorce. You see the same thing in Deuteronomy 22:19. It's like the old song says: "Love and marriage, love and marriage go together like a horse and carriage…. You can't have one without the other." My, how times have changed! We've placed the cart before the horse—with no intention of hooking them up.

In God's Law, is a virgin *always* required to marry the man who took her virginity? Let's read Exodus 22:16-17 and see what it says.

16 If a man seduces a virgin who is not engaged, and lies with her, he must pay a dowry for her to be his wife.

17 If her father absolutely refuses to give her to him, he shall pay money equal to the dowry for virgins.

According to the whole counsel of God, comparing scripture with scripture and seeking out everything the Law has to say on this issue, there is an alternative to marriage. According to these verses in Exodus, what is it?

THE QUESTION OF SAFE SEX

That fourth scenario in Deuteronomy 22—where the woman is not engaged—is most common to our day, isn't it? And yet the instruction for the two to be married has been abandoned—and the man involved rarely pays a penalty for his actions.

Our society generally accepts sex under any circumstances—

    whenever,

        however,

            whatever,

                with whomever.

Sex among singles is no longer a covert affair. Society has abandoned purity in favor of "safe" sex!

And yet, according to God, is there any such thing as safe sex if you're not married? It's a valid question in light of a culture that really doesn't know what God says on the subject, isn't it? So many are at risk because all they know about this issue is what other people think or believe. Since sex is God's invention, it's not safe or wise to rely on the opinions of people. They're like the grass of the field—here a relatively short time, then cut down as a whole new culture is cultivated.

God, however, is eternal and immutable. He never changes, and someday we all shall stand before Him. In light of that, we certainly need to know what God says about sex outside marriage. Is it ever safe?

First Thessalonians 4 has our answer. However, before we look at it, let me tell you something about the times in which Paul wrote this letter. I think having a little background will help you appreciate and better understand why the issue is addressed.

The Greco-Roman world in New Testament times—in the first century A.D.—was a society that held pretty much the same sexual standards we have today. In other words, virtually none! Though our depravity is not yet quite as blatant, we nearly rival the Roman Empire, and we will soon find ourselves on totally equal footing. Unless, of course, the church wakes up and turns from its apostasy, and we revive our understanding of what sex is according to the Bible, begin to live accordingly, and proclaim His truth "in season and out of season," as Paul said in his second letter to Timothy.

Considering where most of the world stands today morally, to call for purity in our sexual conduct is most certainly "out of season"! Our modesty is gone, nudity is in. Just watch television, pick up a magazine, observe the latest in fashion. Our morals have disintegrated. Men in the public eye—especially athletes, rock stars and other music artists, and actors—have individually slept with hundreds of women. This is common knowledge because it's often talked about by the men themselves. The marriage bed has been defiled. Marriage is no longer honored as a covenant. In our society's twisted thinking, it's best to be sure you're sexually compatible with someone before you bother building a relationship. And even many of those who aren't "sleeping around" believe that it's better to live together before marriage, just to be sure the relationship is going to work.

Like the United States today, first-century Rome had turned away from the moral values it once embraced as an empire. Sex not only hung heavy in the air, its dust had settled everywhere. There were no restraints. Here's what one historian has to say:

> Roman literature, written by its own authors such as Juvenal, Ovid, Marial, and Catullus, indicates that sexual activity between men and women had become highly promiscuous and essentially depraved before and during the time that the Christians appeared in Roman society. By the first and second centuries after Christ, undefiled sexual intercourse, along with marital faithfulness, had essentially disappeared. Not only were adultery and fornication common, but people engaged in all sorts of sexual methods, many of them obscene. These sexual practices were shamelessly illustrated on household items such as oil lamps, bowls, cups and vases.[3]

Heterosexual acts were depicted on mosaics, drawings, and other artifacts. Oral and group sex—two men with one woman, two men and two women copulating—were there for all to view, even the children of Roman society.[4] Another historian noted, "There was nothing in which they [the Romans] did not indulge or which they thought was a disgrace."[5]

These depraved sexual practices were as prevalent in the lives of the Roman emperors as they were among the general population. You may be familiar with the Roman saying *qualis rex, talis grex*—"like king, like people." It reminds one of the Clinton administration, when the whole world discovered that the president of the United States had oral sex with a White House intern. And how did America in general respond? They decided that what he did in his private life was of no concern to the nation. By declining to remove President Clinton from office, our officials sent a message that immorality doesn't matter. America condoned this man's sin for a variety of reasons, one of which was that Americans live just as immorally as the president—and they didn't want anyone judging their behavior.

They didn't realize that Someone already has judged it.

Let's get back to the culture in which Paul wrote his epistles to the Thessalonians. Sex not only permeated their society, it was an integral part of their religious worship. They believed that the gods who governed the yield of their crops would be more generous if worshipers visited their temples and engaged in sex with the temple prostitutes, male and female.

Then the message of Christianity invaded this Gentile world, bringing the teachings of the Old Testament and the commandments of Jesus Christ spoken through His apostles. The two worlds clashed like cymbals. Men and women who came to know Jesus Christ discovered that God had clear moral standards for them, and because they were now set apart for God, the old life with its immorality had to go. They had been delivered from the kingdom of darkness; now they were to walk in God's light. They were no longer to live as they had before, but the principles and commandments that bound them were difficult to understand and seemed out of place in Rome's culture.

Thus Paul wrote to the church he established in Thessalonica, a city in Macedonia, now part of Greece. In this letter—the New Testament book of 1 Thessalonians—Paul commended the new believers for the example they set in Macedonia and Achaia and many other places where the news of their conversion resounded. Paul and his ministry partners, Silvanus and Timothy, were filled with joy because their new converts had withstood the persecution that came their way because of the gospel. Such endurance, despite affliction, was proof to these three men that their labor among the Thessalonians was not in vain. The Thessalonians had turned to God from their idols and were serving the living and true God, waiting for His Son to return to earth from heaven. Their faith held; it was genuine!

Now Paul wrote to urge the Thessalonians to excel even more in their walk with Christ. It is in this exhortation that we learn about the importance of one's sexual conduct as a child of God.

Read 1 Thessalonians 4:1-8, printed out for you below. As you do, either circle or color in a specific color of your choosing every *you* or *your* as it refers to *the Thessalonians*. In doing this you'll see not only what God said to them but also what He says to you. This is the purpose of the Word of God; it's our textbook for life. Through its pages you and I can know truth—what is real and certain—so we can live accordingly.

1 THESSALONIANS 4:1-8

1 Finally then, brethren, we request and exhort you in the Lord Jesus, that as you received from us instruction as to how you ought to walk and please God (just as you actually do walk), that you excel still more.

2 For you know what commandments we gave you by the authority of the Lord Jesus.

3 For this is the will of God, your sanctification; that is, that you abstain from sexual immorality;

4 that each of you know how to possess his own vessel in sanctification and honor,

5 not in lustful passion, like the Gentiles who do not know God;

6 and that no man transgress and defraud his brother in the matter because the Lord is the avenger in all these things, just as we also told you before and solemnly warned you.

⁷ For God has not called us for the purpose of impurity, but in sanctification.

⁸ So, he who rejects this is not rejecting man but the God who gives His

Holy Spirit to you.

What did you see in marking these references to *the Thessalonians?* In the space provided, list any *you* or *your* that gives you insight into what we call "the 5 *W*s and an *H*"—who, what, when, where, why, and how. For example, *who* are they? *What* are they doing or *what* are they to do? Does it tell you *when* or *where* something is to happen or be done? *Why*—what's the reason? Is there anything that tells you *how?*

Before we look at what you saw in the text, let me ask if you noticed the word *sanctification?* The words *sanctification, sanctify, saint,* and *holy* all come from the same root word in the Koine Greek, the common language of New Testament times. It simply means "to be set apart, consecrated, and separated for God's use."

Go through the text again and color the word *sanctification* in a way that it can be quickly seen and identified. If you want to use a symbol, use a halo like this: ⬯. Also mark every reference to anything that has to do with their sexual behavior, such as *sexual passion* or *sexual immorality.* Pick a color such as red, or mark it with a big **S.** When you finish, list below what you learn from marking *sanctification* and from marking the references to *sex.* It may seem redundant because of the list you already made from marking the references to *the Thessalonians,* but it will be helpful to write it out again from a different perspective.

It couldn't be any clearer, could it? The will of God for every child of God is that he or she abstain from sexual immorality. The word for immorality in the Greek is *porneia* and refers to fornication or any sexual sin. We will look at the various sexual sins later. Suffice it to say, the child of God is not to live like people who do not know God, in lustful passions of any form. Rather we are instructed to know how to possess our "vessel," our body, in sanctification, holiness, and honor. To act out our desires is to go against the will of God. To act out sexually with another person is to transgress, to go against that person and defraud him or her. When you defraud someone, you take advantage of or violate that person.

That's quite a statement, isn't it? Have you ever thought of having sex with a person to whom you are not married as defrauding the person? According to God, that's exactly what you're doing. You're using that person to gratify your desires, your passions. Sex outside marriage is one of the most self-centered acts you can participate in. You are asking, cajoling, persuading, coercing, or forcing another person to sin against God. And God doesn't like that, my friend. In His eyes it is an abomination.

Yet somehow we get the insane impression that we are exempt from judgment! Our postmodern culture has embraced the lie that we can disconnect the past from the present and the future, that somehow we can avoid the consequences for our actions. Or we think that if by some slim chance a negative consequence follows, we'll be able to handle it.

A DEADLY GAME

As I share this with you, Magic Johnson comes to mind—the beloved basketball superstar whose HIV infection stunned the world in 1991. *Newsweek* told his story:

> Word that Magic Johnson had tested positive for HIV, the virus that
> causes AIDS, whipped around the country last Thursday like a palm-
> stinging Magic Johnson pass. The stages of grief in America now
> move quickly, it seems, from denial to CNN. A few hours after the
> first news leak, the 32-year-old superstar appeared at a televised press
> conference, saying, "Because of the HIV virus I have obtained I will
> have to announce my retirement from the Lakers today." He admitted

having been "naive" about AIDS and added, "Here I am saying it can happen to anybody, even me, Magic Johnson."[6]

After Magic Johnson announced his condition, the National AIDS Hotline lit up with forty thousand calls, more than ten times their usual daily count of thirty-eight hundred. Suddenly others were aware that if it could happen to a superstar, it could happen to them.

Sex outside of marriage is a deadly game of roulette where there are more bullets in the gun than you thought.

"But wait a minute," you say. "We're not being promiscuous. We're only sleeping with each other. It's okay because we're in love and we plan to get married." Then you'd better get married right away and not do anything more sexually until you do. God is very strict about this. I am sure you noticed verse 6 in our passage from 1 Thessalonians: God is the "avenger" of anyone and everyone who gets sexually involved outside of marriage.

Paul is giving the Thessalonians—and you and me—fair warning. A solemn warning. He's letting us know that we can't go against God's Word in the sphere of sex and get away with it. If you are a child of God, you are to abstain—stay away from—sexual immorality.

And what if you don't agree with that? This is not something I came up with, my friend. You saw it for yourself. God said it, and He said it very plainly. Look at verse 8. God will deal with you.

Or what if you share this truth with another person and that person doesn't agree? Whose issue is it? It's that person's and God's. God will deal with him or her.

In light of this I have to ask, Where are you in respect to God's command to abstain from sexual immorality? Is there anything you need to respond to? Anything you need to correct—to change and ask forgiveness for?

After speaking to college students at a Christmas conference for Campus Crusade for Christ, I received a letter from a guy that really touched my heart. Let me share part of it with you.

I was blown away when I heard you speak. I did not realize the extent of your powerful testimony that dealt with sexual immorality. It soon became clear that this issue is close to your heart (God's Word no less), as your words began to pierce my heart like arrows.

You see at the time my girlfriend and I were in a terrible habit of overstepping our boundaries. We set boundaries early on in our relationship that demonstrated our desire to uphold God's best for our relationship. These boundaries lasted for roughly twelve months. As our relationship approached one year in length, we began to struggle much more with our flesh.

After attending the conference in Knoxville, it soon became very clear that the Lord was speaking to my heart. As the conviction took its course, I began to realize that sexual immorality (Galatians 5:19) was not simply having intercourse (or coming close to the action thereof); instead it was compromising God's desire for our bodies to be treated as temples of worship unto him (Romans 12:1-2).

As I brought back to our relationship my convictions from the conference, as well as from tapes of your talk, it became clear to us both that we needed to seek God's redemption and to rely on His strength to obtain purity in our relationship.

In the past eight months we have come to have purity and peace like never before. We have grown in our love and following of Christ as well as our respect for one another. We are now engaged and plan in eight months to share in the sacrament of marriage and unite as one flesh. We have both promised one another, as a sign of our desire for purity until the proper time, as well as simply avoiding the opportunity for temptation, to avoid any and all forms of kissing and physical contact (with the exception of holding hands)....

What an awesome wedding night this couple will have! No guilt. No regrets. Instead, there'll be a beauty, a purity, a special quality about it. They'll enjoy a sweet sense of God's blessing that would be impossible if they had not heard and obeyed God's Word.

How odd this couple may seem in a society like ours. The statistics at the turn of the millennium showed that those who considered themselves Christians, born again, were as immoral as those who didn't even claim to know God. Can you imagine how obeying just this one passage of Scripture would change the church and impact society? The world would see that purity until marriage—and within marriage—is possible, and very rewarding.

Do you realize that those who live together before they get married have a higher divorce rate than those who wait until marriage? Could it be that if we'll just listen to God, we might be onto something about a marriage that lasts?

So what is the answer to the question I asked just before we studied 1 Thessalonians 4—Is there any such thing as "safe" sex? How would you answer, as you listen to what God says about sex?

Finally, because I care about you, I have to ask, How are you going to live in light of what God Himself has to say on the subject? It would be good to write down your thoughts or commitment.

4

Beware of Taking
Forbidden Fruit

Why Does Sex So Often Bring Shame and Guilt?

I s it enough to say sex is for marriage and leave it at that? Say nothing
more? Wrap it up and tag it like a Christmas present, "Do Not Open Until
Marriage"?

Unfortunately that isn't enough, because of an incident that occurred
almost six thousand years ago. It's recorded in the book of beginnings, Genesis. Believing a lie from the devil, Adam and Eve, the mother and father of us
all, thought they could shake God and become like God themselves. When
they didn't heed God's instruction, choosing instead to eat the forbidden fruit
of the tree of the knowledge of good and evil, hell literally broke loose. The
lake of fire created for the devil and his angels would now also be occupied
by man.[1]

Adam and Eve sinned; they chose to walk their own way, to do their own
thing, to disobey God. They didn't listen to Him. Having become like God,
knowing good and evil for themselves, they would now decide if, when, and
to what degree they wanted to honor God as God in their lives. It was a fateful day.

The Bible tells us that sin entered the world through one man, Adam,
and death through sin, so that death spread to all men because all men
sinned.[2] Although Adam and Eve were made in God's image,[3] the children
they bore were just like dad, bearing Adam's image.[4] Adam and Eve gave
birth to little sinners, and they in turn gave birth to sinners.[5]

Sin spread like the plague, invading humanity's gene pool. King David would write, "In sin my mother conceived me" (Psalm 51:5). What was the solution? How could humanity, left to its own devices, be kept from self-destructing? By means of the Law.

The Law not only set boundaries to protect and restrain people, it also defined unacceptable behavior and set forth the consequences of choosing to transgress God's holy commandments. This is the reason the Bible has more to say about sex than that it's only for the married. As with any responsible manufacturer, God put warnings on the label and described what was to be done if they weren't heeded. God is well aware of the power of the sex drive, of the weakness of our flesh, of the desires stirred by the eyes, and of the passion, the images, and the perversions that can be conjured in minds schooled by those who do not fear God.

Therefore God addresses the subject of sex throughout His pages of Holy Writ, giving us exactly the information we need, but no more. Too much information can sometimes be destructive because it leads your thoughts where they don't need to go, where it isn't healthy to go. This is what is happening with sex education in our schools. One of my grandsons told me that the sex education curriculum introduced him and his classmates to things they had never thought about or been curious about. Officials in Britain reported that all their efforts at sex education have not increased the use of condoms or decreased the number of abortions. Rather, they believe that teaching children and teens about sex has resulted in increased sexual activity.

True sex education involves simply teaching what is right and what is wrong—according to God's Word—and the consequences of one's actions. Anything less will not deter us from immorality.

So what does God say about sex, beyond the fact that it should be reserved for marriage? Let's begin with the Law where God lays out the parameters and spells out clearly what is not acceptable in sex.

GOD'S PERSPECTIVE ON ADULTERY AND COVETOUSNESS

When God summarizes the Law in the Ten Commandments, it's evident He understands the battles we face as we live in these bodies of flesh. The nation of Israel, to whom He gave these commandments, lived among people whose gods not only permitted promiscuity and infidelity but also, according to their legends, participated in these things themselves. If you study world religions, you'll see that no god is as strict as the one and only true God. The gods of men's devising are so like men.

Two of the Ten Commandments recorded in Exodus 20 deal with our sexuality. The first is the seventh commandment: "You shall not commit adultery" (verse 14). The Hebrew word translated as "adultery" is *na'ap*. The root of the word represents "sexual intercourse with the wife or betrothed of another man."6 In Ezekiel 16:38, the *King James Version* translates *na'ap* as the verb "break wedlock."

Wedlock—what a word! It's quite a picture, isn't it? In old English, *wedd* refers to the vow. Marriage locks us into our mate by a vow separating us from all others sexually. Figuratively, *na'ap* means "to commit apostasy," which is interesting because apostasy implies turning away from something you once embraced. How aptly these definitions show us the gravity of violating a marriage covenant.

The tenth and final commandment also deals with our sexuality. Read it aloud; hearing its words will help you remember them: "You shall not covet your neighbor's house; you shall not covet your neighbor's wife or his male servant or his female servant or his ox or his donkey or anything that belongs to your neighbor" (Exodus 20:17).

To covet means to delight in something. God doesn't want us delighting in what is not ours. Have you ever done that? I have. In my pain, my emptiness, my loneliness, I'd find myself admiring a man, appreciating his character and abilities, finding him attractive, delighting in him. Then I'd begin wondering what it would be like to be married to him.

What was happening? Coveting. As children of God, you and I are not to go there. It's sin. It's violating God's commandment and putting ourselves in a most dangerous place.

And don't think, *There's no way. Not me!* Consider what one pastor wrote:

> I thought it was innocent at the time, so we spent a lot of time
> together. She'd sit in my office, and we'd talk. At times she told me
> about the difficulties in her marriage, and I counseled her. But I
> should have stopped right there; I was filling a need I had no right to
> fill. We never touched, we never kissed, we never even verbalized our

underlying feelings. But there was a definite attraction, and I liked
that vibe. For me it was all in my mind, but it progressed from there.[7]

God knows that when we begin coveting, we begin imagining. Then we
begin toying with the situation, getting close just to be close until eventually
we are seduced by our desires, our emotions, our dreams, our supposed
needs—and we break the seventh commandment by committing adultery.

Turning to someone who is not ours, rationalizing it all the way, building our case, justifying our actions—none of that will stand in the court of
heaven. The gods of men do things like this, but the One who is absolutely
righteous strictly forbids the lusting after and the taking of another person's
mate.

It's interesting to read what happened after the commandments were
given. Let's look at it. When you read these verses look for the word *test* and
underline it when you come to it.

EXODUS 20:18-20

[18] All the people perceived the thunder and the lightning flashes and the

sound of the trumpet and the mountain smoking; and when the people saw it,

they trembled and stood at a distance.

[19] Then they said to Moses, "Speak to us yourself and we will listen; but let

not God speak to us, or we will die."

[20] Moses said to the people, "Do not be afraid; for God has come in order

to test you, and in order that the fear of Him may remain with you, so that

you may not sin."

How was God testing them? The commandments are a test. They let you
know what God requires, then leave the choice to you. The test is passed, the
grade made when you do what God says. When you choose to disbelieve—
which is synonymous with disobedience—you fail the test. Such behavior
shows you don't fear God, trust Him, honor Him, respect Him. We fear God

when we do what He says regardless of how His commands clash with our desires, our rationale. It's the fear of God that keeps us from sin. Such respect, such fear is very healthy, for sin always brings death in its wake.

As I write this, file folders full of tragic stories of adultery lay strewn across my desk, the floor, the chair. Stories of lives shattered like the window on a car door, broken into a hundred tiny pieces that can never be whole again. Pieces of all shapes and sizes clinging pitifully together but ready to collapse at a breath. Stories of betrayal, the rage of anger, the lashing back or cowering under the bullying accusations. The sense of failure, of guilt that sends you rummaging through the attic of your mind, opening boxes of the past, sorting through one memory after another in a flurry of emotion, digging deeper and deeper, grabbing, groping, trying to find out where it began, why it began. Mumbling to yourself, *What did I do? What was I thinking? How could I be so stupid? If only I…*

Then you sit down in a heap, bombarded with darts of guilt because of your affair: *What about the children? The children! Oh, dear Lord. And our parents? The neighbors? What will they say to each other? Our friends—whose friends will they be? And what about the people at work? at church?*

Oh, the tragedy of adultery, of desiring another and giving way to your passions. Passions so fleeting! Passing pleasures that will last only for a season, because "fornicators and adulterers God will judge" (Hebrews 13:4).

Never forget, beloved: Sin is always a choice—a choice for which you and I will be held accountable. When you choose not to obey, not to respect God, remember Whom you are going against, finite one.

In Leviticus, God calls His people to be holy, for He is holy. To be holy is to be consecrated to God, sanctified, set apart for His pleasure. From Genesis to Revelation, God stresses over and over that He is the Creator of the heavens and the earth and all that is in them. God created us. We exist because of Him, we exist through Him; therefore we ought to be set apart to Him.

WHAT ELSE IS FORBIDDEN?

So the Law tells us that to desire another person's mate or to have sex with a married person is a transgression of God's commandments. Further limitations to our sexual activities and preferences are recorded for us in the twentieth chapter of Leviticus, a portion of which is printed out on the following page.

As you read this biblical text, underline everything that is forbidden and put a drawing of a tombstone like this ⌂ over every reference to *death*, just as you did earlier.

Read this passage aloud, carefully. It's critical that you know for yourself what is written in the Bible. God is a perspicuous God. *Perspicuous* means "plain to the understanding because of the clarity and precision of the presentation." God really wants you to understand Him, to know exactly what He says. And of course He wants you to believe Him. And rightfully so, because God never lies.

LEVITICUS 20

7 You shall consecrate yourselves therefore and be holy, for I am the LORD your God.

8 You shall keep My statutes and practice them; I am the LORD who sanctifies you.

9 If there is anyone who curses his father or his mother, he shall surely be put to death; he has cursed his father or his mother, his bloodguiltiness is upon him.

10 If there is a man who commits adultery with another man's wife, one who commits adultery with his friend's wife, the adulterer and the adulteress shall surely be put to death.

11 If there is a man who lies with his father's wife, he has uncovered his father's nakedness; both of them shall surely be put to death, their bloodguiltiness is upon them.

12 If there is a man who lies with his daughter-in-law, both of them shall surely be put to death; they have committed incest, their bloodguiltiness is upon them.

Let me interrupt your reading for a moment. I want to be sure you and I understand the terminology God uses. *Incest* is having sexual relations with a person you are related to by bloodline or through marriage. The Hebrew word used here expresses the idea of a mixing of unnatural elements. For instance, a father using his daughter or his son for his sexual satisfaction or a brother engaging in sexual acts with his sister—both of these are unnatural. Since incest is a major problem all over the world, we will deal with it in a more thorough way later in the book. Right now we're gaining an overview as to what is unacceptable to God.

13 If there is a man who lies with a male as those who lie with a woman, both of them have committed a detestable act; they shall surely be put to death. Their bloodguiltiness is upon them.

Obviously, this describes homosexuality, which, according to Romans 1:26-27, would also include women with women, lesbianism. We'll also talk about this in greater depth later.

However, if you are involved in homosexuality or lesbianism, you'll want to take an objective look at the Bible. You need to discover for yourself what it says about this, rather than relying on another person's interpretation, because according to the verse you just read, it could be a matter of life and death. You certainly don't want to leave that in another person's hands.

14 If there is a man who marries a woman and her mother, it is immorality; both he and they shall be burned with fire, so that there will be no immorality in your midst.

There's that word *immorality* again. The Hebrew word for it is *zimmah,* which means "wickedness." In the New Testament the word translated as *immorality* is *porneia,* which, as we saw earlier, refers to any illicit sexual activity outside of marriage.

¹⁵ If there is a man who lies with an animal, he shall surely be put to death; you shall also kill the animal.

¹⁶ If there is a woman who approaches any animal to mate with it, you shall kill the woman and the animal; they shall surely be put to death. Their blood-guiltiness is upon them.

Sex with animals is called *bestiality.* The term *incest* is also sometimes used to describe bestiality, since the root meaning of *incest* is "not being pure," a mixing of elements.

¹⁷ If there is a man who takes his sister, his father's daughter or his mother's daughter, so that he sees her nakedness and she sees his nakedness, it is a disgrace; and they shall be cut off in the sight of the sons of their people. He has uncovered his sister's nakedness; he bears his guilt.

Let me stop for a minute and explain this term "nakedness" or "uncovering the nakedness" of a person. The word *uncover—galah* in Hebrew— means "to denude someone," uncover them, especially in a disgraceful sense. Sometimes this would be done to captives to utterly humiliate them.

Nakedness, ervah, carries the idea of exposing the genitals of another, their sexual organs. Therefore uncovering the nakedness refers to the indecent, shameful exposure of someone. Such exposure is acceptable only in the marriage bed, and there it is to be delighted in. Later we'll discuss the Old Testament's Song of Solomon, and you'll understand what I am saying.

So what does the reference to "uncovering nakedness" tell you about bare-it-all clubs with so-called exotic dancing, pornography on the Internet or anywhere else, nudity in the movies or on television, magazines like *Playboy* and *Hustler,* and other forms of "entertainment" that focus on the human body? This scripture begins to set some very definite parameters, doesn't it?

[18] If there is a man who lies with a menstruous woman and uncovers her nakedness, he has laid bare her flow, and she has exposed the flow of her blood; thus both of them shall be cut off from among their people.

[19] You shall also not uncover the nakedness of your mother's sister or of your father's sister, for such a one has made naked his blood relative; they will bear their guilt.

[20] If there is a man who lies with his uncle's wife he has uncovered his uncle's nakedness; they will bear their sin. They will die childless.

[21] If there is a man who takes his brother's wife, it is abhorrent; he has uncovered his brother's nakedness. They will be childless.

[22] You are therefore to keep all My statutes and all My ordinances and do them, so that the land to which I am bringing you to live will not spew you out.

So what is forbidden in these verses? Adultery. Incest. Homosexuality. Bestiality. It's quite a lineup, isn't it? But are they problems today? All of them? Yes, they're often friends, calling each other to join their salacious party. Each is being practiced today in ways and forms you and I probably could never conceive of.

The question I have to ask you out of loving concern is this: Are you battling any of these things? Possibly you've been involved in one of these sexual activities. Or maybe it's a matter of your mind. You've let your thoughts dwell on what such experiences might be like, allowing your imagination to feed your desire.

Is this why you're reading this book? Because you want to know what to do with the feelings you have? the passions boiling within? the preferences you're drawn to?

Maybe you or a friend has been told it's all right, that your behaviors or inclinations are acceptable—it's just the way you're made. But you wonder…

Why does it bring shame, guilt, bondage?

Why doesn't it satisfy anymore?
    Why, deep down inside, am I repulsed by myself?
        Why do I have to go to such extremes to get satisfied?
    Why is society so divided over some of these sexual practices or
preferences?
        Why are those who oppose various sexual preferences called
        "phobics" of one sort or another?

Well, my friend, let's stop for just a moment and think about what you have seen in Exodus and Leviticus.

If you were to go strictly by what you read just in these few verses, if you took them at face value, what would you have to say about how God looks at these sexual expressions? Look at them and write out your thoughts.

What does God say about them?

Are there any consequences to this behavior? Count the tombstones. What names are on the tombstones?

The message is pretty clear, isn't it? It needs no special interpretation. There are no hidden meanings here, no symbolism to be deciphered. God has spoken very plainly. This is His mind, His heart in respect to these sexual behaviors: Death for adulterers. Death for those committing incest. Death for homosexuality. Death for bestiality.

It sounds so harsh, doesn't it? And it is. It is. But what does it tell you about the seriousness of these things? The consequences are grave. However, you need not despair. If you're involved in any of these, there's good news: There *is* a way out, a way of escape. We'll come to it soon, so keep reading.

HOPE FOR THE CAPTIVE

If a relative has violated you in an act of incest, I know it must be a relief to know that God does not condone or support such behavior. It's an abomination to Him. Just know, however, that if you are the victim of someone's sexual aggression, *you* are not guilty, even if the act brought you pleasure. We must remember that our bodies are designed to respond to stimulus. However, just because we feel pleasure doesn't mean we are guilty. The guilt is upon the instigator, the perpetrator—not the victim.

And what if you or a friend or a family member has participated in these things willfully? Does reading what God says put fear into your heart? That's a good sign. Does it make you feel lost, condemned, damned? Do you believe you're without hope? helpless? Do you wish you could undo what you've done?

Oh, beloved—may I call you that on God's behalf? It's a legitimate call because God *does* love you right where you are, even though you're involved in these things and He hates them because they will eventually destroy you. Beloved, there's some good news I want to share with you from 1 Corinthians 6:9-11.

Let's look at it. As you do, mark every *you*.

9 Or do you not know that the unrighteous will not inherit the kingdom of God? Do not be deceived; neither fornicators, nor idolaters, nor adulterers, nor effeminate, nor homosexuals,

10 nor thieves, nor the covetous, nor drunkards, nor revilers, nor swindlers, will inherit the kingdom of God.

11 Such were some of you; but you were washed, but you were sanctified, but you were justified in the name of the Lord Jesus Christ and in the Spirit of our God.

This is such an enlightening passage. List below everything you learn from marking *you*.

Did you see the *were*? It's an awesome word of hope in this context. You'll want to underline it. What does it tell you—or what is its message to anyone else you know who might think there's no hope of ever changing?

God is in the business of setting us *free*! Free from sin and from the bondage it brings to our lives. He's the Redeemer, the One who buys us out of the slave market of sin, never to be sold again! Because He's the Creator, He's able to make us new creations, change our character, make us again into His image. He does it one way and only one way: through His Son, Jesus Christ.

When you truly repent (have a change of mind) and accept Jesus Christ—really believe He is the Son of God, the only One who can save you from sin—then God moves into action.

Just as you saw in 1 Corinthians 6, God washes you, makes you clean, sets you apart for Himself (that's sanctification). He removes all condemnation and declares you absolved of your sin and therefore in right standing with Him (that's justification).

I want you to know all this because anytime you begin to feel there's *no* hope—*no* way out, *no* cure, *no* future, because you see yourself locked in that sexual sin—just know that with God you need not feel despair.

God has a cure. You must listen to Him, not to your feelings. In Romans 5, God tells us that when we were sinners, when we were ungodly, when we were helpless, when we were His enemies, He loved us and moved on our behalf to change all that through His Son. God did it through the death of Jesus Christ in full payment for your sins and through Jesus' resurrection from the dead—His proof that your sins were paid for in full and therefore you can live with Him forever.

COURTING GOD'S JUDGMENT

Now let's get back to Leviticus. This time let's look at chapter 18, where you'll find the same sins as those we saw in Leviticus 20, but in this passage you gain a deeper understanding of God's perspective on these sins and the impact immorality has on a nation.

In Leviticus 18 God uses some terms not used in Leviticus 20: *abomination* (abominable), *perversion,* and *defile* (defiled). Mark these three terms, or any variations of them, each in a distinctive way. Put a big **A** over *abomination(s)* and draw a big **D** over each occurrence of *perversion* and *defile.*

LEVITICUS 18:22-30

²² You shall not lie with a male as one lies with a female; it is an abomination.

²³ Also you shall not have intercourse with any animal to be defiled with it,

nor shall any woman stand before an animal to mate with it; it is a perversion.

²⁴ Do not defile yourselves by any of these things; for by all these the

nations which I am casting out before you have become defiled.

²⁵ For the land has become defiled, therefore I have brought its punishment

upon it, so the land has spewed out its inhabitants.

²⁶ But as for you, you are to keep My statutes and My judgments and shall

not do any of these abominations, neither the native, nor the alien who

sojourns among you

²⁷ (for the men of the land who have been before you have done all these

abominations, and the land has become defiled);

²⁸ so that the land will not spew you out, should you defile it, as it has spewed out the nation which has been before you.

²⁹ For whoever does any of these abominations, those persons who do so shall be cut off from among their people.

³⁰ Thus you are to keep My charge, that you do not practice any of the abominable customs which have been practiced before you, so as not to defile yourselves with them; I am the LORD your God.

Now look at the words *abomination* and *perversion* that you marked. What sins does God characterize with these terms? List them below.

This kind of sexual behavior perverts what God intended for sex; it is unnatural and therefore an abomination. The Hebrew word for *abomination* is *tow'ebah,* which means "morally disgusting." Such things are abhorrent to God and should be to us—not only because of what an individual does to himself by sinning in this way but also because of what it does to society, because sin does not stand still. Stop and think for a moment about all the lives taken by AIDS spread through immorality. What about sexually trans-mitted diseases?

Now go back and look in Leviticus 18 at every place you marked *defile* or *defiled.* What do you see?

According to this passage, it's not only God's chosen people whom He deals with in this way. Read verses 24 and 28 again. What do you see? Write it down.

God said He would use Israel as His rod of judgment against the Canaanites and would drive them from the land because of their sexual perversions. But it wouldn't stop there; He would do the same to Israel if her people became involved in these sexual perversions.

And that's exactly what happened! Israel didn't listen to God. Her people entered into spiritual and physical idolatry and adultery. Consequently, God raised up the Babylonians against them, and they devastated the land of Israel and deported the people. Israel was spewed from their land. Not once, but twice! In A.D. 70, Titus, the legendary Roman general, razed Israel to the ground. How ironic that God used an immoral general of an immoral empire to drive them out!

God will not tolerate the perversion of what He meant to be beautiful and sacred. Thus He pronounces death for the individual unrestrained in his lusts. God wants the abomination stopped before the person becomes a predator upon others and the abhorrent behavior eventually spreads throughout the nation, requiring God's judgment upon all the people. Look at the prime example in the destruction of Sodom and Gomorrah.

DESTROYED BY A LIE

For decades now, America has been courting God's judgment for its tolerance of sexual perversion, and increasingly so since Alfred Kinsey's work on *The Sexual Behavior of the Human Male* in 1948 and *The Sexual Behavior of the Human Female* in 1953. Kinsey's published "findings" laid the foundation for a revolution in society's views on sexuality—but those findings were seriously flawed.

In her book *Kinsey: Crimes and Consequences,*[8] Dr. Judith A. Reisman reveals the depths to which people will go in order to satisfy and justify their perversions. This thoroughly documented, irrefutable work unveils the skewed and fraudulent research that was endorsed by Indiana University's Kinsey Institute.

Dr. Reisman's research revealed that Kinsey conducted human experiments in a soundproof laboratory built to his specifications at Indiana University and that the sexual abuse of at least 317 infants (some as young as five months) and young boys was a scientific protocol for Kinsey's 1948 report. Based on Kinsey's pedophile experiment, children are now considered sexual beings from birth.

In his biography of Kinsey, University of Houston historian James Jones said the sex researcher was not the "dogged, disinterested scientist he claimed to be." Instead, Jones says, Kinsey was a "closeted homosexual and masochist who was obsessed with sex and driven by his own sexual demons to free his fellow citizens from the grip of Victorian repression."[9] Our nation's descent from morality to sexual anarchy finds its impetus in Kinsey's agenda, which, according to his associate Pomeroy's book in 1973, was to undermine the Judeo-Christian ethic.[10] American common law contains within it the biblical principles of God's law, but Kinsey wanted to free man from God's protections.

Conceived in hell's test tube, Kinsey's pseudoresearch not only spawned the sexual revolution of the 1960s, it continues to destroy the moral fiber of this nation through its influence on our educational and judicial systems. His distorted research became the basis of the laws that have been and are still being enacted in the state legislatures and justice systems of America. The laws have been so altered that they free the sexual offenders and jeopardize the innocent. "Kinsey's more than 6,000 citations in law, social science and science journals attest to his considerable influence."[11] But they do not indicate the extent to which key change agents have taken his research and called for a change in U.S. law regarding sex.

Using Kinsey's misleading data, one public authority drew the following conclusion:

> These pre-marital, extra-marital, homosexual and animal contacts, we
> are told, are eventually indulged in by 95 per cent of the population
> in violation of statutory prohibitions. If these conclusions are correct,
> then it is obvious that our sex crime legislation is completely out of
> touch with the realities of individual living.[12]

Thus, laws were altered to protect the basest of men while jeopardizing the welfare of men, women, and children who would be their prey! Until Kinsey perpetrated his deception, sex offenders were the ones in danger because the law protected the innocent and vulnerable. It is just the opposite today. How long will it be until the land spews us out, until a holy God is fed up and brings His rod of judgment on our nation in an even greater way than He has now?

Think of how many people have been victimized by this man because they believed a lie, because they didn't understand what God prohibits in respect to sex! If you were born after 1948, then in all probability you have been either infected or affected in some way by Kinsey's teaching on human sexuality, unless you were raised to know God's Word for yourself and what He says about our sexuality.

Can you see how essential it is that we understand exactly what God says about sex? If we don't understand it, we'll be deceived and destroyed by a lie. Beloved, sex outside God's parameters is a forbidden fruit that will keep you out of His garden, the only place you will find the Tree of Life.

Do you remember the pastor whose story I shared with you earlier, the one enticed in his mind by the woman who was a member of the church staff? Let me finish his story, for in it is a lesson for all of us.

> For me it was all in my mind, but it progressed from there. I started thinking about her on weekends. I kept telling myself, *I can handle this. It hasn't gone too far; it's okay.* But it could have; the opportunity was waiting for me.
>
> Occasionally, I got scared. I'd think, *I don't want to do this. I have a great wife; I have a family. I don't want to go down this road.* And while it was somewhat "fun" knowing I was getting away with something, it also gnawed at me. I knew it wasn't right. Then one day I was on the phone in my office, when she came up behind me and pinched my rear end. That's when fear finally kicked my senses back into my head.
>
> "I'm going to talk to my wife about this," I told her.[13]

He did. He also told the senior pastor. Although nothing happened physically, he knew what was happening in his mind and the danger of where it was all heading.

Oh, beloved, if you've begun playing with fire, drown it with the water of God's Word. If you don't, regardless of who you are, your sins will find you out. God is a holy God; He must judge sin. Guilt, shame, and a nagging conscience are precursors to impending judgment, warning signs to stop and experience God's cleansing power before it's too late.

When I kept silent about my sin, my body wasted away
Through my groaning all day long.
For day and night Your hand was heavy upon me;
My vitality was drained away as with the fever heat of summer. *Selah.*
I acknowledged my sin to You,
And my iniquity I did not hide;
I said, "I will confess my transgressions to the LORD";
And You forgave the guilt of my sin. *Selah.*
Therefore, let everyone who is godly pray to You in a time when You
    may be found;
Surely in a flood of great waters they will not reach him.
You are my hiding place; You preserve me from trouble;
You surround me with songs of deliverance. *Selah.*
I will instruct you and teach you in the way which you should go;
I will counsel you with My eye upon you.
Do not be as the horse or as the mule which have no understanding,
Whose trappings include bit and bridle to hold them in check,
Otherwise they will not come near to you.
Many are the sorrows of the wicked,
But he who trusts in the LORD, lovingkindness shall surround
    him. (Psalm 32:3-10)

5

The Snare of Seduction

What's the Big Deal About Sowing a Few Wild Oats?

The song of the sirens—carried by the wind, skimming the surface of the sea, captured in the sails of the ship—lured many a captain and his sailors to change their charted course. Powerless to resist the sirens' mesmerizing song, the bewitched men set their sails for the sirens' shore, unaware that, beneath the surface of the sparkling waters that danced along the coast, jagged rocks awaited. Blinded by lust, some didn't wait for the inevitable shipwreck but flung themselves into the waters and swam toward shore, only to be devoured by the sirens. The sirens' seductive attire cloaked a cannibal appetite that savagely consumed their victims' flesh.

In Homer's *Odyssey*, we read of the mythical hero Odysseus, also known as Ulysses, and his adventures as he returned home from war, including an encounter with the sirens.[1] Circe, the enchantress with whom Odysseus had an affair, warned him of the lure of the sirens' song. As his ship neared the island, he ordered his sailors to fill their ears with wax to prevent their being seduced by the sirens. But Odysseus, his curiosity aroused, longed to hear their glorious voices. He instructed his crew to lash him to the mast of the ship and warned that, no matter how fervently he begged, they were not to untie him until they were far from the shores of the sirens' island.

How right Circe was, how wise Odysseus to listen. The song of the sirens was so seductive, his death was certain if he could have freed himself from the straps that bound him.

This tale from Greek mythology serves as a warning to those who would linger near dangerous shores, drawn by the lust of the flesh. And like the sirens, the "strange women" described in the book of Proverbs offer a tale of caution for those who want to experience sex according to God's plan.

Proverbs, written by King Solomon of Israel, is a textbook of wisdom and instruction that urged his son to flee from the evil woman, from the smooth tongue of the adulteress.[2] As Circe warned Odysseus, so Solomon warned his son. But the wisdom offered by Solomon was God's wisdom—truth, not myth—counsel sent from the very throne of heaven.

Listen to the father's concern for his son, recorded in Proverbs 6:20-29. These are timeless words of wisdom, recorded and preserved for all generations. As you read, why don't you put a drawing like this [⌂] over every reference to the *commandments,* including the word *teaching* and any pronouns.

PROVERBS 6

²⁰ My son, observe the commandment of your father, and do not forsake the teaching of your mother;

²¹ Bind them continually on your heart; tie them around your neck.

²² When you walk about, they will guide you; when you sleep, they will watch over you; and when you awake, they will talk to you.

²³ For the commandment is a lamp and the teaching is light; and reproofs for discipline are the way of life

²⁴ To keep you from the evil woman, from the smooth tongue of the adulteress.

Now stop and reflect on what you've marked; it will be well worth your time. List what you learn about these commandments—where they came from, what they are, what was to be done with them, and the promised benefits of obeying them.

The commandments of this father and mother were not frivolous orders tossed at their son without purpose; they were words that, if heeded, would keep him from shipwrecking his life, destroying it on the hidden reefs of ignorance and naiveté.

The son of the king was urged to continually bind these teachings upon his heart, tie them around his neck. These truths would provide direction, give him instruction, and protect him from the consequences of ignorance. If he would listen and obey, he would avoid the snare of the sirens' song—the strong lure of temptation, the passion of his flesh—the source of destruction for young and old, small and great, naive and learned. The father knew a man's eyes cannot help but see and then beckon the mind to imagine, the flesh to touch, to taste, to feel, to know—and he wanted to protect his son from the inevitable ruin that would follow such seduction.

The wise father goes on to say,

25 Do not desire her beauty in your heart, nor let her catch you with her eyelids.

26 For on account of a harlot one is reduced to a loaf of bread, and an adulteress hunts for the precious life.

An adulteress! A harlot! This is a woman on the hunt, when God meant man to be the hunter. This is a woman who is skilled at seduction, calling him to her shores, luring him into her snare, taking captive her prey and devouring all his substance.

She would destroy all that distinguished him,
all that could make him a man among men,
a man of character,
one whose life was worthy to be imitated,
whose sons would want to walk in his footsteps,
whose daughters would delight in his moral strength
and snuggle in the security of his integrity.
In exchange for his compromise of integrity,
this siren would bankrupt him of godlikeness
and reduce his worth to the price of a loaf of bread.

The adulteress on the hunt is not a myth; sadly she trades in seduction every day, leading many young men to their destruction.

A couple who leads Precept studies in Canada told me of an incident involving their seventeen-year-old son. He and his buddies spent a day at Canada's Wonderland, which is something like Walt Disney World in Florida. A young girl of about sixteen struck up a conversation with the boys as they waited in line. She hung out with them for the rest of the day. Through casual conversation the girl learned the young man's name and the city he was from.

The following Saturday she stood at their front door, ringing the doorbell. She had ridden the bus fifty miles to spend the day with their son—without invitation and without warning. The whole family was in shock, but none more so than their son.

She was dressed, as Proverbs says, in "the attire of a harlot"—a short-cropped top, low-cut neckline, and very tight jeans. Wanting to be polite, hesitant to turn her away, the family spent an awkward day entertaining her, then took her to the bus.

A week later as my friend sorted the mail, she noticed a letter addressed to her son, a letter from their unexpected visitor. In relating the story to me, she said, "Kay, as I held the letter in my hand, I knew there was a condom inside the envelope." She prayed about how to approach her son. When he arrived home she handed him the letter and warned him of what she suspected. And she was right! "When he opened the letter there was a colorful condom with a note saying she was sending this in preparation for her next visit. My son was embarrassed to death. Until this point in his life he had never seen a condom 'up close and personal.'"

When you read a story like this, you may have a tendency to think it's an unusual incident. How often does this sort of thing really happen? How many women are out there on the hunt? Tragically, this story is much more common than most of us realize. Many a man knows that sex is easy to get if you're interested. Women on the prowl write them notes, show up unexpectedly, call the house or the office. At parties they practically throw themselves at men, making it clear that anything the man wants is available with a simple answer to the question, "My place or yours?"

²⁷ Can a man take fire in his bosom and his clothes not be burned?

²⁸ Or can a man walk on hot coals and his feet not be scorched?

No! No! He cannot. He will be burned. He will be left scarred. Callous. Unfeeling.

²⁹ So is the one who goes in to his neighbor's wife; whoever touches her will not go unpunished.

The Risk and Reward of Obedience

The eyes of God test the heart of man.

You say you could not help it. You heard the sirens' song. It was irresistible, and you yielded. "Who could resist?" you argue with your Maker. "It was too much to bear. Surely you cannot punish me, God. I'm a sexual being; we're built this way. It's expected of us. Surely You'll let me go without chastening me."

When you think this way, remember that in the very first book of the Bible, God gives us a role model in Joseph, whose master's wife approached him day after day to beg him to lie with her.

The circumstances of Joseph's life were very bitter. He was in the house of Potiphar, an Egyptian officer of Pharaoh, because his brothers hated him and had sold him as a slave. God had told Joseph through a dream that his brothers would bow down to him, but they hadn't. God's word hadn't come to pass! Joseph was separated from his parents, his brothers, his land, and from the people who worshiped his God—so why shouldn't he take advantage of this opportunity for a little pleasure? Joseph was young and virile! As a slave, he had little hope of marrying. Surely God would understand—and even if He didn't, why should Joseph care? God should have protected him from being in this position to begin with.

Isn't that the way we often rationalize our response to temptation? My needs, my desires, my appetites—I've got to look after myself.

Let's look at how this role model responded to the situation.

GENESIS 39:7-9

⁷ It came about after these events that his master's wife looked with desire at Joseph, and she said, "Lie with me."

⁸ But he refused and said to his master's wife, "Behold, with me here, my master does not concern himself with anything in the house, and he has put all that he owns in my charge.

⁹ "There is no one greater in this house than I, and he has withheld nothing from me except you, because you are his wife. How then could I do this great evil and sin against God?"

Did you notice his response? Underline it for emphasis. What an awesome answer for anyone who presses you to engage in sex outside of God's plan: "How then could I do this great evil and sin against God?" What a way to share the truth about God and the salvation He offers.

Salvation that brings with it the power to say no…

>not because you might get caught, contract a sexually transmitted disease, or conceive a child,

>>but because it is a sin against God.

>>Salvation that enables us to remain steadfast in our convictions even though our refusal might provoke anger or resentment.

Saying no to sin is not necessarily an easy choice. Joseph's refusal to sleep with Mrs. Potiphar involved great personal risk. She would not take no for an answer. Day after day she pursued him with the same offer. Day after day Joseph refused. He would not be worn down by her persistence. Even when she trapped him alone in the house and—catching him by his loincloth—again asked him to lie with her, Joseph ran, leaving his garment behind.

He fled as the Word of God tells us to do. Joseph would not weaken or compromise. He had determined not to sin against God by having sex outside of marriage—and he suffered for his obedience. He ended up in prison when Mrs. Potiphar decided to seek revenge for the rejection she had suffered. She claimed he had tried to compromise her. Of course, Potiphar reacted just as Proverbs says any husband would act.

> Men do not despise a thief if he steals to satisfy himself when he is hungry; but when he is found, he must repay sevenfold; he must give all the substance of his house. The one who commits adultery with a woman is lacking sense; he who would destroy himself does it. Wounds and disgrace he will find, and his reproach will not be blotted out. For jealousy enrages a man, and he will not spare in the day of vengeance. He will not accept any ransom, nor will he be satisfied though you give many gifts. (Proverbs 6:30-35)

Potiphar was furious. Scripture says, "His anger burned. So Joseph's master took him and put him into the jail, the place where the king's prisoners were confined; and he was there in the jail" (Genesis 39:19-20).

It seems unfair, doesn't it, that a sovereign, omnipotent God wouldn't reward Joseph's virtue? Why would He allow him to be treated so cruelly? Does it make you wonder if it pays to be moral, to do what is right, no matter the cost? Rest assured, beloved, obedience pays great dividends. God always rewards goodness and virtue—but in His time, in His way.

Joseph stayed in prison for at least two years, but at the end of those years almighty God moved His servant Joseph from the prison to the palace, where he ruled over all Egypt under Pharaoh. None was higher than Joseph—and in the end his brothers did come and bow down before him, just as God had promised in the dream He gave this faithful man.

THE WOUNDS OF SEXUAL SIN

By the way, did you look closely at the Proverbs 6 passage quoted earlier? Let's look again at verse 33:

> Wounds and disgrace he will find, and his reproach will not be blotted out.

The Hebrew word translated in this passage as *wounds* is *nega*, meaning "stroke, plague, disease."[3] *Nega* comes from the root word *naga*, which essentially means "to touch" or "that which pertains when one thing (or person) physically contacts another."

Think with me. What are sexually transmitted diseases (STDs)? They are diseases transmitted by *physical contact* in the act of sex. In 1 Corinthians 6:18 when God tells us to "flee immorality," as Joseph did, He goes on to warn us that "every other sin that a man commits is outside the body, but the immoral man sins against his own body."

Romans 1:27 also sounds a warning. In the context of God's giving men over to degrading passions, including lesbianism and homosexuality, the Word refers to "men with men committing indecent acts *and* receiving in their own persons the due penalty of their error."

Following are descriptions of various STDs and their effects. You do not want to gloss over this section. Read it carefully, my friend, and note the "wounds" these diseases cause. See if you think they are really worth a sexual tryst outside the marriage bed. Could this also be part of what God is talking about in Hebrews 13:4: "Marriage is to be held in honor among all, and the marriage bed is to be undefiled; for fornicators and adulterers *God will judge.*"

- Chlamydia and gonorrhea can cause sterility for both men and women.
- Syphilis can result in heart disease, blindness, brain disorders, dementia, and death.
- Genital herpes, with its incurable outbreaks, requires medication for life. Herpes simplex virus type 2 eruptions are now being found above the waist, whereas it used to be that type 1 was always found above the waist, type 2 below. These type 2 eruptions "can be attributed, in part, to an increase in oral-genital contact."[4]

  Do you see the connection between this and oral sex, which many teenagers have turned to as a substitute for sexual intercourse? Take warning! This infection has also brought a rise in herpes simplex keratitis (HSK), an infection of the eye that is "the second most common cause of corneal blindness in the United States, second only to trauma. This is not only occurring in adults but in newborns as the infection migrates up the genital tract following rupture of the amniotic sac."[5] In lay terms this means that when a pregnant woman's water breaks, her baby is infected with the virus she is carrying.

- Human papillomavirus (HPV) can cause cancer of the penis and anus in men. Women can suffer premalignant changes in their sexual organs that are difficult to eradicate.
- Hepatitis B brings severe liver damage, which can eventually lead to cancer of the liver and cirrhosis.
- Pelvic inflammatory disease (PID) affects only women and can cause ectopic pregnancies and sterility.
- HIV (human immunodeficiency virus) enters the body through the lining of the vagina, vulva, penis, rectum, or mouth during sex with an infected partner. Some would be upset with me for not saying "unprotected sex," but the truth is that condoms often do not protect.[6] Those who already have an STD are more susceptible to getting an HIV infection during sex with infected partners.

   HIV can also be transmitted through contact with infected blood or a contaminated needle. It can also be spread to a baby during pregnancy and birth and through the breast milk.
- AIDS (acquired immunodeficiency syndrome) is a nearly inevitable result of the HIV infection. AIDS breaks down the immune system and is almost certain to end in death.

Do you realize that next to the common cold and the flu, STDs are the most common infectious diseases in the United States? As we entered the third millennium, every day an estimated thirty-three thousand Americans were becoming infected with at least one of these diseases. What does that tell you about our society and our morals?

According to Dr. C. Everett Koop, the former U.S. surgeon general, "When you have sex with someone, you are having sex with everyone they have had sex with for the last ten years, and everyone they and their partners have had sex with for the last ten years."

Don't be "void of sense," as Proverbs says. Listen to Wisdom. Embrace her.

How blessed is the man who finds wisdom and the man who gains understanding. For her profit is better than the profit of silver and her gain better than fine gold. She is more precious than jewels; and nothing you desire compares with her. Long life is in her right hand; in her left hand are riches and honor. Her ways are pleasant ways and all her paths are peace. She is a tree of life to those who take hold of her, and happy are all who hold her fast. (Proverbs 3:13-18)

Adultery ruins a man, destroys the family, and demoralizes a nation. Don't go there. Don't trim your sails. Listen instead to the gentle rain from heaven. Lift your face, let the word of God from heaven run down over your eyes, your mouth. Taste its sweetness. Let it soak your clothes, wash your soul. God's words bring life, not death.

As an Ox to Slaughter

As we turn back to Proverbs once more, we see that the Spirit of God prods Solomon to continue, binding his son to the masthead of God's Word, securing him with truth so that he might not give in to the sirens' song. He's saying, "Let me tell you what I saw, what happened, that you might not walk the same path."

As you continue in chapter 7, reading aloud, underline every reference to a certain *young man* Solomon saw—every pronoun, every synonym. Then circle or color every reference to the *seductress*.

PROVERBS 7

¹ My son, keep my words, and treasure my commandments within you.

² Keep my commandments and live, and my teaching as the apple of your eye.

³ Bind them on your fingers; write them on the tablet of your heart.

⁴ Say to wisdom, "You are my sister," and call understanding your intimate friend;

⁵ That they may keep you from an adulteress, from the foreigner who flatters with her words.

⁶ For at the window of my house I looked out through my lattice,

⁷ And I saw among the naive, and discerned among the youths a young man lacking sense,

⁸ Passing through the street near her corner; and he takes the way to her house,

⁹ In the twilight, in the evening, in the middle of the night and in the darkness.

Take a good look at this man. List what you observe about him so far.

I'm sure you saw it. Here is a young man who lacked sense, who wouldn't flee his youthful lusts, who put himself in the path of temptation, who sailed too close to the shores of certain destruction. Here is a man who thinks he can walk in the darkness—just to see what it's like—and escape being taken in. His heart is deceived; he's unaware of his masculine vulnerability, his naiveté. He thinks the night will cloak his actions. Little does he realize that when we think, "Surely the darkness will cover me," the darkness is not dark to God. The night is as bright as the day. Darkness and light are alike to Him.⁷

¹⁰ And behold, a woman comes to meet him, dressed as a harlot and cunning of heart.

She's cunning. Immorality knows the power of the lust of the eyes. She's lingered before the mirror, turning this way and that to be sure she's presenting a visually enticing package. She has chosen her clothing as a careful accompaniment to her siren's song. She knows men are turned on by sight.

The following story from a coauthor of *Every Man's Battle* gives testimony to the power of the eyes. Read this carefully, even if you're a woman. This is not written by some dirty old man; it's the true experience of a man like those you pass day after day.

My eyes…were ravenous heat-seekers searching the horizon, locking on any target with sensual heat. Young mothers leaning over in shorts to pull children out of a car seat. Soloists with silky shirts. Summer dresses with décolletage. My mind ran…wherever it willed. This had begun in my childhood, when I found *Playboy* magazines under Dad's bed. He also subscribed to *From Sex to Sexty,* a publication filled with jokes and comic strips with sexual themes. When Dad divorced Mom and moved to his "bachelor's pad," he hung a giant velvet nude in his living room, overlooking us as we played cards on my Sunday afternoon visits.

Dad gave me a list of chores around his place when I was there. Once I came across a nude photo of his mistress.

All this sexual stuff churned deep inside of me, destroying a purity that wouldn't return for many years.[8]

Eventually all this led to his having "sex with anyone at any time."[9] And what were many of these women like? Solomon describes them:

[11] She is boisterous and rebellious, her feet do not remain at home;

[12] She is now in the streets, now in the squares, and lurks by every corner.

She knows your path, and she waits around the corner. Maybe you believe your paths crossed by chance, but she's executed her plan with care. Your paths *will* cross, you *will* catch a glimpse of her as she walks provocatively down the street, pausing, twisting, turning, catching your eye, smiling…

[13] So she seizes him and kisses him and with a brazen face she says to him:

¹⁴ "I was due to offer peace offerings; today I have paid my vows.

¹⁵ "Therefore I have come out to meet you, to seek your presence earnestly, and I have found you.

¹⁶ "I have spread my couch with coverings, with colored linens of Egypt.

¹⁷ "I have sprinkled my bed with myrrh, aloes and cinnamon.

¹⁸ "Come, let us drink our fill of love until morning; let us delight ourselves with caresses."

Her hands are on your shoulder...moving to your chest. Her words entice you. Your imagination runs deliciously wild, your passions burn. "It's just for one night," she promises. A night of love...in the dark...alone...

¹⁹ "For my husband is not at home, he has gone on a long journey;

²⁰ He has taken a bag of money with him, at the full moon he will come home."

No one will know. Her husband is far, far away...you're safe. Her words go on and on...soft, seductive...promising a night of nights...calling you...beckoning you...bewitching you.

²¹ With her many persuasions she entices him; with her flattering lips she seduces him.

"Why not? No one will know."

If she's on the Internet, no one will know. If she's on the television screen in your hotel room, no one will ever know. There'll be no physical contact. Only in the mind will you touch her, and no one will ever know—except God the Father, God the Holy Spirit, God the Son...and you.

[22] Suddenly he follows her as an ox goes to the slaughter, or as one in fetters to the discipline of a fool,

He does not know that he is about to shipwreck; he cannot see the hidden reefs. He only hears the song. Like the sirens of Greek mythology, she will lure him to the shores of her pleasure, her desire.

[23] Until an arrow pierces through his liver; as a bird hastens to the snare, so he does not know that it will cost him his life.

It began with an e-mail…then Internet pornography…then chat rooms. Until then, no one knew. Then came the invitation to meet. At first he resisted, but the invitation came again. He went and left feeling dirty. Now *she* knew, but he wouldn't contact her again. His secret would be safe.

Then came another invitation from another woman. He went…and it developed into an affair that ended his marriage. He lost his wife, but surely not the children…they were his life—at least that was what he told them when they were growing up.

Then came another e-mail, this one from his nineteen-year-old daughter:

I cannot comprehend the sincerity of anything you say anymore, Dad. You say that you love me, yet you knowingly hurt both me and my family. You say that you would die for me, but you were unwilling to live for me. You say that you miss me, yet it is you who left and abandoned me. I am learning that words are a cheap commodity…especially, your words.

I am angry with you for living a life of deception and for going against everything you have ever taught me to be true and right. I disrespect you as a man, a husband, and as a father. You are a coward for not being willing to sacrifice something for the love of your own children. More than anything, I pity you. I pity you for throwing your life away for lust. You had every earthly thing a man could ever dream of: a loving family, two adoring children, a wonderful job, respect in our

community, and all the possessions you could ever want. Yet you had
a void in your life. Instead of filling that void with Christ, you allowed
sin to fill it. You are caught inside a cloud of deception. I hurt for you
because I know that one day, you will look back at your life and realize all that you lost…for nothing. And I am afraid for you because I
know that God will deal with your sin in His time and that it will be
far worse than any earthly punishment or grief you could encounter.
You are in a dangerous position by not fearing the Lord.

I cannot allow you back into my life until you have a change of
heart. As much as it hurts me to push you away, I believe that it is
necessary for my healing. I don't believe that my brother and I are
really a necessity in your life as you claim. I recall the many times,
while growing up, that you convinced us that a parent could not desire anything more than love from his own children. Obviously, you
have changed your mind—if you ever really meant those words in the
first place. You seem to have no problem trading us for a replacement
person. No matter how many times you say that you love me, I cannot believe the words without seeing the actions.

As disappointed and upset as I am, I will not cease to pray for
you. I will pray that God will soften your heart. I will pray that you
will not find the true peace or contentment until you are right with
God. I will pray that one day, before we die, you will have a change
of heart and lifestyle and that our relationship can be renewed. I will
pray that, in time, God will grant me the grace to forgive you.

In the meantime, I will learn to live again. I will learn to trust
and depend on the Lord to be my Father. I am thankful that God is a
Father who will never betray, deceive, or hurt me. Life will be different
and difficult, at times, but I am confident that God will provide for
Mom, my brother, and me. Each day will get a little easier and a little
less painful to face.[10]

And what about you, my friend? Are you about to reset your sail, to aim
for the shores where the beckoning vision awaits? Don't. Put wax in your ears
and listen to that still small voice calling from within. If you will listen carefully, the fear of God will keep you on course.

Let's go back to the words of Solomon in chapter 7 of Proverbs.

24 Now therefore, my sons, listen to me, and pay attention to the words of my mouth.

25 Do not let your heart turn aside to her ways, do not stray into her paths.

26 For many are the victims she has cast down, and numerous are all her slain.

27 Her house is the way to Sheol, descending to the chambers of death.

My dear brother Bob Reccord tells in his book *Beneath the Surface* of the sirens' song that wafted into a hotel room where he, a pastor, was all alone:

> I flipped on the TV and began surfing. I avoided certain channels because I've learned their danger, but I did land on HBO. It took me a few moments to figure out what the program was. Suddenly, it dawned on me that there, on a major network, was a special on exotic dancers—with nothing left to the imagination.
>
> My heart told me to flip the channel—now! But another voice inside said, "Stay…just for a while. You'll enjoy this…it'll only get better!"
>
> Like Joseph (in Genesis 39), I was faced with a decision that only I could make. Thankfully, long ago I had decided what my course of action would be when faced with such enticements. So the channel was changed—and quickly! But not without tempting second thoughts.[11]

If you say you cannot help yourself—that you are melted butter in the heat of passion, that you never hear God's voice calling you away from temptation—could it possibly be that you are not His child?

God says, "Do not be deceived; neither fornicators, nor idolaters, nor adulterers, nor effeminate, nor homosexuals, nor thieves, nor the covetous, nor drunkards, nor revilers, nor swindlers, will inherit the kingdom of God" (1 Corinthians 6:9-10).

If this is what you are—note the word *are*—if this is your character, your current and continuous lifestyle, then you are lost. You will self-destruct. But if you want out, if you want to change, God will change you. He can take up residence within, bringing His Son and His Spirit. All you have to do is ask God to move in, and He will give you the wisdom and power to say "No!" to sin and walk away from it in His strength.

STRANGE WOMEN AND DUMB MEN

Before we go any further, let's go back and read through these verses from Proverbs once more. Although obviously written to men, Proverbs 6 and 7 offer valuable insight about "strange women," as the *King James Version* calls them, and the "dumb men," as I call them, who are seduced by strange women. The Bible uses the word *naive*. I call them "dumb" because these men have no idea what's about to befall them!

This time list what you learn from marking the references to the man. I promise you it will pay off someday. If you're a man, these truths will be planted in your mind for the Spirit of God to recall any time you are tempted to "play dumb." If you're a parent, studying this will help you raise your sons, teach them how to avoid being naive or dumb when it comes to women on the hunt.

Now, let's look at that "foreign woman" or "strange woman." List everything you learn about her from these same verses in Proverbs.

Study these truths well. Hide them in your heart, for they will tie you to the mast when the storms of temptation blow—or help you choose a wise course when you see a seductress coming onto the path of your son or husband. Many a wise wife has rescued her man from a woman who would destroy him. Men are often so oblivious to the wiles and intentions of the seductress, but another woman often reads them well. A wise man will heed his wife's warning and set his sails in the opposite direction.

In the days when I discovered that sex was like a can of Drano and was teaching this subject to teens as well as adults, Jack and I agreed that our teenage sons could not date until they were sixteen and could spot a strange woman. Why? Because my dear husband and I didn't want any "dumb men" in our house. We wanted our sons to know the characteristics of a "strange woman"—an adulteress on the make!

As you read back through these verses, you saw that she uses her tongue to seduce him, to flatter and soften him until he is putty in her hands. She builds his ego in order to bring him down into her bed. Proverbs 5:3-4 tells us, "The lips of an adulteress drip honey and smoother than oil is her speech; but in the end she is bitter as wormwood, sharp as a two-edged sword."

Her words are seductive, her speech suggestive. No propriety. Of course that was lost in our society years ago. Romance is a lost art, propriety a discarded social grace. Nothing is private anymore, not even the most intimate of issues. There is no modesty, no delicacy of speech. Women's words today are brazen, blunt, and unfortunately, as it says in the book of Jeremiah, we no longer blush.[12] Nothing is sacred—especially not sex, even though God meant it to be.

It's easy for me to spot a seductress; I simply watch her eyes, especially around men. A woman's eyes are the windows of her soul. You might think it a game to seduce a man with your eyes, but if you do, my dear, you will answer to God. Know this: It's a fearful thing to fall into the hands of the living God.[13]

As I pointed out earlier, you can hear the sirens' call; the strange woman is on the hunt. Oh, girls, in our aggressiveness we rob men of their masculinity. Men love the hunt! The conquest! There's an innate nobility in the hearts of many men—the desire to protect, to cherish, to care for a woman as the weaker sex—and we have almost made it extinct with our killing feminist ways. This strange woman bought into a lie; she thought being sexy, seducing man after man, demonstrated her power and proved her femininity.

This woman is not a homebody; she wants to be out there on the streets, in the middle of the action. She's loud and boisterous; she's going to be heard, noticed! There's a brazenness about her sexuality. Her goal is to bed the man!

Why? It could be that the poor woman craves love and thinks it will come by giving herself away. Or possibly she hates herself, feels worthless, and expects to be used. Maybe she was inducted into this life because of the sexual abuse she suffered as a child or as a young woman. Maybe she ended up here because of alcohol, drugs, or poverty. There can be a dozen different reasons, but all of them are wrong and my heart aches for her. I want to take her in my arms, call her beloved, tell her she is precious to God and that this is not what God intends for her, that this is not how a woman finds fulfillment.

Proverbs 5:6 tells us she is not a thinking woman. She lives for the present—or is entangled by her past. "She does not ponder the path of life; her ways are unstable, she does not know it."

THE SEARCH FOR LOVE, POWER, AND FREEDOM

I recently heard of a high school where fourteen- to sixteen-year-old girls are offering themselves to the guys in their school—for a price!

Remember when "bad girls" were in the minority—whispered about and shunned as an oddity? You have to wonder why women have made a U-turn regarding sex. I believe one of the major reasons is the breakup of the traditional family unit. When young women don't have strong moral fathers who love, nurture, and protect their daughters, they are going to seek someone else to fill that void! Sometimes it's another woman, sometimes it's a man. And if it takes sex to get him or keep him, it's a price they willingly pay for the hope of feeling loved.

The most famous example of a woman like this is Marilyn Monroe, the sexual icon who took her life at age thirty-six, having never found the one thing she tried to buy with her sexuality: love. Though there can be only one Marilyn, thousands and thousands of others have stories as tragic as hers. One of these is a thirty-two-year-old I'll call Donna, who wrote me to share her story.

When Donna was five she was touched by one of her father's best friends—constantly.

> I didn't know what was going on then, but now I do. I find I can't forgive him. My older brother used to come in my bedroom at night and have oral sex with me. I was scared, I really didn't know what oral sex

was. I was only nine or ten years old. I didn't turn him away because I was afraid of him. I have been in love or thought I was in love with a guy when I was fifteen years old. He told me he loved me, and I believed him. I came to realize that he didn't really love me, but it was too late. I had become pregnant. My family forced me to get an abortion. My life has been a mess. I am a Christian woman now, but most of my life I have been very promiscuous. I was allowing myself to be violated because I wanted to be loved. I thought sex was a way of showing love....

How short a letter to summarize a lifetime of pain. How I wish I could hold her in my arms, talk with her, and help her see the depth of love she will someday know when she sees her heavenly bridegroom, the Lord Jesus Christ, face to face. All her tears will be wiped away and every wrong done to her will be taken care of.

The sexual revolution—the demise of moral absolutes—is another reason for the increase in sexually aggressive women. When immorality came out of the closet, blatantly dressed as a harlot, it signaled the end of decency and appropriate shame. The catchy song "Anything Goes" said it all! *Playboy* offered a new perspective on sex and the female physique. Ordinary women with extraordinary bodies became the accepted obsession of sex-hungry men, who no longer had to resort to worn, used prostitutes. These centerfolds became the unfortunate standard for every woman who thought she had to have a body like that to please her man.

On the stiletto heels of all this came feminism, which declared that women didn't need a man's protection or help. Men were an unnecessary weight, and women could get on better without them. Sex became power as women tried to prove they didn't need a ring—or a marriage—to be successful, to feel in control of their lives.

Diane Passno in her book *Feminism: Mystique or Mistake?* explains how the feminist movement distorted biblical teaching about roles and gender, weakened the home and the family, manipulated our language, destroyed standards of morality, devastated same-sex friendships, and became dominated by a lesbian agenda. It resulted in a generation of men who disrespect and use women sexually and made women victims.[14] Our protectors became our predators.

The newfound "freedom" of sexual expression was intended to eliminate guilt trips. Kinsey's biased research allegedly had proven that 95 percent of our society was already indulging their sexual desires, so the conclusion was that we ought to be able to continue doing so without fear of reprisal. Forget God's outdated Law; why should we deny ourselves the pleasure of doing "what comes naturally"?

But consider the abortions that follow immorality, the murder of precious souls whom God brought into existence. Though some would have you believe this is nothing more than the removal of a little unwanted "tissue," the process endangers women's lives, sometimes damages them so they can never bear children, and leaves them with a guilty conscience that just won't go away.

In other cases, children conceived in sin and then abandoned by parents on their own self-centered quests, end up in orphanages, numerous foster homes, and—in many countries—living in garbage dumps or on the streets with no adult care whatsoever. Like scrawny little kittens with bloated bellies and mangy hair, they roam the cities scavenging for food, yet skittish and wary of every hand outstretched to help them. If you and I would stop and listen to their stories, hear their pain, then put ourselves in their small, worn-out, dirty shoes, we would rise up in indignation against all those who for a moment of unbridled licentiousness helped create such hell on earth. This is the fruit of our so-called sexual freedom.

When we replaced the "outdated" Word of God with the "scientific" research of man, we were blindsided by the devil. We unwittingly bought the murderer's lie. We ate the forbidden fruit without realizing we were banishing ourselves from the garden. In our exile we are missing out on the joy and security not only of virtue but also of family and, consequently, a safe and healthy society where women and children are valued and protected, where they can walk and play in the streets without fear.

Please hear me when I say that giving away your body for anything other than marriage leads to an empty, lonely, dissatisfying, frustrating life. What hope can the future hold? What will you have left when your beauty fades, when your breasts and bottom hang low and loose, and your waistline thickens—and you've forgotten or missed the joys God intended for you as a woman? What happens when you're replaced by the next available generation, when you can no longer sing the sirens' song?

Who can find a virtuous woman? Oh precious one, Jesus can make you a virtuous woman if you will only come to Him…

> even as the Samaritan woman who had five husbands and was living with a man she wasn't married to.

>> even as Mary Magdalene who had seven demons, all cast out by Jesus.

>>> even as the woman who sinned much and came to wash Jesus' feet with her tears and found her sins forgiven.

Your worth is above blood-red rubies; God paid for you with the life of His Son. What more could God give, what more could He do to prove His love to you, precious one? Listen to His love song of salvation; let its music fill your heart.

The song of the sirens has a sequel in the story of Jason, a character of Greek mythology who was brought up and educated by the centaur Chiron. Jason, too, heard the sirens' song as he sailed his ship, the *Argo,* past the infamous island of the sirens and their destruction. Unlike Odysseus, however, Jason would not plug the ears of his men, the Argonauts, nor would he bind himself or them to the mast of the ship. Instead, Jason commanded Orpheus, a musician of extraordinary talent, to play his music—the most beautiful music he had ever created. As they sailed past the island, the men never heard the sirens' song wafting toward them on the waves of the sea; they were enraptured by the transcendent beauty of another's music.[15]

Like the music of Orpheus, the song of the Lord transcends all others, and if you will listen to it carefully, if you hide it in your heart, it will deafen you to the sirens' music of death and destruction.

For the LORD GOD is my strength and song, and He has become my salvation. (Isaiah 12:2)

And His song will be with me in the night, a prayer to the God of my life. (Psalm 42:8)

6

Consider the Cost

If We're Discreet, Who Are We Really Hurting?

He slipped into the center back pew of the church just as the christening ceremony began. Looking toward the front, he could see that the whole family—except for him—filled the first two pews on the right. What a fine bunch! They clearly were comfortable together: arms laid lightly across each other's shoulders, children sitting close to their parents, looking up every now and then to receive a pat, sometimes cuddling closer. The teenagers looked so young, so virile.

He recognized the back of his wife's head; he had always loved the way her hair cut around her neck. Though no husband sat at her side, she obviously was not alone. Their redheaded daughter sat on one side of the pew with her children squeezed comfortably between her and their grandmother. Their son, looking well dressed and successful, sat on the other side with another grandchild snuggled between them. He caught the smiles, the joy exchanged in glances as the minister presented the grandson to the congregation, walking back and forth across the platform while everyone took delight in the baby's squints and coos as he discovered the crowd and wiggled approvingly.

He had planned on leaving after the christening, but he stayed through the morning service. Although it was painful, he just wanted to sit there and gaze at all of them together. His times with them had been few in recent years—bits and pieces, awkward, in a hurry. The whole of family life was what he missed. He lingered in the foyer of the church after the service and then, seeking one last look, he went into the sanctuary again. Martha was standing there, bending over the pew, a grandchild at her side. His gaze caught hers. Martha smiled. Tears came to his eyes. The forward slant of the aisle seemed to propel him toward her.

Their words were few, but she never forgot what he said: "I've missed so much, so very much. I'm so lonely. How I wish I'd never walked away."

He had missed much—all that comes over the years of growing older, watching the children go away and come home with their mates and then have families of their own. The cycle of family, the second go-round of babies and birthday parties, of school events and sitting in the bleachers, cheering the next generation on.

How had it happened? It was his accountant. Long hours of working together, sharing problems he should have discussed with his wife. The closeness, the mutual sense of accomplishment, the look, the touch…the affair. At the time he thought he'd found what he really wanted. He never stopped long enough to consider the cost. His wife was willing to forgive. His children begged him not to leave. He didn't listen.

Now it was too late. He was too old. The fire of passion had long gone out; the ashes were almost cold. Oh, he and his accountant were still married, still lived together—but they were only two. No family smiled on the periphery of their lives—and it left a big hole right in the middle of his heart.

He hadn't stopped to consider the cost…and neither did David, the king of Israel. One was a commoner, the other royalty. Men of different millenniums, different cultures—yet when it came to sin, consequences followed without regard for personal distinctions. No one breaks God's Law and comes away unscathed.

Let's take a closer look at David's story to learn about the aftermath of sexual sin.

THE PATH TO SIN

As you follow the chronicle of David's life in 2 Samuel, you notice this king, leader of his people, wasn't where he should have been, which is always dangerous! It was spring, the time for kings to go to war, but David stayed home, apparently enjoying the luxuries of his palace. As you read the text from 2 Samuel 11, underline every reference to *David*, including the pronouns that refer to him.

2 SAMUEL 11:1-5

¹ Then it happened in the spring, at the time when kings go out to battle, that David sent Joab and his servants with him and all Israel, and they destroyed the sons of Ammon and besieged Rabbah. But David stayed at Jerusalem.

² Now when evening came David arose from his bed and walked around on the roof of the king's house, and from the roof he saw a woman bathing; and the woman was very beautiful in appearance.

³ So David sent and inquired about the woman. And one said, "Is this not Bathsheba, the daughter of Eliam, the wife of Uriah the Hittite?"

⁴ David sent messengers and took her, and when she came to him, he lay with her; and when she had purified herself from her uncleanness, she returned to her house.

⁵ The woman conceived; and she sent and told David, and said, "I am pregnant."

This one evening…this one act…this one transgression against his God was about to cost David more than he could imagine. Did you notice *what* happened, *how* it happened, *when* it happened, *why* it happened? To make sure you don't miss anything, list what you learn from marking the references to *David*.

Do you find yourself relating to David? Have you seen a beautiful woman you can't get out of your mind? Or are you attracted to a particular man? Do you find yourself tempted, ready to toss caution aside for the sake of fulfilling your desires? If so, I urge you to postpone your decision until you finish this book. You need to understand the gravity of your actions. You need to consider your future.

Or maybe you relate to David because you've followed in his footsteps. If so, you already understand the need for vigilance, don't you?

Now read these verses again. This time mark all the references to *Bathsheba,* then list what you learn about her. Notice that God does not waste words. He wants to make sure we understand that David is aware of who this woman is.

If David had obeyed God's commands in Deuteronomy 17:18-20, then he had a copy of the Torah, written by his own hand. Every king was commanded to "write for himself a copy of this law" and keep it with him to read all the days of his life. Surely David knew the Law. He knew what God said about adultery. So how did David end up with Uriah's wife in his bed? If a king, steeped in the Law, could so blindly choose the path of immorality, what can we learn that might keep us from sin and God's judgment? Let's go back to two passages of Scripture that help us understand how a person gets on the road that dead ends in sin.

Read Genesis 3:1-8 aloud. Mark every reference to *the woman,* including the pronouns and the synonym *wife.*

[1] Now the serpent was more crafty than any beast of the field which the LORD God had made. And he said to the woman, "Indeed, has God said, 'You shall not eat from any tree of the garden'?"

[2] The woman said to the serpent, "From the fruit of the trees of the garden we may eat;

³ but from the fruit of the tree which is in the middle of the garden, God has said, 'You shall not eat from it or touch it, or you will die.'"

⁴ The serpent said to the woman, "You surely shall not die!

⁵ "For God knows that in the day you eat from it your eyes will be opened, and you will be like God, knowing good and evil."

⁶ When the woman saw that the tree was good for food, and that it was a delight to the eyes, and that the tree was desirable to make one wise, she took from its fruit and ate; and she gave also to her husband with her, and he ate.

⁷ Then the eyes of both of them were opened, and they knew that they were naked; and they sewed fig leaves together and made themselves loin coverings.

⁸ They heard the sound of the LORD God walking in the garden in the cool of the day, and the man and his wife hid themselves from the presence of the LORD God among the trees of the garden.

Now, just so you don't miss it, underline the verbs in verses 6-8 that detail the progression of the woman's actions. What do you see? How did that forbidden fruit get into Eve's mouth—and Adam's?

Let's look at one more passage before we move on with David's story, because each of these accounts—David with Bathsheba, Eve and the forbidden fruit, and the sin of Achan at Ai—reveals the path to sin, and you need to know how to avoid that route!

Let me give you the setting of these next verses we want to look at in Joshua. The children of Israel are about to conquer Jericho. God is going to bring down the walls, and the Israelites are going to take the city. God, however, has put the city under the ban, which means the Israelites are to take no spoils of war.

Read the text that follows and mark two things: Draw a box like this ☐ around the words *under the ban* and underline every reference to *Achan* (who fought against Jericho), including pronouns.

JOSHUA 6:17-18; 7:20-21

¹⁷ The city shall be under the ban, it and all that is in it belongs to the LORD; only Rahab the harlot and all who are with her in the house shall live, because she hid the messengers whom we sent.

¹⁸ But as for you, only keep yourselves from the things under the ban, so that you do not covet them and take some of the things under the ban, and make the camp of Israel accursed and bring trouble on it….

⁷:²⁰ So Achan answered Joshua and said, "Truly, I have sinned against the LORD, the God of Israel, and this is what I did:

²¹ when I saw among the spoil a beautiful mantle from Shinar and two hundred shekels of silver and a bar of gold fifty shekels in weight, then I coveted them and took them; and behold, they are concealed in the earth inside my tent with the silver underneath it."

Look again at verse 21 and underline the verbs. Note the sequence of what happened, what Achan did.

Now, my friend, let's look at these three passages together: the accounts of David, Eve, and Achan. What do they have in common?

Is there any similarity in the actions or activities of David, Eve, and Achan? What? What is the path to sin?

Do you see it? David *saw* Bathsheba, a woman who was not his wife, and he *desired* her and he *took* her. Just as Eve *saw, desired,* and *took.* Just as Achan *saw, desired,* and *took.* Eve didn't have to sin; she knew what God said. Achan didn't have to sin; he had heard God's orders. David didn't have to sin; he knew the Commandments, what God had said about adultery.

Not only did David not have to sin, he could have quenched the fires of desire simply by calling one of his wives to his bed. He could have been satisfied by the breasts of his wife and exhilarated by her love as Proverbs 5 says.

Yet at that moment—that fateful moment—David wanted what he saw, and he decided to take another man's wife even though he knew it was wrong. He heard his servant's words, "Is this not Bathsheba, the daughter of Eliam, the wife of Uriah the Hittite?"

David knew the answer. David knew God's answer. As I said, David had his own copy of God's Law. He could not claim ignorance.

The Web of Deceit

David chose to sin, and God chose to open Bathsheba's womb. David was caught and he knew it. He had just slept with the wife of one of his valiant men, part of his elite fighting force. Uriah, the husband of the woman he had just violated, was at war, where the king should have been. What could David do? How could he cover his sin?

Read 2 Samuel 11:6-27. Underline every reference to *David* and circle every reference to *Uriah.*

6 Then David sent to Joab, saying, "Send me Uriah the Hittite." So Joab sent Uriah to David.

7 When Uriah came to him, David asked concerning the welfare of Joab
and the people and the state of the war.

8 Then David said to Uriah, "Go down to your house, and wash your feet."
And Uriah went out of the king's house, and a present from the king was sent
out after him.

9 But Uriah slept at the door of the king's house with all the servants of his
lord, and did not go down to his house.

10 Now when they told David, saying, "Uriah did not go down to his
house," David said to Uriah, "Have you not come from a journey? Why did
you not go down to your house?"

11 Uriah said to David, "The ark and Israel and Judah are staying in tempo-
rary shelters, and my lord Joab and the servants of my lord are camping in the
open field. Shall I then go to my house to eat and to drink and to lie with my
wife? By your life and the life of your soul, I will not do this thing."

As you read this portion, what did you learn about David? What was
happening in this scene? Think it through and record your insights.

And what did you learn about Uriah?

Think about Uriah's situation. Surely he has missed his wife. Here is a woman David has craved because of her beauty, so wouldn't her husband be longing to sleep with her? At the prime of life, a man is ready for sex at least every two days simply because of the accumulation of semen in his body. Here is Uriah's opportunity to enjoy a night with his wife—yet he doesn't take it. You saw why: Uriah is a man of principle.

Have you ever watched someone take the path of virtue when you wanted to do what you knew was wrong or less than honorable? And how did you feel? What did you wish about the one who was determined to take the high and sacrificial path? You wished that he or she hadn't shown up. You wished he'd go away—or that you could persuade him to compromise. It certainly would make you feel better!

Listen to what David did. He wasn't about to abandon his cover-up plan. Uriah *had* to sleep with his wife. It was imperative for Uriah to believe that the child Bathsheba carried was his own. The people could not know that the king had sent his men to battle while he stayed home and slept with a warrior's wife!

Every man has his breaking point, a moral Achilles heel—or so David thought. Watch what he does next. As you read the text continue to mark the references to *David* and *Uriah*.

12 Then David said to Uriah, "Stay here today also, and tomorrow I will let you go." So Uriah remained in Jerusalem that day and the next.

13 Now David called him, and he ate and drank before him, and he made him drunk; and in the evening he went out to lie on his bed with his lord's servants, but he did not go down to his house.

It hadn't worked! Here's a man who stood firm on his convictions even when drunk, which is most unusual. I have heard many a sad story of innocence lost in the fog of drunkenness.

14 Now in the morning David wrote a letter to Joab and sent it by the hand of Uriah.

¹⁵ He had written in the letter, saying, "Place Uriah in the front line of the fiercest battle and withdraw from him, so that he may be struck down and die."

Uriah could even be trusted not to open a letter that carried his death sentence!

¹⁶ So it was as Joab kept watch on the city, that he put Uriah at the place where he knew there were valiant men.

¹⁷ The men of the city went out and fought against Joab, and some of the people among David's servants fell; and Uriah the Hittite also died.

David the warrior-king had finally found a way to cover his sin. But had he covered it completely? Watch Joab's response.

¹⁸ Then Joab sent and reported to David all the events of the war.

¹⁹ He charged the messenger, saying, "When you have finished telling all the events of the war to the king,

²⁰ and if it happens that the king's wrath rises and he says to you, 'Why did you go so near to the city to fight? Did you not know that they would shoot from the wall?

²¹ 'Who struck down Abimelech the son of Jerubbesheth? Did not a woman throw an upper millstone on him from the wall so that he died at Thebez? Why did you go so near the wall?'—then you shall say, 'Your servant Uriah the Hittite is dead also.'"

²² So the messenger departed and came and reported to David all that Joab had sent him to tell.

Joab knew what David wanted. He sent the king a return message saying in essence, "The mission was accomplished, but don't put the blame on me."

23 The messenger said to David, "The men prevailed against us and came

out against us in the field, but we pressed them as far as the entrance of the

gate.

24 "Moreover, the archers shot at your servants from the wall; so some of

the king's servants are dead, and your servant Uriah the Hittite is also dead."

25 Then David said to the messenger, "Thus you shall say to Joab, 'Do

not let this thing displease you, for the sword devours one as well as another;

make your battle against the city stronger and overthrow it'; and so encourage

him."

Can you hear the softness of David's voice? the gentleness of his words? the grace he extends to Joab? "The sword devours one as well as another."

What hypocrisy! David not only committed adultery, he ordered the purposeful death of a man who couldn't be persuaded to let go of his righteousness! What webs of deceit we weave, little realizing that the thread from the spindle to the shuttle is wrapped around our feet.

THE RIGHTEOUS JUDGE, THE GRACIOUS JUSTIFIER

David's cover-up was complete. It wasn't exactly as he planned, but he pulled it off. Now he could bring Bathsheba to his house and sleep with her without fear of any reprisal. I'm sure he must have felt relieved, though perhaps a little disheartened that Uriah had forced him to such extreme measures. If only Uriah had gone home to see his wife, he would have lived. But in David's sin-sick reasoning, Uriah was expendable! Isn't that always the way it is when we break our covenant with God and with our mate? We deem their love and respect expendable for the sake of fulfilling our desires.

For David the passion of the moment overpowered a life of integrity and led to even deeper sin—the taking not only of a man's wife but of his life. He would later regret this decision for the rest of his days, but somehow he failed at the time to see that. If only David had stopped to consider his future, if only he had thought his actions through to their logical conclusion, he would have realized that God would never let him get away with sin.

26 Now when the wife of Uriah heard that Uriah her husband was dead, she mourned for her husband.

27 When the time of mourning was over, David sent and brought her to his house and she became his wife; then she bore him a son. But the thing that David had done was evil in the sight of the LORD.

David's adultery was hidden—but not from God! David's murder of Uriah was hidden from all but Joab—and God! Joab could be trusted to keep quiet because of his position in David's service, but God would not remain silent. How we need to remember this. You may swear others to secrecy, but you can never persuade God to be anything but true to His nature. God's eyes are too pure to behold sin and not judge it.

No one—no one—can shield his sin from God's view. "The eyes of the LORD move to and fro throughout the earth" (2 Chronicles 16:9). It matters not, my friend, whether or not you believe God exists; you cannot hide your sin from Him. "Behold, you have sinned against the LORD, and be sure your sin will find you out" (Numbers 32:23).

So what does God do about it? He sends the prophet Nathan with a story for the king. David listens without suspicion and unknowingly pronounces his own judgment! As you read the account in 2 Samuel 12, mark the references to the poor man's *ewe lamb*. (A ewe is a female, just in case you're not into animal husbandry.)

1 And he came to him and said, "There were two men in one city, the one rich and the other poor.

² "The rich man had a great many flocks and herds.

³ "But the poor man had nothing except one little ewe lamb which he bought and nourished; and it grew up together with him and his children. It would eat of his bread and drink of his cup and lie in his bosom, and was like a daughter to him.

⁴ "Now a traveler came to the rich man, and he was unwilling to take from his own flock or his own herd, to prepare for the wayfarer who had come to him; rather he took the poor man's ewe lamb and prepared it for the man who had come to him."

⁵ Then David's anger burned greatly against the man, and he said to Nathan, "As the LORD lives, surely the man who has done this deserves to die.

⁶ "He must make restitution for the lamb fourfold, because he did this thing and had no compassion."

The man had taken only a lamb, yet David in righteous indignation says he deserves to die! The story has been told, the judgment passed, and David never makes a connection until a proverbial finger is stuck in his face:

⁷ Nathan then said to David, "You are the man!"

Reality dawns: *The man's only lamb...Uriah had only Bathsheba, while I have many wives! Bathsheba was all Uriah had, and he cherished her. In my lust I took her from him when I could have had one of my own wives! I violated her. I violated Uriah. Then I purposefully brought about the death of others, ordering defeat for my men and Joab, just to cover my sin.*

The gravity of it all comes home as Nathan delivers God's message:

⁷ "Thus says the LORD God of Israel, 'It is I who anointed you king over Israel and it is I who delivered you from the hand of Saul.

⁸ 'I also gave you your master's house and your master's wives into your care, and I gave you the house of Israel and Judah; and if that had been too little, I would have added to you many more things like these!' "

Listen to those words again: *"and if that had been too little, I would have added to you many more things like these."*

Choosing sex outside of God's parameters means missing what could have been. David could have had more, much more, if only he had not committed adultery. If only he had confessed his sin instead of trying to cover it. Sin always takes you farther than you wanted to go.

In the heat of his passion, David never stopped to consider what one moment of illegitimate sex would cost him. David would confess his sin—cry out to God, groan in his bed day and night, wetting his pillow with his tears—but it would not alter the consequences of his willful disobedience. David had despised the word of the Lord.

How descriptive of our culture today. Every time we participate in sex outside the boundaries of God's Word, we are despising what God has said. Every time we go against the revealed will of God as written in the Bible, we despise the Word of the Lord. We despise God as God!

Read what Nathan tells David. Watch for every occurrence of the word *despised* and underline it.

⁹ " 'Why have you despised the word of the LORD by doing evil in His sight? You have struck down Uriah the Hittite with the sword, have taken his wife to be your wife, and have killed him with the sword of the sons of Ammon.

¹⁰ 'Now therefore, the sword shall never depart from your house, because you have despised Me and have taken the wife of Uriah the Hittite to be your wife.' "

Joab put Uriah in the front of the battle. Joab ordered the other warriors to withdraw from him. A son of Ammon killed Uriah. Yet God says that *David* is his murderer. David broke three of God's Ten Commandments in a matter of days: He coveted his neighbor's wife, he committed adultery, and he murdered.

What the courts of law would have to say, whatever verdict they might pass would not matter. The righteous Judge had reached his decision: GUILTY!

And how would David be sentenced? What would be the just punishment for his sin?

First, the sword would never depart from his house. There would always be war, death, and destruction until he died.

Second, "Behold, I will raise up evil against you from your own household" (2 Samuel 12:11). There would be conflict in David's home. One of his sons would rape his daughter, another son would try to steal the kingdom from him...the tragedies go on and on.

Third, "I will even take your wives before your eyes and give them to your companion, and he will lie with your wives in broad daylight. Indeed you did it secretly, but I will do this thing before all Israel, and under the sun" (verses 11-12). In the not-too-distant future Absalom, David's son, would sleep in a tent with David's concubine. A tent purposefully pitched in the sight of all Israel! What disgrace! What open rebellion!

How many men today know the grief of a son's adulterous ways as he follows in his father's footsteps? The father commits adultery; the children live with their sex partners before marriage—sometimes just to spite the parent who hurt them and destroyed their family.

Fourth, David's child by Bathsheba would die. Though David fasted and prayed, pleading with God to spare the child's life, he did not change God's mind.

Judgment for immorality comes in a multiplicity of ways, but it always comes—and its repercussions don't always stop with the offender. You might object and say, "God, that's not fair," but how can you call God unfair? God says we're to obey, and if we do, we won't have to go any further in our argument. You and I are to do what God tells us, not sit as His judge!

In the case of the ewe lamb, the king declared that the rich man deserved to die. But the final sentence he pronounced found its source in Exodus 22:1, which decrees that any man who steals a sheep must pay back four in return. David, as judge, declared that the man was to repay fourfold what he had taken.

Then David, as a defendant convicted of his crime, had to take the punishment he had meted out to the fictional rich man. He owed a fourfold debt for his sin. It's interesting that David would lose four of his sons after committing adultery with Bathsheba and putting Uriah to death. Whether this in itself constituted the fourfold punishment or whether the sentence was carried out in the events Nathan foretold, David's punishment was grave.

All David could do was repent, agree with God, call his actions what they were—*sin*. And that's just what David did. He said to Nathan, "I have sinned against the LORD" (2 Samuel 12:13). Later in Psalm 51 he would write, "Against thee, thee only, have I sinned" (verse 4, KJV). Oh, if we could only understand that all sin is ultimately against God, even when it involves human victims—for man is God's creation.

What was the response to David's immediate repentance? Listen to Nathan's words, "The LORD also has taken away your sin; you shall not die" (2 Samuel 12:13).

The man sent to confront David in his sin was the same man who declared to him God's forgiveness. What an awesome picture of our God— *just* in dealing with sin and the *justifier* of those who repent.

Only a God of utmost grace could offer such forgiveness when David— the writer of Psalms, the king of Israel—had by his actions "given occasion to the enemies of the LORD to blaspheme" (verse 14). But then God always has been a God of grace—lavish, extravagant grace. Where sin did abound, grace did much more abound.[1] From the seed of David would come the Messiah, the redeemer of David's sin and yours and mine, beloved.

THE CONSEQUENCES OF ADULTERY

We've seen the consequences of adultery for David; what about for the rest of us?

First, *adultery breaks a covenant* because it violates the unique oneness of flesh shared by a husband and a wife. Remember, the one who joins himself to a harlot (prostitute) becomes one flesh with her, as we read in 1 Corinthians 6.

I received such a sad letter from a woman whose husband committed suicide. He had battled manic depression and wouldn't take his medicine. He also battled immorality, and he wouldn't take his medicine for that either. His adulteries were numerous, as were those of his father, his grandfather, and his great-grandfather—and they all were pastors! Her husband did not have "affairs"; he had repeated "sexual encounters with nameless and faceless women."

She tried and tried to hold the marriage together, but he wouldn't stop. So she moved out with her sons. If only he had believed, if only he would have clung to God "as the waistband clings to the waist of a man" (Jeremiah 13:11), he could have walked in victory, one step at a time.

But because he instead held tightly to his sin, he missed what could have been—and so did his family. When this precious woman wrote of her pain and guilt, wondering if she could have done more, if she should have stayed, if it might have kept him from suicide, my answer had to be, "No, dear, you should not have stayed. Your husband's repeated adulteries broke the marriage covenant." Manic depression, like any other mental illness, is a physical problem, but it's not a free pass into the game of immorality.

Second, *adultery brings judgment*—the judgment of the Almighty who "has been a witness between you and the wife of your youth, against whom you have dealt treacherously, though she is your companion and your wife by covenant" (Malachi 2:14).

Are you a little incredulous at God's punishment of David? A bit put off by all He did to His chosen king? Do you want to say (even if you have to whisper it under your breath),

"But, God, David confessed! Why did You judge him so severely?

Why does David have to miss what could have been,

the 'more' that You would have done for him?

I just don't understand!"

If these are your thoughts, you're right: You don't understand! You need a fuller appreciation of the character of God and of the gravity of sin. Sin has become too common and grace too cheap.

When we think of grace, we often think of getting off scot-free, with no consequences. We think a simple "I'm sorry, God" will return everything to the way it was before. But that's not grace. Grace is not license to sin; rather it is power to keep you from sin. Grace doesn't mean we don't reap the consequences. Grace is favor; it is everything that God has made available to us, but as I just said, it doesn't remove the consequences.

You can have sexual intercourse, then tell God you're sorry, and in grace God will forgive you. But His forgiveness will not obliterate the consequences of your actions. It doesn't mean you won't contract a sexually transmitted disease if your partner was infected, or that you won't get pregnant if the "seed" was sown.

When we sow to the flesh, we reap the consequences. And in reality the consequences are for our good, to teach us to abhor sin and fear God.

David understood all this. There's no record of his being bitter toward God. He bore his punishment as a man of God should, and from that came some of the most encouraging and inspiring words of hope mankind will ever possess, the Psalms. Some psalms were written after David's sin with Bathsheba. One of these is Psalm 51, which we'll look at later. It will bring such hope.

The third consequence of adultery is that *it gives biblical grounds for divorce.* Not that divorce is recommended; on the contrary, God wants to see repentance and forgiveness. But according to Jesus' teaching in Matthew 19:9, sexual immorality breaks the physical oneness of your covenant and thus gives the violated party the right to divorce.

I won't go into the subject of divorce because, though it's a crucial matter, it isn't the topic of this book. You can study this subject inductively from A to Z (or should I say from Alpha to Omega?) and learn what the Bible teaches about divorce by getting our Precept course *A Marriage Without Regrets.* I also cover the topic in a book from Harvest House Publishers, also titled *A Marriage Without Regrets.*

Fourth, *adultery causes a child to stumble.* It gives the wrong example, a distorted picture to our children, the next generation whom God says we're to help come to Him. Malachi 2:15-16 says if you are seeking godly offspring, you don't divorce your mate and you don't cover your garment with wrong. In Exodus 34:7, God warns us that the sins of the fathers are passed on to the next generation. It becomes a sickening cycle: Immorality leads to divorce, divorce to immorality, and immorality to divorce...

Fifth, *immorality puts your children in a vulnerable position.* Their parent *must* be judged and their parent *will* be judged because the Bible says God will judge fornicators and adulterers. Immorality scars or destroys the family unit and puts the child at risk. Even in the best situations, remarriage to someone who is not the child's father or mother brings conflict because of the lack of natural affection. The discipline of the child becomes a topic for disagreement: "Whose child is this anyway?" "My loyalty is to my child!" It also puts your child at risk for physical and sexual abuse when you marry a man or woman who is not the natural parent. My files are filled with heart-breaking stories of lives scarred by abuse from the new parent in the home.

Can you see what happens? Immorality, adultery breaks the oneness of a husband and wife, which is vital to a child's security and protection. I cannot tell you all the questions on this very issue that Jan Silvious and I dealt with during our five years of a Sunday night live call-in program. The letters we received, the children who were unbelievably traumatized. They missed "the more" that they could have had if their parents had only kept their passions under God's holy lock and key!

Sixth, *adultery hurts God*—truly hurts Him. Think of that when you're tempted to have your hour in bed, a bed you have no right to be in! In Ezekiel 6:9 God speaks to Israel, His wife by covenant, as He pronounces His judgment on her adultery:

> Then those of you who escape will remember Me among the nations
> to which they will be carried captive, how I have been hurt by their
> adulterous hearts which turned away from Me, and by their eyes
> which played the harlot after their idols; and they will loathe them-
> selves in their own sight for the evils which they have committed, for
> all their abominations.

Rest assured, eventually the immoral, the adulterer will loathe himself in his own eyes. But when he or she stands before God and sees the pain in His eyes as He mourns what might have been, the adulterer will be grieved beyond measure. And it will be too late, for it is appointed unto man once to die and after that the judgment.[2]

Hear the pathos of God's cry when He says to Israel, "You adulteress wife, who takes strangers instead of her husband!" What had she done?

In the passage that follows, listen to her Husband testify. Take note as to what she did and how it affected Him, for there is much to learn here, much to caution us—and, I pray, to put the fear of God in us. As you read, under-line every *you* and *your.*

EZEKIEL 16:15-17,20-21,25-26,28-30

15 "But you trusted in your beauty and played the harlot because of your fame, and you poured out your harlotries on every passer-by who might be willing.

16 "You took some of your clothes, made for yourself high places of various colors and played the harlot on them, which should never come about nor happen.

17 "You also took your beautiful jewels made of My gold and of My silver, which I had given you, and made for yourself male images that you might play the harlot with them....

20 "Moreover, you took your sons and daughters whom you had borne to Me and sacrificed them to idols to be devoured. Were your harlotries so small a matter?

21 "You slaughtered My children and offered them up to idols by causing them to pass through the fire....

25 "You built yourself a high place at the top of every street and made your beauty abominable, and you spread your legs to every passer-by to multiply your harlotry.

26 "You also played the harlot with the Egyptians, your lustful neighbors, and multiplied your harlotry to make Me angry....

28 "Moreover, you played the harlot with the Assyrians because you were not satisfied; you played the harlot with them and still were not satisfied.

29 "You also multiplied your harlotry with the land of merchants, Chaldea, yet even with this you were not satisfied."

30 "How languishing is your heart," declares the Lord GOD, "while you do all these things, the actions of a bold-faced harlot."

What did you learn from marking the references to *you*? What all had God's "wife" done? List these things below.

All her immorality left her unsatisfied, and it will be no different for you if you succumb to the desires of your flesh. The momentary pleasure will leave you gnawingly unsatisfied and God's heart deeply broken because you loved another more than you loved Him.

And not only that, but *adultery gives cause for the enemies of God to blaspheme His name,* as we've already seen in David's case. This is the seventh consequence of adultery.

His enemies can say, in effect, *Ha, God! I slept with Your Son's bride!*

Do you realize that every time we sin—we who call ourselves Christians—it racks up another victory for the Enemy? Our sin leads the world to believe "there's nothing to this 'God stuff.'" And this is a world God longs to bring to Himself! I'm sure you've heard the comments: "Christians aren't any different than us; they just have a lot more rules! What good does it do to be a Christian?"

Our lives, when lived as God says is right, should take away the world's excuse for sin. Yet more often than not, our unrighteous lifestyles provide people with a covering, an excuse for their sin.

You hear the blasphemy all the time, don't you? On television, radio, talk shows, in sitcoms, in cartoons, in print, in the movies, on billboards. Oh that we would live differently! That we would show the world we need not be governed by the lust of our eyes. We can turn away from what we see, so that the desire wanes and we don't find ourselves eating the forbidden fruit of sex, wrecking our lives and those of others.

It *is* possible to be a sexual being and walk in purity! It's a matter of choice, minute by minute, opportunity by opportunity. A choice that will keep you from missing what might have been. Think of what might have been for David. Think then of what happened because David walked by the lust of his eyes, the lust of his flesh, and committed adultery.

This very point—and the fact of what our adultery does to God and to Jesus, our heavenly Bridegroom who desires to receive us as a chaste virgin—has prompted me to renew my vow, made so long ago, that I would keep myself pure no matter what. I don't want to break His heart, and I don't want people scoffing at the Bridegroom and His bride. I'm determined she'll wear white!

That's why I'm so glad we're doing this study together, so we don't miss the "much more" that God longs to lavish upon us.

Oh beloved, don't you long to have all that God wants for you? You can. It comes with obedience out of love for God above all others, including yourself.

Consider your future...

Jerusalem sinned greatly,
Therefore she has become an unclean thing.
All who honored her despise her
Because they have seen her nakedness;
Even she herself groans and turns away.
Her uncleanness was in her skirts;
She did not consider her future.
Therefore she has fallen astonishingly.
    (Lamentations 1:8-9)

7

The Value of Righteous Indignation

Who Are We to Judge What Others Do?

Dorie Van Stone[1] and I were taking a long walk in a neighborhood adjoining Precept Ministries International's headquarters in Chattanooga, Tennessee, where we both live. I'd found a wounded ball discarded in a vacant lot and was kicking it up the hill and across the streets, running to rescue it from driveways and drain holes. I was back and forth across the road, chasing my ball while we walked and talked.

Dorie is one of my very special friends. Deserted by her father, neglected by her mother, she was placed in an orphanage—and later in foster homes—where she was physically and sexually abused before and after she came to know the Lord. The beautiful ending to the story is that she believed God and allowed His Word to heal her, and now she's being greatly used to help tens of thousands. Dorie speaks publicly across North America and in many foreign countries, telling her story and giving hope and help to others who have experienced similar things in their lives or know others who have.

She's also written books about her experience. Her first one, *Dorie: The Girl Nobody Loved,* tells everything about her childhood—except the sexual abuse. Like hundreds of thousands of others, Dorie was afraid no one would believe her and she would be rejected even more. I so well remember the day, the restaurant where we lingered as she spilled the full truth of her story. She's since shared it in her book *No Place to Cry,* but apart from her husband, I was one of the first two people to know about it. Honestly, I wasn't surprised; in fact I surmised that it had probably happened, but I'd never asked.

I recall her first question after she told me of the sexual degradation she had suffered: "Do you still love me?" I knew she wasn't questioning the genuineness of my love as much as she was questioning her worth now that I knew the "real" Dorie. To me it was a crazy question—knowing her full story made me love and want to protect her even more—yet it is a common concern for those who have been sexually abused. The shame and trauma connected with sexual abuse are so hard to grasp if you've never been its victim.

On that neighborhood walk years later, while I was kicking the ball, our conversation turned to what she had suffered, how people responded when they heard her story of abuse, and how we could help other abuse victims. I could hear Dorie—but suddenly I lost sight of her. Stopping the ball with my foot, I turned around to look for her. There she stood, practically yelling, both hands thrown up in the air as she gestured dramatically in typical Dorie fashion, "They've got to know we believe them! They've got to know!"

Like a kid, this woman who is older than I am ran toward me, grabbed my arm, looked up, and with characteristic passion said, "For years they've kept it a secret because they thought no one would believe the sexual abuse they suffered. And they believed that if others knew, they wouldn't want to be around them anymore. They wouldn't love them anymore. They would think they were dirty." Dorie gave me a gentle push. "And they'd say, 'Get away. I don't want anything to do with you.'"

Dorie stood on tiptoe, her flashing brown eyes, almost black with intensity, looking straight into mine. "Oh, Kay, don't you remember when I first told you?"

"I do, Dorie. And I remember your first words when you finished. You asked, 'Do you still love me?'"

"Kay, Kay," she cried as she grabbed my arm, "they have to know we won't reject them."

They have to know we won't reject them!

Think with me, my friend, of the pain that could be assuaged, the wounds healed, the lives saved, the futures rescued, if we would take a walk, so to speak, with the adulterers, the homosexuals, the transvestites, the alcoholics, the drug addicts, the prostitutes, the pedophiles, and listen to their stories. Let them talk. Believe them. And don't reject them because of...

what they've endured,

the lifestyle they turned to in their pain,

their perverted view of sex because of their initiation into its twisted forms,

what they, in their distorted thinking, have done to others,

all because they either didn't turn to God or didn't even know He had a solution—a healthy, healing way out!

Do you realize that one of every three girls has been sexually abused by the age of eighteen? The statistics for boys are not clear because males are so much more reticent to talk about it, but some believe the figure for them may be just as high. Those of us who've never been abused sexually cannot begin to imagine their pain, their shame, their feelings of betrayal, worthlessness, and anger.

And what happens to these young men and women? Many of them will become promiscuous. Others will turn to members of the same sex for gratification. Still others will go into prostitution because they've already been used and see no point in trying to stay pure. Some will become molesters of children themselves.

What would happen if...

we listened with our hearts as we sat beside them, trying to understand how they ended up where they are,

and *only then* shared with them what can become of their lives because God is God?

What would happen if...

we let God pass by and, grabbing their arms, we cried, "The LORD, the LORD God, compassionate and gracious, slow to anger, and abounding in lovingkindness and truth; who keeps lovingkindness for thousands, who forgives iniquity, transgression and sin; yet He will by no means leave the guilty unpunished, visiting the iniquity of fathers on the children and on the grandchildren to the third and fourth generations" (Exodus 34:6-7)...

and *then* we told them of this One who would cleanse and heal their wounds, free them from a guilty conscience, and break the cycle of the iniquity of generations?

What would happen then?

I'm not naive; I realize many of them would not believe and would walk away, continuing down the broad road that leads to destruction. But not all! Some would listen, and God would pour out His lovingkindness upon them. They would hear God's message through us, and in trembling faith they would believe and walk with us through the narrow gate that leads to eternal life.

Beloved, if you're going to discover what God says about sex, you have to look at what the Scriptures say about homosexuality, and other forms of sexual perversion. However, as we do, I want to be sure you understand my heart. If you're involved in *any* of these things, including incest or the sexual abuse of children, it's imperative that you see for yourself what God says and that you understand that you do what you do, not because you were born that way, but because of your wrong initiation into sex…because you didn't know the truth…because of a lie you believed somewhere along the way.

Are you hearing me, my friend? Are you reading this closely? You don't need to agree with me, just hear me. Sexual deviation has been proven to be a learned behavior. Your initiation to sex as a child, a teen, or an adult greatly impacts how you conduct yourself sexually.

Right now I can't take a walk with you and listen to your story, even though I would count it an honor to have you share it with me (and you can do that by letter if you'd like). But may I urge you to listen to God, to listen carefully? Listen with your heart and with your mind, beloved. Let Him speak. Reason with Him. Believe Him in the same way you want to be believed when you're trying to explain something of importance.

Listen in this chapter and in the chapters to come as we discuss other issues you may need to deal with if you've become caught in Satan's snare. And remember, I'm not judging you. It's God's Word that judges us all. I simply want to help you discover what God says about such behaviors in the hope that you will embrace the truth. When you do, God says He will save you from your bondage to sin—not on the basis of the deeds you have done, but according to His mercy, by the washing of regeneration and renewing by the Holy Spirit.[2]

The Sin of Sodom and Gomorrah

I want us to deal first with homosexuality because it's such a major issue in America today.

In the Bible, the first time we encounter men desiring men for sexual purposes is in the account of the destruction of Sodom and Gomorrah. Archaeologists have not yet uncovered these two cities, but Scripture tells us they were numbered among five "cities of the valley" (or plain) in the days of Abraham. They were probably situated in the valley of Siddim, near the Dead Sea. It's likely that the ruins of these cities are now covered by the sea's shallow end toward the south.

At the time of the destruction of Sodom and Gomorrah, Abraham was ninety-nine years old. His wife, Sarah, was eighty-nine and had been barren all her life. Twenty-four years earlier, God had promised Abraham and Sarah a son, but they were still waiting for

the child of the promise,

the child of the covenant,

the child through whom would come a great and unique
nation,

the child through whom would one day come the Messiah,
the Redeemer of mankind.

One day, as Abraham sat beside the Oaks of Mamre in Hebron, he was approached by three men whose identity was unknown to him. The Scriptures, however, reveal that two were God's angelic messengers and the third was a theophany, a preincarnate appearance of the Messiah, the One who in the fullness of time would be born of a daughter of Abraham so He could taste death for all mankind. The three men brought the long-awaited confirmation that, after almost twenty-five years of waiting, Sarah would give birth to the child God had promised Abraham through a covenant.

After they gave this news to Abraham, the three men rose and looked toward Sodom. They intended to visit the city to see if the sin of the people was as great as the outcry against it. As the two angelic messengers left to make their way toward Sodom, the Lord lingered behind to tell Abraham of the impending judgment of these cities. Abraham then began to challenge God about destroying the city and sweeping away the righteous with the wicked. To Abraham, this judgment didn't seem fair. Their discussion continued until the Lord promised that even if only ten righteous persons could be found there, the city would not be destroyed.

And what was the sin of Sodom that brought such a great outcry? Some identify the sin exclusively by what Ezekiel wrote:

Behold, this was the guilt of your sister Sodom: she and her daughters had arrogance, abundant food and careless ease, but she did not help the poor and needy. Thus they were haughty and committed abominations before Me. Therefore I removed them when I saw it. (Ezekiel 16:49-50)

On the basis of these verses, some say God destroyed the city only because its people didn't care for the poor and the needy. Is that true?

By the time Ezekiel penned those words, Sodom and Gomorrah were long gone, swept away in God's destruction despite Abraham's defense, for not even ten righteous could be found in the city. In Ezekiel's allegorical description of the sin of Israel and her sisters, God seems to parallel the sins of the sisters with the sins of Sodom. We don't know exactly the full meaning of this passage, but Genesis 19 reveals the abomination that was being committed in the city of Sodom.

Read Genesis 19:1-13 for yourself and see what you discover. As you read, color or underline every reference to *the men of the city of Sodom,* including pronouns. Also circle or mark in another color every reference to the *two angels* and their pronouns.

¹ Now the two angels came to Sodom in the evening as Lot was sitting in the gate of Sodom. When Lot saw them, he rose to meet them and bowed down with his face to the ground.

² And he said, "Now behold, my lords, please turn aside into your servant's house, and spend the night, and wash your feet; then you may rise early and go on your way." They said however, "No, but we shall spend the night in the square."

³ Yet he urged them strongly, so they turned aside to him and entered his house; and he prepared a feast for them, and baked unleavened bread, and they ate.

⁴ Before they lay down, the men of the city, the men of Sodom, surrounded the house, both young and old, all the people from every quarter;

⁵ and they called to Lot and said to him, "Where are the men who came to you tonight? Bring them out to us that we may have relations with them."

⁶ But Lot went out to them at the doorway, and shut the door behind him,

⁷ and said, "Please, my brothers, do not act wickedly.

⁸ "Now behold, I have two daughters who have not had relations with man; please let me bring them out to you, and do to them whatever you like; only do nothing to these men, inasmuch as they have come under the shelter of my roof."

⁹ But they said, "Stand aside." Furthermore, they said, "This one came in as an alien, and already he is acting like a judge; now we will treat you worse than them." So they pressed hard against Lot and came near to break the door.

¹⁰ But the men reached out their hands and brought Lot into the house with them, and shut the door.

¹¹ They struck the men who were at the doorway of the house with blindness, both small and great, so that they wearied themselves trying to find the doorway.

¹² Then the two men said to Lot, "Whom else have you here? A son-in-law, and your sons, and your daughters, and whomever you have in the city, bring them out of the place;

¹³ for we are about to destroy this place, because their outcry has become so great before the LORD that the LORD has sent us to destroy it."

What did you learn from marking every reference to *the men of Sodom*? List your insights below.

Simply from reading the text, what do you think was the abomination being committed in Sodom—if indeed it was more than the arrogance, the prosperous and careless ease, and the refusal to help the poor and needy that Ezekiel referenced? As you record your answer, write out how you came to this conclusion simply from observing the text of Genesis 19:1-13.

Do you remember when we studied Leviticus 18 and you marked the word *abominations* with a big **A**? Let's look again at those verses. As you read this passage, once more mark each occurrence of *abominations* and *abominable* with a big **A.**

LEVITICUS 18:22-30

22 You shall not lie with a male as one lies with a female; it is an abomination.

23 Also you shall not have intercourse with any animal to be defiled with it, nor shall any woman stand before an animal to mate with it; it is a perversion.

24 Do not defile yourselves by any of these things; for by all these the nations which I am casting out before you have become defiled.

25 For the land has become defiled, therefore I have brought its punishment upon it, so the land has spewed out its inhabitants.

26 But as for you, you are to keep My statutes and My judgments and shall not do any of these abominations, neither the native, nor the alien who sojourns among you

27 (for the men of the land who have been before you have done all these abominations, and the land has become defiled);

28 so that the land will not spew you out, should you defile it, as it has spewed out the nation which has been before you.

29 For whoever does any of these abominations, those persons who do so shall be cut off from among their people.

30 Thus you are to keep My charge, that you do not practice any of the abominable customs which have been practiced before you, so as not to defile yourselves with them; I am the LORD your God.

What sexual practices are defined as *abominations* in these verses?

When God mentions "any of these abominations" in Leviticus 18:29-30, the reference obviously includes the incest and adultery mentioned in the first portion of Leviticus 18. However, do you see any parallel between verse 22 and the incident described in Genesis 19:1-11?

If you were to simply let the texts say what they say, what would you conclude is the abomination of Sodom that brought about its destruction?

The short book of Jude offers interesting insight into what transpired in Sodom. Let's look at it. Although this passage will take a few minutes to explain, I think it will be well worth the time. Jude wrote his epistle to urge those who received it to "contend earnestly for the faith which was once for all handed down to the saints" (verse 3). He wrote because certain ungodly persons had crept in unnoticed among the believers, individuals who not only were denying our only Master and Lord, Jesus Christ, but also were turning the grace of God into licentiousness—moral anarchy. They were saying you could live as immorally as you wanted and still go to heaven.

Jude wanted the believers to understand that God still hates what He has always hated; God's position on sin has not changed. Consequently God has to deal with those who defy His commandments. In this short epistle of only twenty-five verses, Jude speaks of God's judgment seven different times. He tells how God destroyed the angels who did not keep their own domain but indulged in gross immorality and went after strange flesh and how God destroyed Sodom and Gomorrah and the cities around them because they, like those angels, indulged in gross immorality and went after strange flesh. Let's read the verses:

JUDE 6-7

6 And angels who did not keep their own domain, but abandoned their

proper abode, He has kept in eternal bonds under darkness for the judgment

of the great day,

7 just as Sodom and Gomorrah and the cities around them, since they in

the same way as these indulged in gross immorality and went after strange

flesh, are exhibited as an example in undergoing the punishment of eternal fire.

Some scholars believe that these angels who "did not keep their own domain but went after strange flesh" were the "sons of God" in Genesis 6 who, during the days of Noah, came down to cohabit with the "daughters of men." In other words, these scholars believe angelic beings engaged in sexual relations with human beings. Whether you accept this interpretation or not, we do know that God makes it clear that the people of Sodom and Gomorrah and the cities around them indulged in gross immorality and went after "strange flesh."

The men of Sodom in all probability did not realize that these two men whom they wanted to "know" (a word for sexual intercourse) were angels; however, it's obvious from the account that the men of Sodom preferred men to women. The word used in Jude for *strange* stresses the immorality of homosexuality, and Jude goes on to speak of the eternal fire that comes as punishment upon all those who practice it and never repent, just as it comes on adulterers and those who practice other forms of sexual immorality.

The second chapter of 2 Peter parallels the passage in Jude, referring again to the destruction of Sodom and Gomorrah. Read the verses for yourself so you know exactly what they say. Read the passage aloud and underline every reference to *Sodom and Gomorrah*, including the pronouns.

2 PETER 2:4-10

⁴ For if God did not spare angels when they sinned, but cast them into hell and committed them to pits of darkness, reserved for judgment;

⁵ and did not spare the ancient world, but preserved Noah, a preacher of righteousness, with seven others, when He brought a flood upon the world of the ungodly;

⁶ and if He condemned the cities of Sodom and Gomorrah to destruction by reducing them to ashes, having made them an example to those who would live ungodly lives thereafter;

7 and if He rescued righteous Lot, oppressed by the sensual conduct of unprincipled men

8 (for by what he saw and heard that righteous man, while living among them, felt his righteous soul tormented day after day by their lawless deeds),

9 then the Lord knows how to rescue the godly from temptation, and to keep the unrighteous under punishment for the day of judgment,

10 and especially those who indulge the flesh in its corrupt desires and despise authority.

What did you learn from marking the references to *Sodom and Gomorrah* in verses 1-8? List your insights below.

Now go back and read verses 9-10 again. What do you learn about those who indulge the flesh?

I'm sure you also noticed the word *authority* in verse 10. To despise authority is to willfully go against what God lays down in His Word; it's to go against truth, to choose to embrace a lie because you don't want to obey God. If God is God, can a person get away with that?

Eternal Consequences of an Immoral Lifestyle

Let's look for a moment at several passages in the New Testament and see what they teach in respect to those who enter eternal punishment. It will be a little repetitious, but it's necessary if you're going to understand what happens to immoral persons who never repent of their sin and believe in Jesus Christ. Therefore, as you read the following verses, mark all references to *immorality* with a big **I**, not only the word *immorality* itself, but also every word that represents *a form of immorality* or *sexual transgression*.

1 CORINTHIANS 6:9-11

⁹ Or do you not know that the unrighteous will not inherit the kingdom of God? Do not be deceived; neither fornicators, nor idolaters, nor adulterers, nor effeminate, nor homosexuals,

¹⁰ nor thieves, nor the covetous, nor drunkards, nor revilers, nor swindlers, will inherit the kingdom of God.

¹¹ Such were some of you; but you were washed, but you were sanctified, but you were justified in the name of the Lord Jesus Christ, and in the Spirit of our God.

I had to include verse 11 so you would remember that if you're involved in any form of sexual immorality, there is hope. You *can* be forgiven. You *can* change. You can be made new. You can start again. You can experience healing if you'll come to Jehovah-rapha, the Lord God who heals.

However, Jesus said that if we *don't* repent we will perish. Therefore repentance—according to the definition of the word from the Greek—is essential for salvation. The word *repent, metanoia,* means "to have a change of mind." Biblically it means to change your mind and conform your beliefs to what God's Word says about something, especially about sin and our need for a Savior—*and* to recognize who the Savior is. Of course, *repent* is used in other ways, but in the context of salvation this is what it means.

In the additional passages that follow, continue marking every word that represents *a form of immorality* or *sexual transgression*.

EPHESIANS 5:5-6

⁵ For this you know with certainty, that no immoral or impure person or covetous man, who is an idolater, has an inheritance in the kingdom of Christ and God.

⁶ Let no one deceive you with empty words, for because of these things the wrath of God comes upon the sons of disobedience.

REVELATION 21:8

⁸ But for the cowardly and unbelieving and abominable and murderers and immoral persons and sorcerers and idolaters and all liars, their part will be in the lake that burns with fire and brimstone, which is the second death.

REVELATION 22:14-15

¹⁴ Blessed are those who wash their robes, so that they may have the right to the tree of life, and may enter by the gates into the city.

¹⁵ Outside are the dogs and the sorcerers and the immoral persons and the murderers and the idolaters, and everyone who loves and practices lying.

Now take everything you marked in these passages and list what God says about immorality and the consequences of choosing this kind of a lifestyle.

This, my friend, is what God deems sin. And when there's no repentance—no changing of your mind and agreeing with God, no asking Him to deliver you, no calling it what God calls it—sin, an abomination, perversion—then *you* shut *yourself* out of heaven. Of your own free will, you choose to reject God, and in doing so you consign yourself to hell and eventually to the lake of fire, where the worm will not die and the fire will not be quenched.[3] In other words, you will live there forever and ever and ever because you would not agree with God that sin is sin and you would not receive His Son as the One who gladly would have saved you from that sin. You loved your sin and clung to it all the way to hell.

Note what I just said, because it's important to understand that these sins describe the *lifestyle* of these people—*not* their temptations, their battles, or their slip-ups, but a willful lifestyle. These are lifestyles of choice. These people are without excuse before God. They have chosen death over life, when a compassionate, merciful God would have saved them had they not hardened their hearts.

Let's look at Romans 1:18-32, as I believe it will help you understand this even more clearly. As you read this passage, mark every reference to these *ungodly, unrighteous men* who are going to experience the wrath of God. Don't miss a single pronoun!

[18] For the wrath of God is revealed from heaven against all ungodliness and unrighteousness of men who suppress the truth in unrighteousness,

[19] because that which is known about God is evident within them; for God made it evident to them.

[20] For since the creation of the world His invisible attributes, His eternal power and divine nature, have been clearly seen, being understood through what has been made, so that they are without excuse.

[21] For even though they knew God, they did not honor Him as God or give thanks, but they became futile in their speculations, and their foolish heart was darkened.

²² Professing to be wise, they became fools,

²³ and exchanged the glory of the incorruptible God for an image in the form of corruptible man and of birds and four-footed animals and crawling creatures.

²⁴ Therefore God gave them over in the lusts of their hearts to impurity, so that their bodies would be dishonored among them.

²⁵ For they exchanged the truth of God for a lie, and worshiped and served the creature rather than the Creator, who is blessed forever. Amen.

²⁶ For this reason God gave them over to degrading passions; for their women exchanged the natural function for that which is unnatural,

²⁷ and in the same way also the men abandoned the natural function of the woman and burned in their desire toward one another, men with men committing indecent acts and receiving in their own persons the due penalty of their error.

²⁸ And just as they did not see fit to acknowledge God any longer, God gave them over to a depraved mind, to do those things which are not proper,

²⁹ being filled with all unrighteousness, wickedness, greed, evil; full of envy, murder, strife, deceit, malice; they are gossips,

³⁰ slanderers, haters of God, insolent, arrogant, boastful, inventors of evil, disobedient to parents,

³¹ without understanding, untrustworthy, unloving, unmerciful;

³² and although they know the ordinance of God, that those who practice such things are worthy of death, they not only do the same, but also give hearty approval to those who practice them.

As you read the text, I'm sure you noticed the repeated phrase, "God gave them over." Go back and highlight or mark it with a cloud like this 🌥 . Also, with another color or symbol such as a box, mark each time an *exchange* is mentioned—and inside the box include *who* exchanged *what* for *what*. Then stop and notice which came first: God's giving the people over or someone making an exchange?

Now write a profile of these persons (the passage refers to humanity in general—men and women). Put your list in the space provided on the following page. I want to ask you some questions, because it's imperative that you know and understand exactly what God says. You don't need another person's interpretation to get this. God has spoken plainly and clearly. He means what He says, and He says what He means. Nothing is hidden.

What sexual behaviors are mentioned in this passage? (Make sure you go all the way back to verse 24.)

Are these sexual expressions acceptable to God? Is this sex according to God's will? How do you know?

When you look at the profile of these people upon whom the wrath of God will come, you see that they willfully refused to honor God as God

PROFILE OF THE UNGODLY

(verse 21). If you were to tell someone how to honor God, what fundamentals would you set forth? Write your answer here; it doesn't need to be detailed.

Look at the statement "they are without excuse" in verse 20. What makes them without excuse?

Who turned their back first, God or man? How?

For every exchange mentioned in this passage from Romans 1, there's a response from God. List what was exchanged and how God responded:

THEY EXCHANGED...   GOD GAVE THEM OVER...

Look at verse 32. What makes these people so destructive to their culture and their nation?

Sin never stands alone. It always wants company. The fact that others walk in willful disobedience to the express and clear commands of God seems to give credence to what they are doing. Therefore licentious men and women, in their rebellion against God, become contaminants in society. They use others for their satisfaction, or they lure them into their deviant lifestyle, justifying actions that are clearly forbidden in the Word of God. This is why, under the Old Covenant, God said such people were to be put to death. It was not that God didn't love or care for these people or desire that they be saved. Rather, it was because they insisted on breaking His commandments and because their behavior would destroy others. God ordered them destroyed because He had to save and protect His people.

A Time for Anger

I wish you could take a walk with some of the dear broken men, women, and teens who have written to me or to our counselors at Precept Ministries International. I wish you could listen to them, truly listen to their stories without writing them off.

I wish you could travel with Dorie Van Stone and watch what happens when she speaks in prisons, in children's homes, on the campuses of universities and Christian schools, at student gatherings, and in churches, both here and overseas. In place after place you would find people crowding around her, tears of relief filling their eyes, for at last they know someone understands, someone believes them. In Dorie's vulnerability they find comfort and courage. These are the wounded—sexually used and abused for the pleasure of another person—whose lives have ricocheted into immorality, masturbation, pornography, prostitution, homosexuality, pedophilia, depression, suicide attempts, multiple personalities, alcoholism, drugs, bitterness, child abuse. And it began because someone got away with breaking God's commandments regarding sex. In many cases, society tolerated the assault on their innocence—condoned it, protected it, promoted it, propagated it. Or those in a position to help or to rescue simply turned their backs; it was not something they wanted to know about or cared about.

I wonder if we can begin to comprehend the pain that has come because everyone did what was right in their own eyes rather than in God's eyes. God was not their ruler; *they* were!

Our own times seem to mirror the approximately three and a half centuries in Israel's history during the period of the Judges—a period of apathy, apostasy, and anarchy. The final five chapters of Judges describe well this moral climate. In Judges 19, "when there was no king in Israel" (verse 1), we read of a certain Levite and his concubine who are spending the night in the home of a Benjamite. As you read this passage, underline every reference to *the men of the city.*

JUDGES 19:22-30

22 While they were celebrating, behold, the men of the city, certain worthless fellows, surrounded the house, pounding the door; and they spoke to the owner of the house, the old man, saying, "Bring out the man who came into your house that we may have relations with him."

23 Then the man, the owner of the house, went out to them and said to them, "No, my fellows, please do not act so wickedly; since this man has come into my house, do not commit this act of folly.

24 "Here is my virgin daughter and his concubine. Please let me bring them out that you may ravish them and do to them whatever you wish. But do not commit such an act of folly against this man."

25 But the men would not listen to him. So the man seized his concubine and brought her out to them; and they raped her and abused her all night until morning, then let her go at the approach of dawn.

²⁶ As the day began to dawn, the woman came and fell down at the doorway of the man's house where her master was, until full daylight.

²⁷ When her master arose in the morning and opened the doors of the house and went out to go on his way, then behold, his concubine was lying at the doorway of the house with her hands on the threshold.

²⁸ He said to her, "Get up and let us go," but there was no answer. Then he placed her on the donkey; and the man arose and went to his home.

²⁹ When he entered his house, he took a knife and laid hold of his concubine and cut her in twelve pieces, limb by limb, and sent her throughout the territory of Israel.

³⁰ All who saw it said, "Nothing like this has ever happened or been seen from the day when the sons of Israel came up from the land of Egypt to this day. Consider it, take counsel and speak up!"

Do you get the picture? Does it make you sick? angry? If not, why not? What's wrong with you? You ought to be indignant for a number of reasons.

First, it's inconceivable that a Jewish village would tolerate homosexuality. These were God's chosen people, and Benjamin was once a noble tribe. At one time God said that homosexuality was a sin punishable by death! You know that from our earlier study of the Torah, the Book of the Law. Had God changed? Did His Law change as the culture changed? Is something that was once wrong now perfectly acceptable? Of course not! The man who took in the Levite and his concubine told the men of the city that what they wanted to do was wicked, an act of folly.

Second, how could a man offer to hand over his own flesh and blood to a group of men and tell them that they could steal his daughter's virginity? How could a father give men permission to ravish his daughter for their twisted pleasure? Even as I ask that question, I shudder to realize that fathers all over this nation, all over the world, do the same thing day in and day out, night after night. They use their daughters for their sexual gratification and often share their precious children with their friends.

Mothers do the same. I think of one mother who began using her twelve-year-old son to satisfy her sexual appetite after her husband died. The boy grew into a man who was filled with hatred toward the woman who gave him life. She was supposed to protect and nurture him, but instead she had ruined his life. I think of another woman who used her son in this way, and even after he was married sought him out for sex. Twisted. Sick. Destructive. An abomination to God.

You say, "Well, if God is so sovereign and all-powerful and ever-present that nothing escapes His notice, why doesn't He stop it?" I honestly don't know. Right now it's a mystery, but I trust Him. I am not God. I cannot explain Him, but I can trust Him.

I do know, however, that someday the mystery will be understood; it will be finished.[4] His wrath will be poured out. He will repay. Vengeance belongs to Him.[5] The lake of fire is eternal. No human being will simply disintegrate; each of us will live forever either in the lake of fire or on the new earth under the new heaven. Read from the final chapters of God's book, Revelation 19–21. God will make all things new for those who come to Him. Sorrow and pain and death will be gone forever—and God Himself will wipe away all our tears. Then we will know what it's like to live in a world without sin. I await that glorious day when we will no longer look through a glass darkly but have full and perfect understanding.

The third reason the story of the Benjamites makes me angry is that we find a man being protected at the expense of a woman. Man is to be the protector of woman. How could this man offer his virgin daughter? How could a Levite, a man who was supposed to be a teacher in Israel, send his concubine out the door into the hands of such wicked men? How could he tell these men to do what they wished, whatever seemed good in their eyes to these women? How could this "husband" go to bed and not check on the welfare of his concubine until morning? How could he sleep, knowing that he had used her to save his own skin?

We might ask the same question today as we look at conditions in America. How can the men of this nation—a nation that planted it roots in the rich soil of the Word of God and the fear of God—allow women to be mistreated, used, desecrated in a multitude of ways, sacrificed on the altar of men's unbridled lust?

Where are our protectors? Why don't you and others rise up to protect us, to shield us, to care about our welfare and our virtue? Where are those with courage to say, "Enough is enough"?

The Levite got Israel's attention when he chopped the body of his concubine into twelve pieces, addressed one package to each of the twelve tribes of Israel, and asked them what they were going to do about this wickedness. Do we need to do the same? Wrap up the body parts of those who've been aborted, the children and woman who've been used, abused, and murdered, and send them across our land, demanding to know what will be done about it?

When the tribes of Israel received their packages, how did the men of Israel respond? Read on.

JUDGES 20:1-7

¹ Then all the sons of Israel from Dan to Beersheba, including the land of Gilead, came out, and the congregation assembled as one man to the LORD at Mizpah.

² The chiefs of all the people, even of all the tribes of Israel, took their stand in the assembly of the people of God, 400,000 foot soldiers who drew the sword.

³ (Now the sons of Benjamin heard that the sons of Israel had gone up to Mizpah.) And the sons of Israel said, "Tell us, how did this wickedness take place?"

⁴ So the Levite, the husband of the woman who was murdered, answered and said, "I came with my concubine to spend the night at Gibeah which belongs to Benjamin.

5 "But the men of Gibeah rose up against me and surrounded the house at night because of me. They intended to kill me; instead, they ravished my concubine so that she died.

6 "And I took hold of my concubine and cut her in pieces and sent her throughout the land of Israel's inheritance; for they have committed a lewd and disgraceful act in Israel.

7 "Behold, all you sons of Israel, give your advice and counsel here."

Do you know what happened next? Read Judges 20 and 21. The Benjamites refused to deliver up the men who raped and murdered the woman! The nation was divided, and civil war broke out. More than sixty-five thousand men died as a result of the ensuing battles over this incident.

Why? Because just like today, people did what was right in their own eyes. They didn't listen to God.

Oh, beloved, think of the tragedy of it all. The horrific, senseless tragedy! This is what comes when we don't live according to God's Word. It is only going to get worse in this nation, in this world. If our morals don't change, God will judge us in a way we never thought possible.

Judgment is already happening. Did you notice Romans 1:27? Paul spoke of "men with men committing indecent acts and receiving in their own persons [literally, themselves] the due penalty of their error." Sexual immorality brings with it consequences that affect our bodies. What do you think sexually transmitted diseases are? And what about AIDS? I realize that innocent people get AIDS, but where did it start? It started in the homosexual community, and from there it spread to society in general. Judgment is upon us, but even greater judgment is coming if society doesn't have a change of mind regarding sexual immorality.

The question is, what are *you* going to do about it? You're discovering what God says about sex. What are you going to do with that knowledge?

One place you can start is with sharing the message of this book. Why don't you pray about getting some friends together to study and discuss this book and its companion study guide. Challenge your friends to find out what God has to say about sex and to get the message out to others. Think of what could happen as a result. Consider the lives that could be rescued, turned around, salvaged, saved…if emboldened people began to let God's voice be heard and to get active in reversing our culture's decline through prayer and legislation.

We have a lot more to study yet, but why don't you start praying right now and see how God speaks to you. If you don't feel you're the one to lead a study like this, ask God who it should be, then commit to helping that person.

I urge you for heaven's sake to do *something*. If God judged Sodom and Gomorrah because of their wickedness, He will have to do the same to us unless we repent.

Just remember: Before a mind can be changed, it has to be exposed to truth. Take a walk with your friends, and listen to them with your heart. You may be surprised at what you learn, but don't withdraw in shock. Believe them and help them see truth for themselves. Jesus said, "You will know the truth, and the truth will make you free" (John 8:32). Free indeed.

8

Stitching Up the Wounds

Is It Too Late for Me?

What do you do when your experience with sex has happened in a way that is not according to God's plan, either because you've done something you shouldn't have or because someone violated you sexually? Is it really possible to recover and get on with life?

Yes, my friend, it is. There is life after illegitimate sex. We're going to look at the how of it all in this chapter.

If you're one of those wise ones who has handled sex according to God, how I rejoice with you. You're in a blessed minority. However, this chapter is for you as well. Don't skip it, because God wants to use you to help others recover and move forward in victory.

Let me give you a preview of the issues we'll discuss, issues that are critical to any person's well-being and recovery.

First, we'll look at how to get right with God. When you understand this, you're prepared to handle all that follows. Then we'll look at what you do after adultery or fornication, how you relate to the person you "defrauded," as God would put it—or the one who defrauded you. What should you do, if anything, after you've committed adultery? Finally, we'll look at forgiving those who have violated you sexually. It's a difficult topic, beloved, but if there is ever going to be healing in your life—the ability to go on and not live in the gall of bitterness, anger, and demoralizing defeat—you must understand the major role the forgiveness of God plays in the healing of sexual transgression.

In all these things, we'll understand better the healing that God alone can provide. Let me illustrate.

Two days ago my son Mark, who is the chief operating officer of Precept Ministries International, called to tell me that he and Ryan, the younger of his two sons, were home from the Daytona 500 auto races. This is an annual father-son tradition, but this year it was extra special because two of Ryan's friends went with them. As I was catching up on the great time had by all and telling our son that his dad and I had been praying all day for their safe trip home—that they wouldn't be driving as if they were *in* the races—Mark said, "I've got to tell you something."

As his story unfolded, I had to say, "Be still, my heart." On the way back from Daytona, the boys were driving separately in a Jeep, and one of the boys fell asleep at the wheel. Mark watched as the car went past him, hit a guardrail, and rolled. The Jeep was totaled. I'm convinced that God had prompted us to pray, because no one was hurt except our Ryan, who was asleep in the backseat. He was a bloody mess, but only from a small gash above his eye.

At the emergency room, the doctor stitched him up in a hurry—Ryan was eager to attend a special banquet where he and other members of The McCallie School football team would receive their state championship rings. As they left the emergency room, the nurse said, "You may want to have a plastic surgeon check the stitches since it was done in such a rush—but do it right away. Don't wait."

Sure enough, when Mark later took Ryan to the surgeon, he confirmed that the gash hadn't been sewn together well. On the surface all looked good, but a big pocket had been left under the cut; the connecting muscle hadn't been sewn up. Also, because the wound hadn't been thoroughly cleaned, infection had already set in.

Now listen carefully, my friend; don't miss my point in telling this story. If Ryan hadn't gone to the expert to have the wound fixed properly, it would have resulted in poor healing, maybe a serious infection, and without question he would have borne a deep scar for the rest of his life. What a picture this is of what happens when we don't ask the right doctor to take proper care of the wounds of sexual sin. Infection sets in because of inadequate cleansing, and we're left with visible scars because the wound was never dealt with properly.

THE HEALING BALM OF GRACE

One of the names of God is *Jehovah-rapha,* the Lord who heals. King David experienced this healing. Yes, he suffered the consequences of his sin with Bathsheba, as we saw in an earlier chapter, but David didn't want to be scarred for life. So he turned to God for healing. It's all written out for us in Psalm 51.

When you read this powerful psalm, don't miss the introduction, as it sets the context and direction for the passage. Amazingly, the introduction begins by saying this psalm was written "for the choir director." It was supposed to be sung by the people! Then the introduction continues, "A Psalm of David, when Nathan the prophet came to him, after he had gone in to Bathsheba." Why would such a psalm, an emotional record of personal repentance, be sung by the people? Because, my friend, when we put words to a tune and sing it over and over again, the message stays in our minds and is easy to recall.

God wants us to be able to recall this psalm when the memory of our moral failures rears its tormenting, demoralizing head.

While I don't know the original tune for this psalm, I know that the words alone can bring great healing. They've brought healing and comfort to me.

I want us to walk through this psalm together, almost verse by verse. Before we do, I think it would be best for you to first read it aloud—all nineteen verses. As you do so, every time you hear yourself mention *sin, sinners, transgression, evil,* or *iniquity,* color the word brown or mark it with a big **S.**

PSALM 51

¹ Be gracious to me, O God, according to Your lovingkindness; according

to the greatness of Your compassion blot out my transgressions.

² Wash me thoroughly from my iniquity and cleanse me from my

sin.

³ For I know my transgressions, and my sin is ever before me.

⁴ Against You, You only, I have sinned and done what is evil in Your sight, so that You are justified when You speak and blameless when You judge.

⁵ Behold, I was brought forth in iniquity, and in sin my mother conceived me.

⁶ Behold, You desire truth in the innermost being, and in the hidden part You will make me know wisdom.

⁷ Purify me with hyssop, and I shall be clean; wash me, and I shall be whiter than snow.

⁸ Make me to hear joy and gladness, let the bones which You have broken rejoice.

⁹ Hide Your face from my sins and blot out all my iniquities.

¹⁰ Create in me a clean heart, O God, and renew a steadfast spirit within me.

¹¹ Do not cast me away from Your presence and do not take Your Holy Spirit from me.

¹² Restore to me the joy of Your salvation and sustain me with a willing spirit.

¹³ Then I will teach transgressors Your ways, and sinners will be converted to You.

¹⁴ Deliver me from bloodguiltiness, O God, the God of my salvation; then my tongue will joyfully sing of Your righteousness.

¹⁵ O Lord, open my lips, that my mouth may declare Your praise.

¹⁶ For You do not delight in sacrifice, otherwise I would give it; You are not pleased with burnt offering.

¹⁷ The sacrifices of God are a broken spirit; a broken and a contrite heart, O God, You will not despise.

¹⁸ By Your favor do good to Zion; build the walls of Jerusalem.

¹⁹ Then You will delight in righteous sacrifices, in burnt offering and whole burnt offering; then young bulls will be offered on Your altar.

My friend, I obviously don't know the extent of your sin, the tangled web spun by one transgression upon another as you tried in your own strength to extricate yourself from sin's tenacious grip. But I do know that our God is a God of abundant grace. Because of Him, you can experience forgiveness. As we know, David's sin was compounded, sin upon sin, after he committed adultery with Bathsheba, and yet he could write this psalm for all to sing because he knew the character of His God.

Now let's go through this psalm again, more slowly this time, so you don't miss a thing. Watch how David goes about righting what is wrong, seeking restoration so he can get on with life instead of living in the haunted house of sin.

David begins his quest with *God*—with what he knows about Him and His grace.

¹ Be gracious to me, O God, according to Your lovingkindness; according to the greatness of Your compassion blot out my transgressions.

The basis for all that follows is the knowledge of who God is, the attributes that make Him God. This is so crucial, because if you aren't right with God, you won't ever really feel right with anyone. You have to know that, no matter what has happened, it's possible to be right with Him. So often we miss this because we think of God in human terms rather than in terms of His divine character.

David's plea is made...

    according to God's lovingkindness,

      according to His compassion,

        according to His tender mercies.

How I wish you could see this in Hebrew; it's such a picturesque language. For example the word *racham,* translated as *compassion* in Psalm 51, indicates being connected to the womb, as cherishing the fetus. Isn't that interesting, since we come to know God and experience His compassionate forgiveness by being born again!

David's request begins not on the basis of anything to do with himself or his situation, but according to all that God is—His lovingkindness and the greatness of His love and compassion.

As I write this, I think of the letter written by a dear woman after studying my book *Lord, I Need Grace to Make It Today.* To protect her privacy, I'll disguise some of the details of her letter, which tells how sin upon sin entered her life—and finally brought her to her knees.

It began with an illegitimate pregnancy and went downhill when her fiancé called off their wedding the night before the ceremony. Bitterness and hurt took root as she watched the father of their child let them go on welfare. He never acknowledged their child, never offered to support his offspring. Her situation deteriorated even further with the coming of another man, another pregnancy, then yet another man—and finally marriage. But with the husband came drinking and beatings. She filed for divorce four times before she could finally walk away.

After the divorce came a failed suicide attempt. At age twenty-five she married again, this time an acquaintance from childhood. She knew he was an alcoholic, but she thought she could change all that—if she could only transform herself into the woman of his dreams. She changed her hair color and the shape of her nose and her breasts. She changed—but he didn't.

Then she had an affair with a married man, a relationship she wasn't looking for but fell into. All the gentleness, love, and admiration she longed to receive from her spouse was bestowed by the husband of another. Finally she brought the affair to a halt and confessed her sin to her husband. He made sure she paid greatly for her wrong choices, but at least there was no more hiding.

They had another child, then their teenage son was caught—in the church—being immoral with their pastor's daughter. Yet as all this unraveled, my friend experienced grace—grace from the pastor, the father of the girl with whom her son had been caught! He was understanding, forgiving, patient in handling the whole mess. Her husband was furious and her home life was hell—her son and his father were still fighting over it all—but she had seen the grace of God in a man so terribly hurt by his daughter's sin.

My friend decided to go to church for Maundy Thursday services. She listened carefully as the pastor who had extended grace himself stood in the pulpit and proclaimed the grace of God in offering forgiveness of sins because of the death, burial, and resurrection of Jesus Christ. She writes:

> As the pastor gave the gospel I broke down in tears. I cried at the altar for two hours. I was drained when I left. That night I trusted Jesus Christ for forgiveness and His death on that cross. I gave up and trusted Him to do whatever it took.
>
> Out of all my bad decisions, failures, mistakes—God has worked all things together for His good. I don't know at this point what God plans to do with this, but I am willing to do whatever He chooses. Because when I listen to hurting people I know exactly why they are where they are. They never understood the grace and love of our heavenly Father. I stand in awe when I think He can forgive me for all that. For years I hid it as I was so ashamed. I know people who would never speak to me or believe it. Now I understand Paul when he said, "By the grace of God I am who I am."

Grace, beloved. Unmerited, abundant, extravagant grace. It's there for all who will simply ask.

A Cleansing of the Soul

Because of God's grace, David was able to ask for cleansing and know that he would receive it without protest. Listen as David goes on:

² Wash me thoroughly from my iniquity and cleanse me from my sin.

³ For I know my transgressions, and my sin is ever before me.

⁴ Against You, You only, I have sinned, and done what is evil in Your sight,

so that You are justified when You speak and blameless when You judge.

Oh, if we could only see that all sin is ultimately against God. Sin's arrow shot from the bowels of hell doesn't lodge on earth, satisfied with wounding or disfiguring us or piercing those in the path of our sin. No, like Nimrod's rebellion,[1] it pierces men and flies through their wounded bodies into the heavens, not stopping until it strikes the very heart of God. All sin ultimately is committed against God, grieving Him more than we can even begin to comprehend.

It is God's commandment, God's Law that we have transgressed—sometimes unknowingly, other times willfully, blatantly, brashly. Either way it is an affront to the Holy One. Whatever means God would choose to judge David's sin, my sin, and your sin would be justified and rightly executed. God would stand blameless.

David knows his sin. He recognizes his transgressions. His sin is ever before him. He is not trying to hide it. He's not seeking to excuse it, not covering it anymore. Whatever God would say about it, David would agree to.

And what about you, my friend? Do you know your sin? Do you realize it is God against whom you have transgressed, God whom you have hurt? Healing and wholeness will never come until you, like David, confess that you have sinned against God and that He is just in dealing with your sin. It's not a matter of arguing your case. It's a matter of falling before Him and pleading for mercy and cleansing.

David knows whom He has grieved. Now He stands before God in his filth and asks God to wash him thoroughly. He longs to be clean—totally, completely clean.

When this is your heart, beloved, when you come to such a place, then you can know you're standing in the circle of God's forgiveness. You have seen and confessed your sin for what it is. Taking full responsibility for your actions, you stand before Him without excuse.

[5] Behold, I was brought forth in iniquity, and in sin my mother conceived me.

[6] Behold, You desire truth in the innermost being, and in the hidden part

You will make me know wisdom.

You know you are a sinner. We're all born that way: "If we say that we have no sin, we are deceiving ourselves and the truth is not in us.… If we say that we have not sinned, we make Him a liar and His word is not in us" (1 John

1:8,10). When we concur with God as to our natural state, we are embracing truth—and from that comes wisdom. As we embrace reality, we'll find the wisdom to seek cleansing and forgiveness from the only One who can really impart it, the One who knows no sin—God.

⁷ Purify me with hyssop, and I shall be clean; wash me, and I shall be whiter than snow.

How pleasing it is to God, and how healing and restorative to us, to acknowledge that we can be made clean. To know that the stain of sin is not permanent, the garment is not ruined.

Did you notice there's no call here for you to forgive yourself? So many have said to me, "Pray for me. I've asked God to forgive me, but I cannot forgive myself." Forgiving oneself is not where healing is found. Although you may have heard this from the lips of another, you never hear it from the mouth of God. It's a phrase we've picked up, a human-centered thought we've embraced—but it's not a biblical concept. All sin is against God; forgiveness therefore must come from God. Are you greater than God that you must forgive yourself when the Almighty already has declared you forgiven? Presumptuous, isn't it? It reveals a lack of faith. God forgives, dear one, and when you believe and accept this, you'll experience a cleansing tide that brings something more in its wake.

Hear what David said:

⁸ Make me to hear joy and gladness, let the bones which You have broken rejoice.

Forgiveness—cleansing—brings joy. The heaviness is gone. The bones that God has broken in His just judgment will leap with joy.

⁹ Hide Your face from my sins and blot out all my iniquities.

¹⁰ Create in me a clean heart, O God, and renew a steadfast spirit within me.

[11] Do not cast me away from Your presence and do not take Your Holy Spirit from me.

God will never again mention your sins. Others may remind you, shun you, reject you, toss them in your face—but not God. The Almighty turns His face. He blots out your sins with the flesh of the Lamb of God, and you become clean right to your very heart. You will never be turned away from the throne of your Father God. His Spirit is no longer grieved by unconfessed sin; instead, He will keep you steadfast in your resolve. Why? Because you have done exactly what you should have, the only thing you could do to be made clean again: You've repented and sought His forgiveness.

The Return of Joy

After wondering if you could ever hope again, you'll find you are renewed, restored.

[12] Restore to me the joy of Your salvation and sustain me with a willing spirit.

You can know joy, the joy you felt when you were first forgiven and brought to salvation.

[13] Then I will teach transgressors Your ways, and sinners will be converted to You.

Having been restored, having been renewed through the forgiveness you've received from God, you can now show others the way to the same joyous experience.

[14] Deliver me from bloodguiltiness, O God, the God of my salvation; then my tongue will joyfully sing of Your righteousness.

David had caused an innocent man's death. Maybe you can relate to his pain. Perhaps you've caused an innocent baby's death through abortion. David had Uriah killed; you had a baby killed. Abortion is a grievous sin that results in bloodguiltiness. But you *can* be forgiven and experience healing.

"But," you say, "my guilt is overwhelming." I understand, but because God is God, you must not be overwhelmed. Through Jesus' death for your sins, your guilt is taken away. You're still alive because God isn't finished with you. God still has a purpose for your life—and in the light of these truths you must go forward.

It's true that no matter what you do, you cannot bring the dead to life; only God can resurrect. And that day is coming. You must trust God as God. Don't compound sin by *not* listening to Him, *not* believing Him and obeying. You must have faith. You must take Him at His Word and go forward in the strength and the joy of your salvation. Demonstrate the restorative, renewing power of His grace. Don't permit yourself to live in the torment of sins past.

Let your life be a testimony of His lavish, extravagant grace. Pray as David prayed:

15 O Lord, open my lips, that my mouth may declare Your praise.

16 For You do not delight in sacrifice, otherwise I would give it; You are not pleased with burnt offering.

17 The sacrifices of God are a broken spirit; a broken and a contrite heart, O God, You will not despise.

This is what God wants—a heart that beats in unison with His, broken by the things that break His heart. When God sees your godly sorrow, which leads to genuine repentance as 2 Corinthians 7:9-10 says, He knows everything will be all right. Your sorrow, your brokenness will cause you to abhor what He abhors, to flee what He forbids. This is why He does not despise a broken, contrite spirit. God places a high value on those who value Him.

THOSE AFFECTED BY YOUR SIN

The last two verses of this psalm are so interesting. At first you may wonder what these verses have to do with seeking God's forgiveness. But it all makes sense when you realize that sin never stands still. It's never isolated. This is why David prays for favor for Zion, for the building of the walls of Jerusalem. Sin impacts a family, a church, a community, a nation.

[18] By Your favor do good to Zion; build the walls of Jerusalem.

[19] Then You will delight in righteous sacrifices, in burnt offering and whole burnt offering; then young bulls will be offered on Your altar.

As David prayed for Jerusalem, so you ought to pray for those affected by your sin. Pray that God will bring favor upon them and that the walls of protection dismantled by sin will be built again.

As I mentioned earlier, once you take care of your sin with God, you must make it right with others. If you've committed adultery, the first place you go is to God. Then you need God's wisdom in dealing with your relationship to your mate.

Adultery is a grievous sin and must be dealt with accordingly.

You've broken God's commandment.

You've broken a covenant agreement.

You've put your marriage at risk; divorce is now permissible, although it's not the best resolution.

You've put your mate at risk of AIDS or other sexually transmitted diseases.

You've put your children at risk, jeopardized their future.

You've failed as a role model.

You've sinned against your own body.

You've defrauded another person and caused him or her to come under the judgment of God.

You've sinned against the church, the body of Christ.

You've sinned against the community; the land has again been defiled.

What you have done is worthy of death under Old Testament Law. This cannot be treated lightly, brushed aside with an "I'm sorry." You must take stock of the enormity of your sexual transgression and treat it accordingly.

So what do you do? You've confessed your sin and received God's forgiveness. Now you must go to your mate and seek his or her forgiveness— and be prepared for the consequences. Proverbs tells us that jealousy enrages a man, and the same is true for a woman. God understands; His name is *Qanna*, "jealous." When we play the harlot spiritually, it grieves the heart of God, for we have chosen another above Him.

Listen to what Proverbs 6 says:

PROVERBS 6:32-35

32 The one who commits adultery with a woman is lacking sense; he who would destroy himself does it.

33 Wounds and disgrace he will find, and his reproach will not be blotted out.

34 For jealousy enrages a man, and he will not spare in the day of vengeance.

35 He will not accept any ransom, nor will he be satisfied though you give many gifts.

Do I personally advise that you always confess? To God? Absolutely. Nothing will be right until you do. To your mate? No, not always. If it was a single transgression, an unpremeditated one, and it's not likely to be discovered, I would not suggest that you put your spouse under the awful burden of such knowledge. I realize you may disagree with me about this, and obviously that's fine. I don't claim to have all the answers or to fully understand each of God's precepts.

The reason I would not counsel the unfaithful party to confess is for the sake of the offended one. As Proverbs 6 says, adultery can bring rage and jealousy. Knowledge of such betrayal could create a wound that may never heal, especially if the person is the type who would constantly pick at it. If the person doesn't know God or is insecure and jealous, would such knowledge only make matters worse? I've dealt with so many who feel they need to confess simply to get relief for themselves, but what about the defrauded husband or wife? What if their wounds aren't stitched up properly?

If you do choose to confess, be sure you take into account the grievousness of your sin. Make certain your heart is broken and your spirit contrite, just as you read in Psalm 51. Then confess what you've done, name it for what it was, and agree with God that it's worthy of death. Don't go into details, don't excuse yourself, don't place the blame anywhere but upon yourself. Be sure you come in godly sorrow, in genuine repentance, and be prepared and eager to do whatever is necessary, within the bounds of Scripture, to heal the situation.

When you do this, beloved, you should expect your relationship to be different. In Hosea 3, after the prophet buys back his harlot wife and brings her home, he shuts her up for a while. He doesn't go in to her as his wife. He allows a time of healing, an opportunity to show and express love apart from sex. It is so important that you recognize the devastating effects of your betrayal and deal with them gently. Later the time will come to unite as one flesh, to promise fidelity from this point on.

And what if your mate will not take you back? Whether your mate forgives and restores you or not, you must fill your life with God. When you do this, there is great hope for restoration and a stronger foundation for restructuring your marriage.

And what if you sexually violated someone to whom you aren't married? You must confess what you have done. Talk about it with no other, but go to that person and name your sin for what it is. Don't downplay the gravity of what you've done. Remember, God tells us that if we cover our sins we won't prosper, but if we confess and forsake them, we'll find compassion[2]—mercy from the offended one hopefully, but certainly from God—and therein lies your strength.

The act of confessing your sin to God, as we see in Psalm 51, will prepare you to deal with others and with the consequences of your sin—whatever they may be. However, if you haven't sought God's absolution through your confession, as 1 John 1:9 says, then you have no foundation on which to build any other relationship. Remember: "Against You and You only, I have sinned..."

If your sin was committed against a child or if it constituted rape—something violent or something that occurred without full mutual consent—then you must pay the consequences. You cannot expect to go free, nor should you. Take your sentence as from God and use your circumstances to become the man or woman God would have you be from that day forward. God grants forgiveness, but as we saw earlier, this does not negate the consequences of your sin.

WHEN YOU ARE THE VICTIM

And what if you are the victim? Perhaps you've been misused sexually—abused, raped, betrayed. Or what if the adulterer is not you, but your husband or your wife? What do you do when the sexual transgression has been against you?

Beloved, you have a choice to make.

You can be bitter, you can be angry, you can rage, you can hate, you can seek revenge—yet none of these will ever take care of the person's sin against you. Instead of punishing the perpetrator, you will punish only yourself—and once again become that person's victim.

If you choose instead to handle it God's way, you'll know a healing and freedom you may never have thought you would experience again.

Like others who have written on this topic—people such as Marie Chapian, Dan Allender, and Dorie Van Stone—I've received incredible letters from those who have studied my book *Lord, Heal My Hurts* and have experienced healing when all else failed. The healing is not something I attribute to my writing but to the power of God's Word, a power that's activated when we're confronted with truth and respond accordingly.

A woman who had been sexually molested by her father when she was a child so beautifully demonstrates the power of God's Word when it is studied and obeyed:

From the day I walked into my first Precept study the Holy Spirit began to convict me of things in my life that were not like Him. Some of those things remained in my life as a direct result of my ignorance. Some things lingered on because I yet had unforgiveness, hatred, anger, and bitterness in my heart.

I was sexually molested by my father when I was a young girl, and I made it my business to make him pay for what he had done to me. I made sure he knew I hated him, and I did not respect or honor him as my father. I felt I had a right to be treated with kindness and love, so I made it my business to right the wrong my dad had done. But I learned that I had no rights except to serve God and then that isn't a right but a privilege.

I realized I would be forgiven only to the extent I forgave others.[3] I recognized that I was to love as God loved me: unconditionally and unselfishly. Love was an act of my will. I chose to love and expect nothing back in return. Revenge is never sweet. We say that revenge gives us satisfaction, but it satisfies temporarily at best.

I asked Dad to forgive me for my wrong attitude and actions toward him, and I began to honor him and share the gospel with him as I didn't want him to spend eternity in hell. One day we were talking, and God revealed my dad's heart to me. I began to tell him things only God could have made known to me, and my heart was overwhelmed with love and compassion for him [that] only God could give.

I remember my dad's words to this day, "B_____, I know there is a God, because you of all people have forgiven me." My dad sobbed loudly over the telephone, and I felt a wall between us come tumbling down. Dad later told me God must have revealed everything he was going through and feeling at that time.

Kay, who truly knows the heart? Only our One and True God. I have continued to witness to my dad long distance. I see God cleansing him and drawing him into His arms. Last week Dad phoned to say he has been sober for almost three weeks now. He smoked marijuana daily for twenty to twenty-five years, but now he gives God glory and praise for taking the desire away to stay high. Daddy recognizes that only God could do that. I will continue to thank God for what He has done, and I will stand firm on God's promise that He will save me and my whole house.

I believe God's Word brings genuine and complete healing. I love Psalm 107:20, where God tells us how He sent His word and healed them and delivered them from all their destructions. How my heart echoes the cry of faith preserved for us forever in Jeremiah 17:14: "Heal me, O LORD, and I will be healed; Save me and I will be saved."

While this book is not written for the purpose of healing, I simply cannot fail to mention the importance of not only receiving forgiveness from God but also extending it to those who have abused or misused you sexually.

When I mention forgiving the perpetrator of your pain, I know you may shake your head and say, "Never! Never in a thousand years!" I understand. I have grieved with too many not to understand. However, when I mention forgiveness, please know that forgiving does not mean the offender goes free and escapes the just judgment of God. Rather, when you forgive as God in Christ Jesus has forgiven you, you simply remove yourself from a role you aren't suited for anyway, that of Judge and Executioner.

This is God's role toward those who will never bow the knee to Him or allow Him to take control of their lives. Believe me, God will do His part. While you say you could never forgive them in a thousand years, God says they shall suffer forever and ever. Read Revelation. Read of the days when His wrath is poured out on the unbelieving, the unrepentant.

The sexually immoral make their bed in hell. Listen to the fate of those who never turn from their sin: "The cowardly and unbelieving and abominable and murderers and immoral persons and sorcerers and idolaters and all liars, their part will be in the lake that burns with fire and brimstone, which is the second death" (Revelation 21:8). These persons will never escape torment—while you, by receiving the forgiveness of God, shall never die. God will wipe away your tears, while, in contrast, they will never cease to cry, "Why? Why didn't I believe?"

To forgive is to give up your right to punish, and when you do this, it annuls every excuse the person offers for their sin. When you tell them you will forgive them, name the sin they committed. It needs to be said, to be identified. Then tell the person you forgive them—that you are sending their sin away and leaving it with God, because ultimately, all sin is against God. When you do this, you bring that person face to face with God, because, beloved, you have just demonstrated Him to the person you have forgiven. Now that you are out of the way, the person is God's to deal with!

This, beloved, is what salvation is all about—the kingdom of heaven and the forgiveness of sins. When we don't forgive, then, according to Jesus, we're turned over to the torturers.[4] Refusing to forgive, clinging to your resentment holds you in bondage to the one who violated you.

Please understand that forgiving someone does not mean you must act as if he or she never violated you. You're to love that person with God's *agape* love, to desire his highest good, which is that he be saved. However, you can demonstrate *agape* love without spending time with that person or extending affection. God loves the world and sacrificed His Son for everyone, but that doesn't guarantee the world a relationship with Him. Jesus loved the rich young ruler, but He let him walk away because the man preferred his riches to the kingdom of God.

If your violator or covenant breaker does not confess his or her sin and ask your forgiveness, there can be no relationship and no valid reason for a relationship. This is obvious in Scripture. No one can have fellowship with God—share anything in common with Him—until there's an acknowledgment of sin, a verbal agreement that what was done was wrong.

This is made clear for us in 1 John 1. Let's take a moment to read verses 4-10 and mark *sin* with a big **S** and *fellowship* with a symbol like this: ⛵ . (*Fellowship* means "to share in common"; it's like two fellows in a ship!)

1 JOHN 1:4-10

4 These things we write, so that our joy may be made complete.

5 This is the message we have heard from Him [the Him refers to Jesus Christ as the previous verses show] and announce to you, that God is Light, and in Him there is no darkness at all.

6 If we say that we have fellowship with Him and yet walk in the darkness, we lie and do not practice the truth;

7 but if we walk in the Light as He Himself is in the Light, we have fellowship with one another, and the blood of Jesus His Son cleanses us from all sin.

⁸ If we say that we have no sin, we are deceiving ourselves and the truth is not in us.

⁹ If we confess our sins, He is faithful and righteous to forgive us our sins and to cleanse us from all unrighteousness.

¹⁰ If we say that we have not sinned, we make Him a liar and His word is not in us.

Can you see how important, how imperative it is that sin be recognized and confessed as sin? God says that those who cover their sins will never prosper. Without confession, there can be no healing. Therefore it's crucial that sin be exposed. It needs to be brought out in the open and dealt with accordingly.

When men or women get away with immorality, they'll only continue to misuse God's gift of sex and seduce others to do evil. Surely by now you realize that sex apart from marriage is sin, and sin is evil. It belongs to the kingdom of darkness. All things become light when they're exposed, as Ephesians 5 says.

As you get into the Word of God, I believe you'll understand these things for yourself and also find God's direction for you as an individual.

If you're tortured because of sexual immorality, seek God's forgiveness today. It will become a day of days, I promise! Then begin the process of forgiving, even as He has forgiven you. As you do so, you'll find the wound will heal well. There'll be no scar. You'll delight in peace and release that cannot be bought—except by the Lamb of God who takes away the sins of the world.

It is a trustworthy statement, deserving full acceptance, that Christ Jesus came into the world to save sinners, among whom I am foremost of all. (1 Timothy 1:15)

9

In the Heat of the Moment

How Far Can I Go?

Ohhhh, baby…baby…don't make me wait. If you love me, please…
please don't make me wait…"

"We love each other, so it's all right…isn't it?"

"What do I do? I'm about to explode!"

"It's okay to show our love…as long as we don't go all the way,
right?"

Men and women wrestle with these situations and debate these questions
day after day, night after night, date after date.

"I'm single. What am I supposed to do with these urges?"

"We can't get married yet, but we're in love…and sex is about
love, isn't it?"

"How far can I go and still be a virgin?"

"I married the wrong person, but now I've found my soul mate.
How can we express our love to one another and still not commit
adultery?"

"I'm attracted to men *and* to women…why can't other people
accept my bisexuality?"

"I don't desire a gender, I desire a person."[1]

In the previous chapters we've taken a comprehensive look at what God
says about our sexuality—what is permitted, what is prohibited, what is an
abomination to God, and what He calls perversion. We have seen what He
will judge. We have learned how to receive and give forgiveness. We know
the truth about sex according to God. We have searched it out, studied it.

But even with all that knowledge, what do we do with the temptation? How do we handle the passion that taunts our minds and burns in our bodies? What about the conversation in our mind, the inner voice that insists we're incapable of resisting the desires of our flesh? Is it really possible to resist, to win the battle against such inherent desires, to not yield to this natural longing for touch, for expression, for satisfaction?

TURNED ON

No one has to tell us we're sensual beings. God made us that way. Every man and woman is genetically wired to react to sexual stimuli. Almost without exception our hormones kick into full gear before we're ever ready for marriage. And when we live in a sensual, sexual world, how can we help but be turned on by what we see and hear? How can we resist the smells, the sights, the sounds—songs that fill our ears, pictures that tantalize our eyes?

And the drive is always there, whether we're single or married, whether we're young or simply wish we were.

What do we do? What does God expect? How do we handle this?

This was Amnon's problem. Let's walk through his story together as it's told in 2 Samuel 13.

¹ Now it was after this that Absalom the son of David had a beautiful sister whose name was Tamar, and Amnon the son of David loved her.

Let's pause for a moment and put a clock like this 🕐 over that phrase *after this,* because it tells us when this incident is happening. And if God tells us *when,* we ought to pay attention. Everything in God's Word is for a purpose; He wastes no words.

So this scene opens after what? The story of Amnon, Absalom, and Tamar follows David's sin with Bathsheba. The events we want to look at are recorded in the chapter immediately following Nathan's confrontation with David and his pronouncement of the consequence of David's sin.

It seems David had at least six wives when he took Bathsheba. Six wives—

and seven children from these wives. He would later have four more children by Bathsheba plus nine more whose mothers aren't identified. Talk about a blended family! And when a family is blended, especially over a period of years, all sorts of complications arise in the realm of sexual attraction.

Absalom and Tamar were born to David through Maacah, his fourth wife. Amnon was the son of Ahinoam, David's second wife. The text tells us Amnon *loved* his half sister, Tamar. Put a heart over that word in verse 1.

² Amnon was so frustrated because of his sister Tamar that he made himself ill, for she was a virgin, and it seemed hard to Amnon to do anything to her.

Obviously this young man is burning with desire. He cannot get Tamar off his mind. The thought of her is tearing him up. And he knows he cannot take her because she is a virgin. Either the man's conscience is holding him back, restraining him—or his desires are thwarted because virgins were isolated from the eligible young males and it was impossible for him to get near her. Whatever the explanation, his thoughts are killing him. His mind is consumed with knowing Tamar sexually.

³ But Amnon had a friend whose name was Jonadab, the son of Shimeah, David's brother; and Jonadab was a very shrewd man.

⁴ He said to him, "O son of the king, why are you so depressed morning after morning? Will you not tell me?" Then Amnon said to him, "I am in love with Tamar, the sister of my brother Absalom."

Such is the state of Amnon's desire and torment that he can't hide his distress! Can you relate? Have you ever been at a point where you can't shake your desire, you can't get him or her off your mind? You can think of no one else; you can imagine nothing but what it would be like to be together.

If you're a woman, you're not necessarily thinking about the actual act of sexual intercourse as much as a relationship, the romance of it all—being loved, being in love, being together, cherished, kissed, touched. Your dreams are drawn from the emotional scenes you've tucked away with every romance novel, every movie.

If you're a man, however, the thoughts usually go further. Maybe you don't plan to act on your desires until you're married, but still you dream of what it will be like. Maybe you've already undressed her in your mind and imagined that moment when she gives herself to you and you take her as your own, your very own.

So you probably understand that Amnon had Tamar on his mind. Before we look at Jonadab's solution to Amnon's anguish, return to verses 3 and 4 and mark the word *love*.

⁵ Jonadab then said to him, "Lie down on your bed and pretend to be ill; when your father comes to see you, say to him, 'Please let my sister Tamar come and give me some food to eat, and let her prepare the food in my sight, that I may see it and eat from her hand.'"

It seems that Jonadab, the shrewd cousin and friend of Amnon's, comprehends the situation—and he helps plot a wicked solution. We know nothing about Jonadab except the deadly advice he gives his cousin, advice that reveals his character—or lack thereof.

From the first chapter of the book of Proverbs, Solomon would warn his son about men like Amnon: "My son, if sinners entice you, do not consent" (Proverbs 1:10). Later the apostle Paul would warn the Corinthians that evil companions corrupt good morals. Watch whose counsel you follow, because when all is said and done, you cannot pass the blame! Each of us is held accountable for our behavior. With God we can never point the finger to someone else and say, "But he said it was all right…she made it possible…she suggested…he dared me…" Hush. Those excuses won't stand up in the court of heaven.

⁶ So Amnon lay down and pretended to be ill; when the king came to see

him, Amnon said to the king, "Please let my sister Tamar come and make me a

couple of cakes in my sight, that I may eat from her hand."

⁷ Then David sent to the house for Tamar, saying, "Go now to your

brother Amnon's house, and prepare food for him."

Daddy wasn't thinking—and he ought to have been! He ought to have been on high alert after what happened in his own life with Bathsheba. Why didn't he wonder about Amnon specifically requesting Tamar's presence?

Mom, Dad, don't let your children blindside you. Surely you remember when you were a teen, a college student. You aren't over the hill—even if they think you are. Stop and evaluate why they're asking for the keys, checking out your schedule, finding reasons for not staying home, skirting around your words of caution about a certain friend or relationship. Think about what's happening in the minds of your kids!

Don't set up your kids to fall. Do you know how many teens lose their virginity in their own homes? in their bedrooms? Our homes are supposed to be shelters, places of safety and protection where we're secure from the world and all its lusts, where we're taught, nurtured, matured, where we're prepared to handle life. Bedrooms ought to be off-limits for members of the opposite sex, as should dorm rooms and apartments. Clear rules should be set, stating that a child is never to be in the home alone with someone of the opposite sex who's not a family member. Even with family members, it's important to exercise caution, especially when the brother or sister has friends over. No parties without parental supervision. In addition, parents ought to perform periodic reconnaissance missions at unexpected times!

I read of one mother who walked through a bedroom, saw her sixteen-year-old nephew under the sheets with her ten-year-old daughter, and didn't say a word. She just kept walking. Several days later she threw an offhanded statement at her daughter: "You'd better not be doing anything in bed." What kind of parenting is that? The sheet should have been jerked off immediately.

No "home alone" scenes for twosomes of the opposite sex; it just invites trouble. I know I sound totally out of it—believe me, I know. Many will think I just don't understand how things are today—but I do. I've seen the television commercials with the gorgeous hunk borrowing a stick of butter from a luscious girl, the two seeking a reason to be alone together. More in keeping with the java craze is the scene where a guy lingers at his date's door with the question in his eyes: "I've just paid the tab for the evening; aren't you going to reward me?" She hesitates, starts to go in. The camera catches her eyes closing sensually for a moment and her lips forming a gentle knowing smile. Turning back to the guy whose shoulders are sagging with disappointment, she asks ever so invitingly, "Do you want to come in for a cup of coffee?"

No more needs to be said or shown. We all know where it's leading.

8 So Tamar went to her brother Amnon's house, and he was lying down.

And she took dough, kneaded it, made cakes in his sight, and baked the cakes.

And what was Amnon doing? Watching the folds of her dress cling to her body as she prepared his meal…dreaming of taking her to his bed…imagining what she would look like when…

9 She took the pan and dished them out before him, but he refused to eat.

And Amnon said, "Have everyone go out from me." So everyone went out from him.

"Flee…youthful lusts," Paul urged Timothy, his son in the Lord, and he instructed the Thessalonians to avoid the appearance of evil.[2]

A man on death row—which was where Amnon unknowingly was headed—described the power of the lust of his eyes like this: "For me, seeing pornography was like lighting a fuse on a stick of dynamite; I became stimulated and had to gratify my urges or explode."

¹⁰ Then Amnon said to Tamar, "Bring the food into the bedroom, that I may eat from your hand." So Tamar took the cakes which she had made and brought them into the bedroom to her brother Amnon.

Didn't it occur to her what was happening? Didn't she understand the lust that can overtake a man, simply by watching and visualizing the taking of a woman?

From the text, it seems that Tamar was innocent. Like many other women, she didn't recognize the trap that had been set for her.

It reminds me of a letter I read yesterday. Trying to redeem every moment for this book, I read the letter as Jack and I delivered a meal to a member of our staff who recently had surgery. The letter told how this woman's marriage had ended in divorce despite a prophecy from someone in the church that their relationship would be healed. But finally she left. She just couldn't take it anymore—after thirteen years of his infidelity, neglect, cruelty, drugs, alcohol…years in which she'd leave for several months and then come back to begin the cycle again…years of living off and on in a shelter with their several children.

Then a newly divorced man showed up at church. No family of his own. Kind. Charming. He helped her and the children move from the shelter to a house, helped her get the first car she'd ever owned, and even gave her money for the divorce. The man had a lot of excess baggage, but he was there for her.

Yet all the time, he was setting her up, luring her into his trap. When he finally felt it was safe, he made his move. He shared that he was so wounded, so disillusioned with women that the only way he could ever be gratified was to become his own image of a woman. He vowed that if she didn't marry him, he would have the surgery he needed to look and act like a real woman.

Of course you can read the handwriting on the wall: She married a man who wears her nightgowns to bed—and worse. A man, she discovered, who was caught in the snare of pornography at the age of five and has lived in a fantasy world ever since. A world that is totally disgusting to her, yet she stays with him—because "he said if I told anyone at church he would quit the church and disappear…. I want to go to church for counseling but am afraid they will protect him and shun me since he's been in the church family for seven years, in their choir, always seeking public attention from the staff..."

> "Will you walk into my parlor?" said the Spider to the Fly....
> He dragged her up his winding stair, into his dismal den,
> Within his little parlour—but she ne'er came out again![3]

How my heart grieves for this woman, trapped by a sick, manipulative man who may call himself a Christian, but who, according to the Word of God, has no inheritance in the kingdom of God.[4] I know I sound harsh and possibly judgmental, but I'm not the one calling the shots. It's God who has drawn the line—and the line will never move. Man is the one who is to move. When we move to God's side, He gives us the power and grace to escape the bonds of sin, but it will be on God's terms—only through Jesus Christ and faith's response to who He is.

When I responded to the letter from this hurting woman, among other things I told her the line must be drawn. We are not to enable others in their sin. God says, "Do not participate in the unfruitful deeds of darkness, but instead even expose them; for it is disgraceful even to speak of the things which are done by them in secret. But all things become visible when they are exposed by the light" (Ephesians 5:11-13).

SIN NEVER SATISFIES

Let's return to Tamar's tragic story, remembering that, since this incident was deemed important enough by God to include it in His Word, there must be lessons He wants us to learn from it.

[11] When she brought them to him to eat, he took hold of her and said to her, "Come, lie with me, my sister."

[12] But she answered him, "No, my brother, do not violate me, for such a thing is not done in Israel; do not do this disgraceful thing!

¹³ "As for me, where could I get rid of my reproach? And as for you, you will be like one of the fools in Israel. Now therefore, please speak to the king, for he will not withhold me from you."

Interesting, isn't it? Tamar did not reject Amnon. She just didn't want him to violate her—or his reputation. Such behavior would be disgraceful. She knew—as did he—that sex outside of marriage, sex apart from a covenant, is unacceptable in God's eyes. Their father had given in to his passions, and look at the shame it brought. How the enemies of God blasphemed the name of God!

So she suggests that they wait. "Let's go to our father the king. He understands. He won't withhold me from you. I'll be yours. I'm not rejecting you; I'm just asking you to wait, to do what's right, to respect me, to not bring reproach on me."

"Ohhhh, baby…baby…don't make me wait. If you love me, please…please don't make me wait."

James 1:14 tells us "each one is tempted when he is carried away and enticed by his own lust."

¹⁴ However, he would not listen to her; since he was stronger than she, he violated her and lay with her.

Amnon had already taken Tamar mentally; now he had to have her physically. And he wouldn't wait. He wanted her then. Immediately. He would satisfy *his* desire no matter what it cost her. And it would cost Tamar her virginity and her reputation, along with her mental, emotional, and physical welfare.

Amnon violated her. *Violated.* The Hebrew word used here is *anah,* which means "to depress, to bring down." The *King James Version* translates the word as *forced.*

Amnon forced himself on Tamar. "For out of the heart come evil thoughts, murders, adulteries, fornications, thefts, false witness, slanders. These are the things which defile the man" (Matthew 15:19-20).

¹⁵ Then Amnon hated her with a very great hatred; for the hatred with which he hated her was greater than the love with which he had loved her. And Amnon said to her, "Get up, go away!"

Amnon loved Tamar—or at least that's what he thought. He even told his cousin Jonadab he loved her. So what had changed?

In a matter of minutes—or did it only take seconds?—love turned to hate. Did you mark *love* again? And how would you mark *hate*? How about a heart with a slash through it, like this: ⊘.

Love turned to hate, but why? I believe it was because Amnon suddenly came face to face with his lust, and his lust turned to disgust—disgust with himself. Instead of owning the consequences of his actions, instead of begging for forgiveness and seeking to heal the one he had just violated, he looked at Tamar and blamed her for his actions.

"Get up! Go away!"

Tamar has just been ravished. Violated. The blood of her virginity is on his sheets. And *he* orders *her* to get up and walk out of the bedroom, through the house, out the door!

¹⁶ But she said to him, "No, because this wrong in sending me away is greater than the other that you have done to me!" Yet he would not listen to her.

¹⁷ Then he called his young man who attended him and said, "Now throw this woman out of my presence, and lock the door behind her."

Amnon had physically released the throbbing in his loins and now he ordered Tamar, the dream of his life, thrown out of his room! Where was the tenderness of love, the gratitude, the delight, the deep satisfaction that overwhelms a man or woman after they've made love? It's never really there outside the marriage bed. No matter how strong the desire is, sex outside of marriage leaves a nagging guilt deep inside, an unexplainable dissatisfaction, a void that's still not filled.

God knows why. Remember, He's the Manufacturer. He knows His product. He knows what brings total satisfaction—and that the abuse of His product brings only regret and loathing.

¹⁸ Now she had on a long-sleeved garment; for in this manner the virgin daughters of the king dressed themselves in robes. Then his attendant took her out and locked the door behind her.

What incredible shame Amnon brought on the young virgin who came to make a meal for her sick brother. Amnon was ill, very ill—sick with lust and sickened even more because it overcame him.

Anyone, male or female, who cannot control their sexual desires is sick with a malignancy that will lead to certain death if God doesn't become their great physician.

¹⁹ Tamar put ashes on her head and tore her long-sleeved garment which was on her; and she put her hand on her head and went away, crying aloud as she went.

Ashes on the forehead was a sign of mourning, of grieving a loss. Her virginity had been stolen and could never be returned.

²⁰ Then Absalom her brother said to her, "Has Amnon your brother been with you? But now keep silent, my sister, he is your brother; do not take this matter to heart." So Tamar remained and was desolate in her brother Absalom's house.

The Hebrew word God chose in describing Tamar as *desolate* was *shamem,* which comes from a word that means "ruined." Amnon's uncontrolled passion ruined the life of his sister.

I wonder how many so-called Christian brothers have ruined the lives of their "sisters" by taking advantage of the intimacy that comes naturally to fellow believers in Jesus Christ?

Sex outside of marriage is the most self-centered act anyone can perform. What does God think about a man or a woman who would do this to another? Do you think the perpetrator will go free? Escape the just judgment of God? Not according to God's Book! Don't forget Numbers 32:23—"Be sure your sin will find you out"!

You may think you're acting in secret, but your sin is performed in the presence of a holy Trinity—the Father who created you, the Son who died for you, the Spirit who desires to live in you and give you the power to overcome every lust of your flesh, to turn from every temptation.

   [21] Now when King David heard of all these matters, he was very angry.

And rightly so! But what did David do about it? The Bible doesn't tell us, yet Scripture seems to speak even through its silence. Apparently David failed as a father; he didn't confront his children, deal with the issue, pronounce judgment, or bring a just resolution. Had he not learned anything from Nathan?

Was David's failure to act the result of his guilty conscience? Was it because his thoughts were consumed with his own remorse? "How can I say anything? Look at what I've done!"

Sinning—failing God—does *not* mean that we can never open our mouths again or call sin by name and see that it is dealt with. Sin is always to be addressed according to the Word of God, not according to our righteousness or lack thereof! If we cover it up instead of dealing with it, the wound will fester and more damage will be done in the process.

This is why...

    every child molester needs to be exposed and face the just consequences of his or her sin. If not, the sin will continue and others will suffer.

       every immoral failure within the leadership of the church must be addressed; it is not to be hidden or ignored so the person can do it again.

       every rapist must be dealt with.

David should have followed the precepts we studied in Deuteronomy 22, the guidelines God provided regarding the action to be taken in cases of immorality. Amnon should have married his sister. And maybe through doing what was right, noble, and good, Amnon's love for Tamar would have been restored.

As far as we know, however, the situation was never dealt with biblically.

22 But Absalom did not speak to Amnon either good or bad; for Absalom hated Amnon because he had violated his sister Tamar.

Two years later, Tamar's brother Absalom killed Amnon. Death in some form always follows sin. In this incident literal death resulted, but spiritual death is an unavoidable consequence of sin. James 1 sets forth this principle. Let's read it and mark the text. Mark every reference to being *tempted* or *enticed*. By the way, I'd suggest reading the passage aloud. You want to store these verses in your memory bank so you can bring them up on the screen of your mind when you need them.

JAMES 1:13-17

13 Let no one say when he is tempted, "I am being tempted by God"; for God cannot be tempted by evil, and He Himself does not tempt anyone.

14 But each one is tempted when he is carried away and enticed by his own lust.

15 Then when lust has conceived, it gives birth to sin; and when sin is accomplished, it brings forth death.

16 Do not be deceived, my beloved brethren.

17 Every good thing given and every perfect gift is from above, coming down from the Father of lights, with whom there is no variation or shifting shadow.

How about reading it again? This time mark *death* with a tombstone ⌂. Color *sin* brown or black or put a big scarlet **S** over it.

When we sin sexually, it seems so easy to excuse ourselves. "I just couldn't help it! The desire was overwhelming. I'm sure God understands. After all, He made me the way I am!" But will such excuses stand?

List what you learned from marking *tempted* and *enticed*.

And what did you learn about sin?

What about death?

According to this passage, is it a sin to be tempted?

When did Amnon sin? Answer that question strictly according to the account you just read in 2 Samuel and what you observed in James 1, and without reading any thoughts into Amnon's mind or projecting your own opinion into the story.

What died as a result of Amnon's unchecked lust, his yielding to sexual temptation?

The Devil's Design—and Our Way Out

The Greek word translated *enticed* in James 1:14 is quite a picturesque word. It's a hunting term used for setting a trap; it also describes baiting a hook in order to lure a fish out from under a rock.

I'm married to a fisherman, and if there's one thing I know from picking out fishing magazines for him, it's that fish love to hang out under rocks.

And who is *our* Rock, beneath whose shadow we need to hide? You know the answer: It's God, whose name is *Cur*—Rock! We're to hide in the cleft of the Rock, in the shelter of our God. That's where we're safe and secure.

Do you think this might be why the devil took up fishing? Although Satan knows that he can never have us again as his own, he surely desires to wipe us out by getting us to sin and putting us in a position to receive God's chastening.

The devil's strategy is to lure us from our Rock and get us to swallow his bait. One of the most powerful and successful lures in his tackle box is sex. The devil's an expert when it comes to threading that worm on his hook, leaving just enough wiggling tail to get our attention.

Sex successfully lured the family of King David!

David slept with Bathsheba,

    Amnon with Tamar,

        and Absalom would eventually sleep with his father's concubines in full view of Israel!

David. Amnon. Absalom.

They had no one to blame except themselves. We cannot blame our sin on temptation. It comes as a result of feeding our own lust—lust that is strengthened with every look, with every thought.

Just five days ago I traveled to Cleveland, Ohio, to speak at a women's conference for Moody Bible Institute and Radio. At the airport I walked over to the magazine racks, wanting to see if there was anything new on sexually transmitted diseases or AIDS that might contribute to the content of this book. As I passed the "hot" section of magazines—featuring women in all sorts of sensual positions, flaunting their bodies in various stages of undress—I noticed a tall young man standing extremely close to the rack. He was gingerly flipping the edges of one of these magazines, then peeping into a half open page to stare at something that caught his attention. As I passed by, I caught a glimpse of what had captured his interest. I saw only half the picture, but it revealed more than enough. I thought, *Lord, this is what I'm writing about.*

I went over and put my hand on his shoulder, so when he looked up we were practically eyeball to eyeball. "Son," I said, "you shouldn't be looking at that. It will just make you want more and more. It's addictive."

The poor guy looked at me absolutely stunned and murmured, "I know."

I removed my hand from his shoulder. As I turned to walk away, all I could say was, "It's not pleasing to God."

I wish now I had said more. I had spoken gently, lovingly—but I was nervous, and I'm sorry I didn't have more of my wits about me to talk with him a bit longer. All I could do was pray that God would use our encounter in a significant way in his life.

By the way, if you ever see me on television with a black eye, you'll know some guy finally decked me for speaking to him about his morals! But I think, *Lord, someone has to speak out. Doesn't Your love desire another's highest good?* Think of what could happen if this guy listens. And even if there's no immediate impact, he'll remember our conversation every time he goes to a magazine rack to "gaze upon a woman." Maybe the Spirit of God will wear him down.

Wanting to look at that magazine was not this young man's sin; that was merely temptation. The sin was in actually *looking* at the magazine, in yielding to the temptation.

As part of preparing your heart to battle temptation, I recommend you memorize the following verse. I did so right after getting saved, and it's been of enormous help.

1 CORINTHIANS 10:13

13 No temptation has overtaken you but such as is common to man; and

God is faithful, who will not allow you to be tempted beyond what you are able, but with the temptation will provide the way of escape also, that you may

be able to endure it.

It's a good verse to recite at magazine racks. And think about the possible benefit to those who might hear you! Now that you've read it through, why don't you read it again aloud. As you read, mark every occurrence of *tempted* and *temptation*. Then record below what you learn about temptation from marking the word.

Isn't that awesome? God has promised that no temptation will ever be more than you can bear. There will always be a way of escape.

How well this is illustrated even in our story of Tamar and Amnon. Tamar told her brother to ask their father the king and he would give her to him! There was Amnon's way of escape—and a promise of the fulfillment of his longing. If only he had taken it!

But you may say, "He couldn't help it. He couldn't wait, and I know just how he felt. Sometimes I'm certain that if I don't get it then and there, I'll explode!"

But there *is* a way of escape; there always is: Lift your voice, cry to God—yell, if you must—*"I'm going to explode. What do I do? Help me!"*

And He will help. He has to, because He has promised. God cannot lie. God cannot fail. It's when we don't rely on Him, but instead let our lusts hold sway over our decisions and actions, that we get into trouble.

Look at what God says about lust in 1 John 2:15-17. Circle the word *lust* or *lusts* each time it appears.

¹⁵ Do not love the world nor the things in the world. If anyone loves the

world, the love of the Father is not in him.

16 For all that is in the world, the lust of the flesh and the lust of the eyes and the boastful pride of life, is not from the Father, but is from the world.

17 The world is passing away, and also its lusts; but the one who does the will of God lives forever.

What types of lust are mentioned in these verses?

Where are these lusts from?

And what is it that will eventually pass away?

Before we leave these verses, go back and read the text aloud again. This time put a heart around every reference to *love*. Then stop and ask yourself, "What do *I* love—*really* love?"

The lust of the flesh is a powerful thing. When it comes to taking something, having something, participating in something, eating something we shouldn't, you've heard many a person say, "I just couldn't help it. I had to have it!"

Really? Let's see what Ephesians says about that. As you read these verses, mark the words *lust* and *desires* in the same way you marked *lust* previously.

EPHESIANS 2:1-6

¹ And you were dead in your trespasses and sins,

² in which you formerly walked according to the course of this world, according to the prince of the power of the air, of the spirit that is now working in the sons of disobedience.

³ Among them we too all formerly lived in the lusts of our flesh, indulging the desires of the flesh and of the mind, and were by nature children of wrath, even as the rest.

⁴ But God, being rich in mercy, because of His great love with which He loved us,

⁵ even when we were dead in our transgressions, made us alive together with Christ (by grace you have been saved),

⁶ and raised us up with Him, and seated us with Him in the heavenly places in Christ Jesus.

Now go back and read this passage aloud. Every time you come to the word *formerly*, mark it with a symbol like this ⟨*formerly*, and every time you come to the phrase *according to,* underline it.

What did you learn from marking *formerly*? What were these people *formerly,* before God in love saved them by His grace, His unearned favor? Write it out. You'll want to remember this valuable insight.

There's quite a contrast between the first three verses of this passage and the last three. The children of the devil, also referred to as children of wrath, are described in the first three. In the last three you find a description of those who, through the mercy and love of God, are saved from the devil's domain by the death and resurrection of Jesus Christ. And what is so incredibly awesome is that God did this for us when we were dead in our transgressions, when we lived in willful disobedience to His laws.

This revelation is really stunning because, in our salvation, God didn't leave us powerless when it comes to sin. In our identification with Jesus Christ, in uniting us to Him, making us His dwelling place—Christ in us and we in Him—we're now seated in a place of power. We can exercise power over sin and Satan because, as Ephesians 1:18-23 says, our union with Christ actually puts us above Satan and all his demonic host! Now that's worth a "Hallelujah" once you understand it!

Because of this power that is now given us, this *dunamis,* God can give us the following instructions, knowing that we have the strength, through the Holy Spirit, to obey.

EPHESIANS 5:3-12

³ But immorality or any impurity or greed must not even be named among you, as is proper among saints;

⁴ and there must be no filthiness and silly talk, or coarse jesting, which are not fitting, but rather giving of thanks.

⁵ For this you know with certainty, that no immoral or impure person or covetous man, who is an idolater, has an inheritance in the kingdom of Christ and God.

⁶ Let no one deceive you with empty words, for because of these things the wrath of God comes upon the sons of disobedience.

⁷ Therefore do not be partakers with them;

⁸ for you were formerly darkness, but now you are Light in the Lord; walk as children of Light

⁹ (for the fruit of the Light consists in all goodness and righteousness and truth),

¹⁰ trying to learn what is pleasing to the Lord.

¹¹ Do not participate in the unfruitful deeds of darkness, but instead even expose them;

¹² for it is disgraceful even to speak of the things which are done by them in secret.

Did you read those verses carefully? They're full of instruction, aren't they? Why? Because these words are written to those who, according to Ephesians 2:1-6, are no longer children of wrath, walking according to (under the dominion of) Satan, the prince of the power of the air. Those who receive these words are no longer bound to the standards or dictates of the world that lies under Satan's power.

Now, just so you don't miss the gravity of what's being said in Ephesians 5:3-12, let's zero in for a closer observation. Two groups of people are mentioned in these verses—the *sons of disobedience* and those who are called *saints, children of Light.* Put a pitchfork like this Ψ over every reference to the *sons of disobedience,* those who are under Satan's dominion. Draw a big circle like the sun ☼ over every reference to the *children of Light.* As you do this, watch for pronouns and mark them accordingly, either with a pitchfork or a circle. Also watch for and again mark *formerly.* It's a keyword in Ephesians.

Now list below what you learn about...

THE SAINTS, THE CHILDREN OF LIGHT

THE SONS OF DISOBEDIENCE

AN ACTION PLAN

So how do you handle temptation if you're going to walk in light and not in darkness? First Thessalonians 4:4 tells us we're to know how to possess our vessel in sanctification and honor. So what do you need to do in the throes of lust, in the place of temptation? Let's come up with a plan of action.

First, I would suggest that before you put your feet on the floor in the morning, your prayer should be: "Father, lead me not into temptation. Deliver me from evil and the evil one." Let God know that you are choosing not to sin, not even to put yourself in the path of sin. You want to be delivered from evil. What does this mean practically?

Think about what we've talked about in this book, because we've basically covered it. You know your weakness, your particular area of fascination. Whatever it is, you're to separate yourself from it physically. You're to follow the counsel of 2 Timothy 2:22—Flee youthful lusts. And believe me, those lusts can attack no matter how old you are, as even spiritual giants have admitted!

If your attraction to a particular person is drawing you toward sin, avoid going where you know he or she will be. If you have to pass by that person's home or office, don't look. Don't cruise the neighborhood. Change dentists, doctors, lawyers, pastors, secretaries, accountants—whatever it takes to avoid whoever is attracting you. Change jobs if you have to. If you're a married woman and a man at your place of employment is attractive to you, maybe God is telling you to go home to your family and to live on less income!

If you want a way out, God will reveal a path of escape. I can't play God and give you specifics in a book like this, but know this: God will make the way clear if you simply ask for His help and tell Him you'll do whatever He says. Just remember, God never goes against His Word.

So step one is to avoid any hook loaded with the bait most likely to catch you!

Second, you know that sex outside of marriage is absolutely forbidden, so don't light fires that cannot righteously be put out in the marriage bed. This means that besides controlling your eyes and your thoughts, you must also control your hands.

Can you fondle a person to whom you aren't married? How far can you go in respect to groping, petting—whatever it's currently called in your circle of friends—putting your hands all over another person's body to excite you or them?

Let's look for our answer in 1 Corinthians. Mark every reference to the *body*, along with all synonyms and pronouns, including the word *members* as it refers to the various parts of your body.

1 CORINTHIANS 6:13-20

13 Food is for the stomach and the stomach is for food, but God will do away with both of them. Yet the body is not for immorality, but for the Lord, and the Lord is for the body.

14 Now God has not only raised the Lord, but will also raise us up through His power.

15 Do you not know that your bodies are members of Christ? Shall I then take away the members of Christ and make them members of a prostitute? May it never be!

16 Or do you not know that the one who joins himself to a prostitute is one body with her? For He says, "THE TWO WILL BECOME ONE FLESH."

17 But the one who joins himself to the Lord is one spirit with Him.

18 Flee immorality. Every other sin that a man commits is outside the body, but the immoral man sins against his own body.

19 Or do you not know that your body is a temple of the Holy Spirit who is in you, whom you have from God, and that you are not your own?

20 For you have been bought with a price: therefore glorify God in your body.

What did you learn from marking the references to the *body*? List your insights.

Now let's reason together. According to this passage, can you take your hands and the other parts of your body given to you by God and use them to arouse yourself and another when you aren't married? And if you arouse another, how are you going to legitimately put out the fire you started, apart from intercourse? Will you train your body to shut off short of a climax? And what will happen when you get married? Will you find satisfaction only in doing as you've trained your body to do? What if you don't marry the person who stimulated you in these ways? Will your learned behavior affect, distort, or destroy the pleasure God intended you to experience with your husband or wife?

Did verse 18 register with you? You might want to read it again aloud. The immoral man sins against his *own* body! I don't think this *only* refers to reaping the consequence of sexually transmitted diseases! I think it includes programming your body for sex in such a way that it hurts you.

So if you can't touch another person's body until marriage, because it falls under the category of sexual immorality, what about masturbation? It's a difficult word to say, isn't it? Something you usually don't discuss. I understand. Yet because so many participate in this habit, it needs to be addressed. Masturbation is a major problem, especially for men.

I think the issue can be resolved rather quickly, although breaking the habit will be another thing. All we need to understand is why an individual masturbates. Though any number of things may prompt the action, the end result is always the same—sexual gratification. Therefore masturbation is off-limits.

"But I'm single!"

"But my wife or husband won't…can't…isn't around!"

"But if I don't, I'll go crazy. I can't handle it. I'll explode!"

Listen very carefully: Masturbation stimulates your body sexually. The more you do it, the more you want. And the way you masturbate becomes the way you usually want sex. You've figured out the combination of sights, sounds, thoughts, and moves to bring you to satisfaction—and this will carry over into the marriage bed. Remember Pavlov's dog? Ring the bell, feed the dog; ring the bell, feed the dog. Repeat it often enough, and just the ring of a bell will start the dog's saliva flowing! No food is necessary.

Counselors in the secular world (and even some in the Christian world) have assured us there's nothing wrong with masturbation; it's quite natural. We're told the Bible is silent on the subject, so you're free to choose.

But masturbation is *not* natural. It's a learned behavior, initiated in response to a stimulus. And the Bible is *not* silent about it. We looked earlier at God's instructions in 1 Corinthians 7:1 and 7:9. The message is clear: If you burn sexually, get married. This is God's Word, not mine or some psychologist's. God didn't say, "If you're burning and cannot control it, then masturbate." He said to get married.

Reason with me a little further. When a person masturbates, he or she fantasizes sexually. Jesus said in Matthew 5 that this is the same as committing adultery. So what are you to do? "Cut off your hand." Is God saying to literally chop it off at the wrist? No, it's hyperbole. God is making the point that we're to do whatever it takes to stop, because no adulterer has any inheritance in heaven. It's better to do whatever is necessary to stop now than to suffer the torment of hell with your body intact. Jesus is making a strong point with a strong illustration. The question is, did you get it? If not, get on your knees before God and read Matthew 5:29-30, then tell God you want to understand this to the very core of your being.

Finally, can you use your hands to sexually stimulate yourself or another person outside of marriage and claim you are following Colossians 3:17, which says, "Whatever you do in word or deed, do all in the name of the Lord Jesus"? Do you honestly believe this can bring honor and glory to God?

"But," you say, "what about the physical release I need as a man every two to three days?" Remember that God said He will not give you any temptation you can't bear. God always has a way of escape. In regard to a man and his sperm, God has made provision through nocturnal emissions, more commonly called "wet dreams."

Now, after all you've seen in the Word of God, do we really need to talk about oral sex? About the right and wrong of using it as a stopgap measure so you can remain a virgin until you get married? I doubt it. You know from all you've learned in the Word of God that it's wrong. Until fifty years ago, American law declared sodomy (which includes oral sex) a criminal act for the both the married and unmarried. Isn't it obvious that oral sex represents leaving the natural use of God's design, abandoning the beauty of becoming one flesh, for something that is unnatural, something that distorts His beautiful picture of oneness?

Oh, my friend, wait for marriage. Conduct yourself in a way pleasing to God. Pursue peace and the sanctification without which no one will ever see the Lord.[5]

And if you remain single for the rest of your life, stay pure. In your sexual hunger, don't sell your birthright as an heir of God and a joint heir with Jesus Christ for a mess of pottage, as Esau did. He thought he'd die if he didn't get the food his body craved, so he sold all that could have been his...for a dish of red stew! Esau's appetite was satisfied, but his birthright was lost in the hunger of the moment. And though he cried and pleaded afterward, it could never be recovered.[6] He became an angry, bitter man—never fulfilled, never satisfied.

Sex outside of marriage will do that to you, leave you wallowing in bitterness and regret. So how do you walk in sexual purity? Galatians 5:16 tells you that if you will walk by the Spirit, you will not fulfill the lust of your flesh. Notice God did *not* say you would never battle the lust of the flesh; the flesh does have its appetites. But they can be overridden by habitually, continuously choosing moment by moment, temptation by temptation, to walk by the Spirit. Among the ninefold aspects of the fruit of the Spirit are goodness and self-control. You know what God says is good and that He will enable you to live in goodness. He will also, by His Spirit, give you His power to control your flesh at all times. It's simply a matter of choice.

Sexual desires are only exacerbated when you awaken them, feed them, stimulate them. The wonderful flip side to that is, as you choose to walk in the Spirit opportunity by opportunity and to resist the pull of the flesh, temptation will slacken its grip. As you offer the parts of your body to Him as instruments of righteousness,7 your eyes, your mind, and your hands will come under the control of the Spirit of God.

When you choose to live by God's standards of holiness, and not by the world's measure of what's normal or natural, you'll find that "the mind set on the Spirit is life and peace" (Romans 8:6). And you'll experience such a sense of well-being...because you'll feel God's pleasure.

1 0

It's All in Your Head

What Do I Do When My Mind Turns to Sex?

The following story reflects the experience of so many men:

> We were going over a proposal and couldn't make sense of the dollar
> figures. As I sat at the conference table, deeply engrossed in numbers,
> trying to figure it all out, I found my mind drifting from the task at
> hand…captured by the sweet scent of a woman. It caused me to pause
> for a moment, still staring at the figures which seemed so out of place
> with the perfume floating in the air. Its intensity grew and, trying to
> shake myself from the reverie of the moment, I looked up from the
> papers spread on the conference table before me into the softness of
> breasts cradled in lace. My associate was bending over the table, the
> intensity of her perfume overwhelming my senses as she tried to
> explain to me where the mistake was.
>
> "It was over! From that moment on, I couldn't think of any other
> problem than how I was going to get home, get the kids in bed early
> so I could have sex with my wife."

Sex on the brain!
This is a phrase often used by women to describe their husbands—and
men haven't disowned the portrayal. For a man, the ON switch for sex is the
mind. It's as if a sexual stimulator runs from the eyes to the mind to the male
sexual organs. The eyes see it, the mind thinks it, and the body is ready to go.

If you're a man, you not only understand what I'm saying, but you're probably saying "Amen" under your breath. At last a woman understands!

Believe me, God understands. He knows the mind is the most powerful sex organ in our bodies—and that the eyes serve as a catalyst to turn on the mind. This is obviously true for men, and it's true for women as well—although in a different way and to a lesser degree. So whether we're male or female, we need to find out what to do about *sex in the head* before it becomes *sex in the bed* with someone other than your spouse.

DECEIVED BY THE ENEMY

Let's review for a moment. We saw that when sin entered into the world, Satan distorted what God had made beautiful. Consequently sex became one of the devil's major ploys to lead us into sexual immorality, which in turn, and much to the devil's delight, would bring us under the just judgment of God.

For example, when Balak, king of the Moabites, wanted to curse the children of Israel so his people could defeat them, he hired that infamous prophet Balaam. He's the one who was reprimanded by a talking donkey, and we find the first part of his story recorded in Numbers 22–24. Although Balaam wanted the fee Balak offered for his services, the prophet was unable to put a curse on God's people. Every time Balaam opened his mouth, God caused him to bless Israel rather than curse them, and in doing so, Balaam uttered some marvelous prophecies on Israel's behalf. God is like that; He just doesn't permit people to go around cursing His beloved.

However, Balaam was not about to lose his wages. Though he couldn't curse the Israelites, he devised another way to accomplish his purposes. According to what we read in Numbers 31:16 and other verses, he counseled the daughters of the Moabites to invite the sons of the Israelites to their parties, to worship their gods.[1] Soon in typical worldly party style, they were in bed together. Remember, the gods of this earth have no morals! Immorality always follows idolatry.[2]

In Numbers 25 we find God very angry with His people for having joined the pagans both in idol worship and in sexual sin. Filled with righteous indignation, God ordered the leaders of the people to take the men under their charge and slay every one who had joined himself to Baal of Peor.

The last straw came right after the order was given, when a son of Israel brought a Midianite woman to his brothers' tent in the sight of Moses and all the congregation of Israel. Immediately a plague descended on the people, and the only thing that stopped the death toll at twenty-four thousand was the action of Phinehas, the son of Eleazar and grandson of Aaron the priest. This faithful man, horrified by the sin around him, entered the tent where the Israelite lay with the Midianite woman and put a spear through their bodies. God then announced a covenant of peace to the Levite and his descendants, because Phinehas "was jealous with My jealousy among them, so that I did not destroy the sons of Israel in My jealousy" (Numbers 25:11).

You may be appalled at how quickly the Israelites embraced sin, but isn't history repeating itself today? The enemy is weakening the forces of the people of God through sexual immorality. Just look at the statistics of the morally dead in our churches! Look at the immorality, the fornication, the abortions, the adultery, and the divorces. Our depravity as Christians ranks right up there with the world's, and that's not the way it's supposed to be!

The question is why? Why have we allowed ourselves to be deceived, drawn into sexual sin?

Personally I believe it's because we've taken our eyes off the Word of God and put them on the flesh of mankind. We've been tantalized by the world's perfume, so distracted that we don't have time for intimacy with Jesus. We're too busy for personal Bible reading, let alone serious Bible study, yet somehow we find time to watch the world go by—on television, on the Internet, in the movies, in magazines and newspapers, in novels. And when the world struts by, how is she dressed? In the attire of a harlot! And she's wearing the alluring fragrance of sex.

Every summer at our Precept Ministries International headquarters in Chattanooga, Tennessee, we hold ten-day and five-day camps for teenagers and college students. They come from all over the United States, Canada, and even foreign countries to participate. Most of the days are spent learning inductive Bible study skills as the kids dig into the Word of God, book after book. It's awesome to see sharp, consecrated kids like this, young people who take their Christianity seriously.

In my files is a letter written by a gal from Arizona who attended one of these camps. Her story illustrates what can happen when we get our eyes off the world and into the Book of books.

God taught me a lot there about how I should act and who I should spend the majority of my time with. It was tough to admit and to deal with the fact that the way I acted was sinful and not pleasing to God. I resented it for a while, but when I finally admitted it and was able to talk to a counselor for some help, she told me that not only did God love me, but He wanted to fill that void. She said that being intimate with Jesus could satisfy that need in me to get attention from guys. That was so awesome. It works! If I stay close to Jesus, I don't need it anymore.

So I came home practicing my newfound truth and saw the study book *Someday A Marriage Without Regrets* on the shelf and finished it. I had to do the study alone. I sat in my room sometimes three hours and would do the whole week's lessons in one night. I learned soooo much.

This young lady is putting a chain-link fence around her mind, a barrier to keep out any intruders who would rob her blind. How wise she is, for as we think within ourselves, so we are.[3] This is why, as the Bible says, we're to keep our hearts, our thoughts with all diligence, for out of them flow the issues of life.[4]

GUARDING YOUR EYES AND MIND

Let's reason together for a few minutes. What is the major problem among men today, even—perhaps especially—in the church and among pastors? It's pornography, something that should never be a problem for a man of God. Why do I say that? Because the prevention and the cure for this problem are set out clearly in the Word of God. As we saw in the last chapter, the power to resist such temptation is found in the presence of the indwelling Spirit of God. If this is true, why do 40–60 percent of men who claim to be Christians struggle with pornography? Many were introduced to sexually explicit material as boys or young men, and they have never destroyed the roots of this sin.

To understand how pornography becomes such a pervasive problem, affecting many facets of a person's life, let's look at what it involves.

Pornography enlists two very powerful parts of the body, neither of which we usually think of as sexual organs—the eyes and the mind. And what does pornography incite through these vehicles? Masturbation. Imitation. Adultery. Fornication. Incest. Bestiality. Homosexuality. Lesbianism. Group sex. Masochism. Sadomasochism. Pedophilia.

Oh, my friend, beloved of God (and you *are,* no matter what sin has ensnared you), have you been caught in any of these vices, either mentally or physically? Or have you talked with someone who has? If so, you know how destructive these things are. Is there hope? Yes! Because God is the God of all hope.

Let's find this hope as we seek to understand how individuals are drawn into such sin and how they can be set free. Let's begin by looking at what Jesus says in Matthew 15:10-20. As you read this passage, draw an arrow aimed down on every occurrence of *defile,* like this: ↓, and place a heart like this ♡ over each occurrence of *heart.*

¹⁰ After Jesus called the crowd to Him, He said to them, "Hear and understand.

¹¹ "It is not what enters into the mouth that defiles the man, but what proceeds out of the mouth, this defiles the man."

¹² Then the disciples came and said to Him, "Do You know that the Pharisees were offended when they heard this statement?"

¹³ But He answered and said, "Every plant which My heavenly Father did not plant shall be uprooted.

¹⁴ "Let them alone; they are blind guides of the blind. And if a blind man guides a blind man, both will fall into a pit."

¹⁵ Peter said to Him, "Explain the parable to us."

¹⁶ Jesus said, "Are you still lacking in understanding also?

¹⁷ "Do you not understand that everything that goes into the mouth passes into the stomach, and is eliminated?

¹⁸ "But the things that proceed out of the mouth come from the heart, and those defile the man.

¹⁹ "For out of the heart come evil thoughts, murders, adulteries, fornications, thefts, false witness, slanders.

²⁰ "These are the things which defile the man; but to eat with unwashed
hands does not defile the man."

In Jewish thinking the heart is synonymous with the mind. In light of
this, list below what you learned from marking *defile* and *heart*.

The religious Jews of Jesus' day were more concerned about what they
ate than what they thought. What they ate, however, only came and went; it
passed through the body and never altered their character. Meanwhile, their
thoughts—what was on their hearts (in their minds) and came out through
their mouths—were the things that could actually defile them. Did you
notice the specific sexual sins listed in verse 19—adulteries and fornications?
Fornication covers every kind of sexual activity forbidden by God, all those
things I listed before we looked at this passage in Matthew. Did you observe
that these things don't begin with the act but with the thought? They're conceived in the mind, then born in the flesh.

And how do these things get into the mind? Stop and consider what we
learned earlier from observing the biblical accounts of Eve, the warrior Achan,
and King David. Their flesh was activated by their eyes. Each one—Eve,
Achan, and David—saw, desired, and took. In each case, someone else eventually was drawn into their sin. Adam followed Eve; Achan's family helped
hide the things he had stolen; Bathsheba slept with David. And in the wake
of each incident, death followed. Seeing produces desire, and desire, if
unchecked, results in acting out that desire.

As we discussed earlier, the mind is a major sex organ in our bodies—
even for women. What happens when women read the lusty novels, watch

the trashy soaps, let their eyes linger on the guys? The same thing as with men: Their thoughts lead to desire. It's just that men focus more quickly and are stimulated more easily because of how they're physically engineered.

But what if a person merely looks, whether at ads for lingerie or underwear in the newspaper or at the neighbor sunbathing next door or at pornographic pictures of some nameless person? Surely that cannot be a sin, can it? No one has done anything. There's been no intercourse; two have not become "one flesh."

If this is your question, you aren't alone. Many have asked the same thing. Can a man or woman "look and imagine" and not have their thoughts register on the Richter scale of immorality—and therefore escape the judgment of God?

Let's look at Matthew 5:27-30. These verses are from Jesus' well-known and beloved Sermon on the Mount. As you read the text aloud, mark anything that refers to *looking* or to the *eyes*. You might want to draw two eyeballs like this: 👀.

27 You have heard that it was said, "You shall not commit adultery";

28 but I say to you that everyone who looks at a woman with lust for her has already committed adultery with her in his heart.

29 If your right eye makes you stumble, tear it out and throw it from you; for it is better for you to lose one of the parts of your body, than for your whole body to be thrown into hell.

30 If your right hand makes you stumble, cut it off and throw it from you; for it is better for you to lose one of the parts of your body, than for your whole body to go into hell.

Now read through the text again. This time mark the word *adultery* in a distinctive way and circle the word *lust*. When you finish, look at the keywords you marked and list what you've learned on the following page.

ADULTERY

LOOKING AND THE EYE

Now let's revisit the questions I posed earlier about the gravity of look-ing and imagining versus the act of sexual intercourse. Is it all right to look at sexually explicit images, to gaze on someone and imagine sex—as long as you don't physically participate in it? How would you answer?

The Greek tense for the verb *looks* in verse 28 implies continuous or habitual action: "to 'keep on' looking." This indicates that Jesus is not warn-ing us about a thought that invades one's mind uninvited. He's not referring to something that happens as an instant action, where you see something briefly and then let it go. Rather, the verb tense lets us know that Jesus is talk-ing about a deliberate, continuous looking, a purposeful imagining to the point where you take the person to bed mentally. He's making reference to a thought that you welcome with open arms, greedily embrace, and invite to sit and chat awhile. This is a thought that eventually is engraved on your mind.

Jesus makes it clear, doesn't He, that to continue looking at someone with the purpose of taking him or her in your mind is considered adultery by God. Adultery, as you have seen, is sin, transgression of God's Law—and according to Jesus, to look at a woman and lust after her is adultery. It doesn't matter that it's all in your mind, that in reality this is a one-participant event physically and mentally; it still is judged as sin, as committing adultery in your heart.

What happens in your mind has such power! If it involves you sexually, it has the potential to be so dangerous that Jesus tells us to do whatever is necessary to stop it: Pluck out your eye, chop off your hand. If you don't get your thought life under control, it will take you to hell. That, my friend, is how extremely serious this is.

We're so tolerant today of sin and of the weakness of our flesh that we often excuse ourselves and others with a casual, "Oh, it's okay. God understands. We're all that way. Didn't Jesus say, 'Let the one without sin cast the first stone'?"[5]

While we may excuse ourselves this way, we'd better understand that God doesn't! This is why He duly warns us in His Word about the importance of guarding our eyes and our minds. Sex begins in the head; it's a matter of the mind. If you don't stop it, if you aren't careful about what you see and where your mind follows, then imagining sex will result in doing something first with your hands—such as masturbating or groping another—and then your thoughts will take your body where they want to go.

Could this be the reason Jesus mentions first dealing with the eye that offends—the door to the mind—and then with the hand that offends? If it's mental sex, involving only your eyes and mind, it offends God, and you have to bring it to a halt or ultimately you will face hell. If it's physical—using your hands and body—the same is true. You're breaking God's Law in respect to your sexuality.

These are pretty strong statements, aren't they! Do you wonder why God is so adamant that we keep our thoughts pure? It's because what we think is imprinted on the brain. And when it's accompanied by a picture, it leaves an even more powerful impression.

THE DESTRUCTIVE POWER OF PORNOGRAPHY

Psychologist James L. McGaugh at the University of California–Irvine has reported research findings that suggest memories formed at times of emotional arousal (which could include sexual arousal) get "locked into the brain"

by an adrenal gland hormone, epinephrine, and are difficult to erase. Powerful, sexually arousing memories of experiences from the past keep intruding
on the mind's memory screen, serving to stimulate and erotically arouse the
viewer. If a person masturbates to these fantasies or images, he or she rein-
forces the link between sexual arousal and orgasm, with the particular scene
or image repeatedly rehearsed in his mind.[6] This principle explains why
pornography becomes addictive and destructive.

Dr. Victor B. Cline is a psychotherapist specializing in family and marital counseling and sexual addictions. He has written a number of scientific
articles and books, including *Where Do You Draw the Line? Explorations in
Media Violence, Pornography, and Censorship*. As a result of his experiences
and study, he has identified a four-factor syndrome common to nearly all his
clients, especially those with early involvement in pornography. The first
change—and this is so relevant to what God says about the mind—is the
addiction effect. "The porn-consumers got hooked. Once involved in pornographic materials, they kept coming back for more and still more. The material seemed to provide a very powerful sexual stimulant or aphrodisiac effect,
followed by sexual release, most often through masturbation. The pornography provided very exciting and powerful imagery which they frequently
recalled to mind and elaborated on in their fantasies."[7]

Let's stop here for a moment and review what we've just seen from
Matthew 5 about looking "at a woman with lust for her." Doesn't that parallel pornography? The person described by Jesus in this passage sees a woman,
lusts for her, and in his mind commits the act.

Playboy's Web site, which offers free teaser shots of its Playmates, averages
five million hits per day.[8] Think of the battles going on in the mind, think of
the wounded and dying strewn on pornography's battlefield. Many, unless
they come to know Jesus Christ, will be maimed for life, only to then suffer
the eternal torment of hell and the lake of fire. Dr. Cline says that when the
wave of desire hits sex addicts, "nothing can stand in the way of getting what
they want, whether that be pornography accompanied by masturbation, sex
from a prostitute, molesting a child or raping a woman." And it started with
what they permitted their eyes to see!

The second factor or phase in sex addiction is escalation. More and more
is required to satisfy. It's like drug addiction. "Over time there is nearly always
an increasing need for more of the stimulant to get the same initial effect....

Their addiction and escalation were mainly due to the powerful sexual imagery in their minds, implanted there by the exposure to pornography." Pornography almost always diminishes a person's capacity to love and express affection to their mate in their intimate relations. One woman tearfully told Dr. Cline that her husband preferred to masturbate to pornography rather than make love to her.

The third phase is desensitization. "The sexual activity depicted in the pornography (no matter how antisocial or deviant) became legitimized. There was increasingly a sense that 'everybody does it' and this gave them permission to also do it, even though the activity was possibly illegal and contrary to their previous moral beliefs and personal standards."

If you were born before the 1960s and the sexual revolution, you've seen this phase played out in the cultural mores of our times. What once was totally unacceptable and kept hidden is now performed openly, without any fear of reprisal. And it all came to pass because our thinking changed. The mind is the battleground where wars are fought and losers are taken into captivity of the cruelest sort.

Following addiction, escalation, and desensitization comes the fourth phase: "an increasing tendency to act out sexually the behaviors viewed in the pornography that the porn-consumers had been repeatedly exposed to, including compulsive promiscuity, exhibitionism, group sex, voyeurism [peeping], frequenting massage parlors, having sex with minor children, rape, and inflicting pain on themselves or a partner during sex. This behavior frequently grew into a sexual addiction which they found themselves locked into and unable to change or reverse—no matter what the negative consequences were in their life."[9]

The National Victim Center has estimated that at least one woman is raped in the United States every forty-six seconds.[10] A study of adult sex offenders found that 86 percent of convicted rapists said they were regular users of pornography, with 57 percent admitting direct imitation of previously viewed pornographic scenes while committing their rapes.[11]

Dr. Cline concludes "that most or all sexual deviations are learned behaviors, usually through inadvertent or accidental conditioning. There is no convincing evidence, to date, suggesting the hereditary transmission of any pathological sexual behavior pattern such as rape, incest, pedophilia [use of children for sex], exhibitionism, or promiscuity."[12]

"Learned behaviors." Doesn't this convince you that it's crucial to listen to God, to understand His precepts, His standards and parameters for life—and to live accordingly? The psalmist wrote, "From Your precepts I get understanding; therefore I hate every false way" (Psalm 119:104).

THE KEY TO VICTORY

So what is the understanding you and I need as we study the role of the mind in our sexuality? It's to remember that the will of God is our sanctification, that we abstain from sexual immorality. Therefore we must vow not to let our eyes rest on what is forbidden by God, and we must not permit our minds to think on these things, no matter how much our flesh craves them.

So what must you do? What can you do to be free of the bondage of sexual sin—or stay free—and live victoriously? If you're addicted to pornography, you may need more help than I'm able to give you in this book. You may need an accountability partner to walk through this with you[13] or you may want to seek more teaching on the subject.[14] However, I believe, the biblical principles for victory will be the same.

First, you need to realize that if you're going to win the battle for the mind, you cannot fight in your own strength. Look at Romans 13:12-14 with me. In fact, why don't you read it aloud?

[12] The night is almost gone, and the day is near. Therefore let us lay aside the deeds of darkness and put on the armor of light.

[13] Let us behave properly as in the day, not in carousing and drunkenness, not in sexual promiscuity and sensuality, not in strife and jealousy.

[14] But put on the Lord Jesus Christ, and make no provision for the flesh in regard to its lusts.

Read these verses aloud a second time and this time underline every *us* and put a big **S** over every reference to *sexual immorality*.

Finally—bear with me!—read the passage aloud one more time and circle the word *lusts*.

Now what did you see from all your reading and marking? What is the admonition for *us*? List every instruction in these three verses. They're important because these are orders from God, which, if obeyed, will bring you victory.

Did you see that the only way to guarantee total victory over your eyes and your mind, over temptation and sin, is to wear Jesus Christ? In this passage Paul is writing to Christians living in Rome, the capital of debauchery, the home of every sexual perversion you might imagine. People could observe any form of depravity, including bestiality, performed live on stage. In a previous chapter I shared what it was like in the first century—much like our times, only a little worse.

In the cultural context of Paul's day, when talking about our salvation, he likened our relationship with God to changing clothes, putting off the old man (what we were before we became genuine Christians) and putting on Christ. Paul repeats this concept in Romans 6 (which tells us what happens at salvation) and in Ephesians 4 and Colossians 3, where we're urged to "lay aside the old self, which is being corrupted in accordance with the lusts of deceit" and to "put on the new self, which in the likeness of God has been created in righteousness and holiness of the truth" (Ephesians 4:22,24).

If this is unfamiliar territory to you, take a moment and ask God right now to help you understand. He will! Believe me, He would love to. Everything I'm going to tell you comes straight from the Bible, though I'm not going to specifically mention each passage I'm drawing on. I'll string truths together like a garland of popcorn, one kernel of truth after another. So as you read, simply tell God you want to hear and understand what He is saying.

When Jesus became a man, a genuine human being like you and me, God's purpose was to take His Son and offer Him on a cross so that Jesus might die in our place for our sins. Jesus came to taste death for every person who would ever live. He had to do this because someone had to take the punishment for our sin if we were going to move from spiritual death to life and not be consigned to eternal torment in the lake of fire, which God initially prepared for the devil and his angels.

Jesus could not be born a sinner and still die in your place, as your substitute. If He had been one of Adam's descendants in the same way you and I are, He would have had to die for His own sin. Instead, Jesus was born of a virgin through God's seed, which God placed in the womb of a virgin named Mary. Although He was man, Jesus was different from all other people who have ever been born. He was born without sin, without a sin nature.

During His whole life on earth, Jesus lived in such a way as to always and only please the Father. Though tempted in every way that we have been tempted, Jesus never gave in. Therefore He could have lived forever. Instead Jesus chose to pay for our sins by dying in our place.

He died after being nailed to a cross. While He hung on that cross, God His Father took your sins, my sins—the sins of the whole world since the beginning of time—and placed them on Jesus. Jesus, who knew no sin, was made sin for you. Being made sin, He had to die, because the wages of sin is death. It's as if Jesus went to the electric chair for you and died in your place so you could go free.

Because Jesus never sinned, God's holiness was satisfied through the offering of the body of Jesus Christ once for all. As a result, God raised Jesus from the dead, never to die again.

Jesus conquered sin and death, and through Him, God offers to everyone who desires it the free gift of salvation—the forgiveness of sins and the promise of eternal life with the heavenly Father. But forgiveness of sins and eternal life can come only one way—through Jesus. There's absolutely no other way to escape hell and the lake of fire, and if you don't believe that, you're deceived by the father of lies, the devil. Though the world says all religions are equal as long as they lead us to God, Jesus said He was "the way, and the truth, and the life; no one comes to the Father but through Me" (John 14:6).

When anyone repents—has a change of mind with respect to personal sin and the need for a savior—and believes in his or her heart that God raised

Jesus from the dead, that person is saved. Jesus then spiritually moves into the person's body, and he or she is clothed in Christ. This is what it means to "put on Christ," to become a new creation in Christ Jesus. Christianity is simply "Christ in you, the hope of glory" (Colossians 1:27).

Consequently, as children of God not only are we forgiven of our sin, but we *have the power to say no to sin, to say no to wrong thoughts and desires.* Sin's power is totally broken. It's true for everyone who believes, because that's what always comes in the real salvation package. But the power is released and realized only as we appropriate it need by need.

When the flesh cries out for the "old days" and wants to satisfy its desires, you don't yield because you remember that you've put off the old man and have put on Christ. You make not one single provision for the flesh, because you know you would bitterly regret it later. Rather, you resist the enemy, remembering that Jesus, who is in you, is greater than the enemy who is in the world. You always deal with the enemy from your position of strength, which is Jesus.

However, don't miss the point, beloved: You cannot win the battle *if* you have not received Jesus Christ as your Lord, your God, your Savior.

YOURS FOR THE ASKING

Let me share a story with you. Once again it's in the form of a letter, written by a woman who attended one of our annual women's conferences here at Precept Ministries International in Chattanooga, Tennessee. She writes,

> The day after I got home my husband confessed to me that he had been involved in pornography…looking at magazines and on the Internet. Strangely, I stayed calm. I knew that God had prepared me for this by allowing me to come to the conference. My husband told me that he was going to resign as deacon and I suggested that he resign from any other kind of leadership role in the church also.
>
> The next day I was having a quiet time and God very clearly spoke to me (not audibly) and told me to pray for my husband's salvation. I was taken aback, but it all started to make sense. I dug out all my notes from the conference and pored over all the verses about the ungodly and all the verses about the fruit of the Spirit. God made it

very clear to me that my husband was practicing sin, and at his so-called conversion there was never a change. He cleaned up his act, but there was never a hungering and thirsting for righteousness, no self-control and certainly no peace.

On the following Sunday my husband asked me out of the blue if I thought someone could be saved and still continue in their same sin pattern and never have a change. I confidently said, "No." He confessed that he had had some doubts about salvation, and he had struggled with pornography of some form since he was eleven years old. I simply told him that he needed to ask God to make it clear to him where he stood with Him. I suggested he get his Bible and God would show him.

Kay, I have a new husband. I feel like I have been saved all over again because such a burden and load has been lifted from me. Instead of one who never desired to be in the Word, he now gets up at 5:00 every morning to study his Bible.... It is such a blessing to watch him see things in the Word he has never seen before. He even noticed that we have a lot of good Christian books on the shelves in our den. His thought life is controllable. He may have bad thoughts, but they are fleeting. And he can't stop talking about the peace that came over him when he prayed to receive Christ. He is planning to be at the Men's Conference in February and he can't wait!

As you noticed, my friend's husband still has to deal with bad thoughts that come his way, but he's having victory because of the intimate relationship he's maintaining with the Lord in His Word. Once he truly believed in his heart and received Christ, he found the Spirit-driven power to resist temptation.

The question is, Have you truly believed and received Christ? Has there been a genuine change like the one you read about in my friend's letter? If not, then will you receive Jesus Christ as your Lord, your God, the only Savior there is?

If so, simply tell Him now, aloud. Call on the name of the Lord, telling Jesus that you recognize that He's the Son of God—God in the flesh—and that you want to live a life pleasing to Him. Tell God you want Him to save you...and you *will* be saved.

It's not necessary, but if you want to write out your prayer, do so in the space provided. It will become a permanent record of your transaction with God. Even if you don't want to write it out, you may want to record the date below.

On the day of our Lord _____ (month, day) in the year of our Lord _____,
I repented and received Jesus Christ as my God, my Lord, my Savior.
I believe in my heart that Jesus died for me a sinner and was raised from the dead.
And I thank You, my God and my Father, for clothing me in Your Son,
the Lord Jesus Christ, and giving me the gift of eternal life.
How awesome to think I will live with You forever!

All these words aren't necessary, beloved. I simply wrote them out for you as a statement of your faith. A place to turn to as a reminder. Your spiritual birth certificate. A declaration of your faith and commitment. In fact, the only words necessary are to confess Jesus Christ as your Lord. There's no mantra, no magical combination of words for salvation. We simply believe the truth about Jesus Christ and about our status as sinners apart from Him, and we're born again. This is the beginning of a new life—an awesome, exciting, challenging, rewarding life that gives you the ability, the power to overcome sin.

Oh how I wish I could say all this to you in person so you could hear my voice, my passion, my excitement. It's a life where Christ is in you and you are in Christ, never to be separated from one another. Your body now becomes His temple, His dwelling place, and everything in His temple is now to glorify Him, to give an accurate reflection of the One who lives in you. Sanctification is a process, but it *will* happen as you feed on the Word of God and seek to live by every word that comes out of God's heart. His greatest desire for you is to "establish your hearts without blame in holiness before our God and Father," to sanctify you entirely so that your "spirit and soul and body [will] be preserved complete, without blame at the coming of our Lord Jesus Christ" (1 Thessalonians 3:13; 5:23).

A Covenant with Your Eyes

Once you understand where your ability, your power, and your authority lie so that you can control your eyes and your mind, what's next? You still live in a body of flesh with eyes that see and a mind that thinks. So how do you live in a world that hasn't changed, although you have?

Let's see what God intends for you to learn from a man named Job. As you read the following passage aloud, mark every reference to the *eyes* as you previously marked references to *looking*.

JOB 31:1-12

¹ I have made a covenant with my eyes; how then could I gaze at a virgin?

² And what is the portion of God from above or the heritage of the Almighty from on high?

³ Is it not calamity to the unjust and disaster to those who work iniquity?

⁴ Does He not see my ways and number all my steps?

⁵ If I have walked with falsehood, and my foot has hastened after deceit,

⁶ Let Him weigh me with accurate scales, and let God know my integrity.

⁷ If my step has turned from the way, or my heart followed my eyes, or if any spot has stuck to my hands,

⁸ Let me sow and another eat, and let my crops be uprooted.

⁹ If my heart has been enticed by a woman, or I have lurked at my neighbor's doorway,

¹⁰ May my wife grind for another, and let others kneel down over her.

¹¹ For that would be a lustful crime; moreover, it would be an iniquity punishable by judges.

¹² For it would be fire that consumes to Abaddon, and would uproot all my increase.

As you marked the *eyes,* did you notice the references to the *heart,* to *lust?* You might want to read the passage again—aloud—and draw a heart over the references to the *heart* and circle any references to *lust,* including any synonyms, such as *enticed* and *lurked* in verse 9.

At this point in the book of Job, this dear man, tested by Satan with God's permission, is defending his integrity to his three skeptical friends. As you read this passage, note the arenas in which he defends his integrity. List them below:

It's evident, isn't it, that Job defends his sexual behavior. Job had a wholesome fear of God. He knew a holy God had to judge sin; thus Job determined to live righteously before Him, not just in a show or profession of righteousness but with purity of heart. Job understood the omniscience and the omnipresence of God. Job realized that God saw all his ways, numbered his steps, and knew what was in his heart. God would know what was on his mind and whether or not he allowed himself to be enticed by a woman—by the smells, the sounds, the sights of womanhood. Job knew God would read his thoughts when he visited his neighbor and his wife; He would know whether or not Job coveted another man's wife in his heart.

And what do you learn from Job's vindication of himself? You see that if you allow your heart, your mind to be enticed by a woman, by someone to whom you aren't married, this is a sin. When attraction raises its lustful head, it is to be decapitated immediately. It's to be shown no mercy, given no trial. This is sin, and sin warrants judgment. Judge yourself so you won't have to be judged by God.[15]

Job also said he didn't hang around other men's wives, lurking in their doorways. He agrees with God that these are lustful crimes, iniquity that should be condemned and punished by judges. Sins of the heart, of the mind, become like fires out of control, consuming everything and licking at your heels all the way to Abaddon, the place of destruction. Sins of the mind, if unchecked, will cost you everything, leave you with nothing.

And where would such sin find its beginning? With the eyes! This is why Job made a covenant with his eyes. He would not look on a woman, would not gaze at her and desire her in his heart.

It's a covenant every man and every woman should make with their eyes. What purity of heart it would bring! What unclouded vision and under-standing of God! Did not Jesus promise us, "Blessed are the pure in heart, for they shall see God" (Matthew 5:8)?

Oh, beloved of God, may I challenge you to pause now and spend time with God. Let Him purify your heart. Pour everything out to the One who sees all your ways and knows every thought, every issue of your heart and mind. Then make a covenant with your eyes, as Job did. Tell God that you'll look away from anything that would seduce you sexually, anything that would cause you to lust, to desire what is not legitimate.

But listen carefully: This is not something to be entered into lightly. Once a covenant is made, God becomes the sovereign Administrator of that covenant—and He will hold you to it. Remember, a covenant by its very essence is a solemn and binding agreement made by passing through pieces of flesh.[16] When you came to God, Hebrews 10 tells us, you came to Him through the rent veil of the flesh of the Son of God. Therefore if you make this covenant with your eyes, tell God you are doing so on the basis of Jesus' blood that purchased you for God.

Remember, your body is now the temple of the Holy Spirit, and you want to be holy. You want everything in His temple to say "holy to the Lord"; therefore, you will choose to turn your eyes from anything that is not pleas-ing to Him and is lustful to you.

If you'll do that, then write your commitment out to God in your own words and date it. Keep this book so you can pick it up from time to time and reread all you have written. Review God's precepts on sex. We constantly need to be reminded of these things.

The Weapons of Our Warfare

Now then, day by day, situation by situation, what do you do when your eyes see what they shouldn't see and your desires are suddenly aroused or your imagination sparked? Let me help you develop a battle plan for keeping your covenant commitment.

First, immediately *turn your eyes* from whatever sparked your desire. Don't keep on looking, because you've a made a covenant not to do so.

But what if a lustful thought, triggered by something you saw or heard, runs charging into your mind? Without even knocking, it's there! What are you to do now?

That leads us to the second thing: *Bring every thought captive* to the obedience of Jesus Christ, just as 2 Corinthians 10:5 says. Let's read it in context:

2 CORINTHIANS 10:3-5

³ For though we walk in the flesh, we do not war according to the flesh,

⁴ for the weapons of our warfare are not of the flesh, but divinely powerful for the destruction of fortresses.

⁵ We are destroying speculations and every lofty thing raised up against the knowledge of God, and we are taking every thought captive to the obedience of Christ.

You are in warfare. The battle is for your mind. If a delivery man came to your door with a huge box filled with poisonous snakes addressed to you, would you sign for the package and take it into your house? Of course not! Would you assume they came from a friend? Ridiculous! You know no friend is behind that shipment. So what would you do? You would have the man take the box and "return to sender."

And if the delivery man begged you just to keep the box overnight so he wouldn't have to go back to the warehouse, would you let him talk you into it? Not if you're in your right mind. What's in the box is deadly, and you don't want it anywhere near you. You would insist that it be returned to the sender.

Well, my friend, where do you think immoral thoughts come from? A friend? Absolutely not! Don't let them in your mind for a minute. Get rid of them. They're sent from the pit of hell by the destroyer, the serpent of old, the devil.

Don't allow anything to slither into your mind that's against the truth or contrary to what you know about God, no matter how difficult the circumstance. Immediately destroy that thought. It isn't reality. It's an empty imagination, an immoral thought that goes against all you know about God, about His Word, His will, His holiness. Crush that emissary of the devil underfoot. Hold its poisonous mouth firmly closed; don't listen to a word. Then bring that captive thought to Jesus. Tell God it showed up and you will not entertain it. It's out the door, under His authority. You choose to be holy even as God is holy.

After I was saved it seemed I continually battled with immoral thoughts and dreams. I cried, I prayed, I read before I went to sleep, but still my thoughts and dreams tormented me, leaving me feeling very unclean at times. I honestly didn't want them, but there they were. Then one day I realized these thoughts weren't coming from me but from the devil. They were just disguised as my thoughts. Once I realized this, I learned how to stamp the box "Return to Sender." The battles grew fewer and fewer, but sometimes they would come at the most unexpected times.

Years ago in my beginning days of travel, I was in an airport, headed down the stairs to a smaller plane, when a handsome man passed me on the stairs—and a filthy thought flew into my mind. I know the Enemy was trying to convince me that if I had thoughts like that I shouldn't be out teaching the Word of God. At that point, however, the devil was tangling with someone who had studied warfare, and I knew I wasn't to be ignorant of his tricks or devices. Immediately I simply said under my breath, "I rebuke you in the name of Jesus Christ and by the blood of Jesus Christ"—and went my way rejoicing in the Spirit.

You may need to do a study on warfare if you're being persistently bombarded with evil thoughts.[17] Just rest assured that God always causes us to triumph through Christ Jesus our Lord.[18]

But even after you've taken the thought captive and turned it over to Christ, the battle isn't won. You cannot turn away the enemy and leave your mind vacant. Something will occupy your thoughts. This leads us to the third and final step of our battle plan: *Let your mind dwell on the things of God.* Once you've turned the lustful thought over to God, you purposefully turn your mind to any thought or consideration that meets the description set forth in Philippians 4:8:

> Finally, brethren, whatever is true,
> > whatever is honorable,
> > whatever is right,
> > whatever is pure,
> > whatever is lovely,
> > whatever is of good repute,
> > if there is any excellence
> > > and
> > if anything worthy of praise,
> > > dwell on these things.

You make a definitive choice to think the way God wants you to think. You aren't a slave to your thoughts; rather, you're to enslave them, take them captive. Anything that doesn't measure up to who you are in Christ and who Christ is in you is to be booted out.

You're to purposefully think on things that are *true* and *honorable.* Immoral desires are not true; they're fantasies you want to come true, but they can't and shouldn't because they are not honorable but base. Replace them with things that have honor, dignity, worth, value. Things such as marriage, which is to be honored by all. In your mind, be a man, a woman of honor and dignity. Take the high road, the noble way.

Think of what is *right* and envision yourself in that role. There was a day when men and women wouldn't compromise what was right for anything. Think about people like this. Think about doing what pleases God.

Replace impure thoughts with *pure* thoughts. As a child of God you have the mind of Christ. Would Jesus allow impure thoughts to dwell in His mind? Of course not.

What's *lovely*? Think about it; it will change your whole mood. Purposefully direct your eyes and your mind to what is lovely rather than that which is sordid, dirty, twisted, perverted, or destructive.

If it's *reputable*—if it has worth, goodness, virtue—then dwell on it. Think about how these qualities can be built into your family and friendships and how you would live them out.

Aim high; think of *excellence,* excelling, doing your best, doing what is right.

If it's *worthy of praise*—worthwhile, of value—think about it.

Think what is right. "Above all else, guard your heart, for it is the wellspring of life" (Proverbs 4:23, NIV). Think of what Jesus would do or say and how pleased He would be to have you follow His example.

I would encourage you to sit down and spend time with the Lord and ask Him for specific scriptures or thoughts to turn your mind to. Get a battle plan. And when the attack comes, if you're where you can do so, start conversing out loud with God.

David said he consulted with himself; you can do that also. Give yourself battle orders; speak as a four-star general to a sergeant.

There it is, beloved of God. Put on Jesus and make no room for the flesh with its desires. You'll be so thankful you did. You'll go from strength to strength, from victory to victory—and if you lose a skirmish, get up, clean up by confessing, and move forward.

> For this is the love of God, that we keep His commandments; and His
> commandments are not burdensome. For whatever is born of God
> overcomes the world; and this is the victory that has overcome the
> world—our faith. Who is the one who overcomes the world, but he
> who believes that Jesus is the Son of God? (1 John 5:3-5)

1 1

Return to the Garden

Can Sex Truly Be Beautiful?

My friend and I had been discussing this book, and she turned to me as she walked out the door. "My kids"—they're in their twenties—"would never buy it. They would laugh at it. It is so contrary to what they believe, where they live—"

"I know," I interrupted, "and it breaks my heart. A lot of people will never buy its content. But I had to write it so at least people—teens *and* adults—would know what God says, what can be theirs if they will only listen to Him and believe what He says."

She hesitated, then asked, "Do you really believe people think sex is beautiful? Most of the people I know don't."

In her words I heard the emptiness of a thousand generations who wished sex *were* beautiful and yet didn't really want to hear that it could be…because they had never found it so.

Last night after putting the final edits on the previous chapter, I turned on the television while Jack and I ate dinner. One of the networks was advertising a two-hour special on the subject of whether or not gay couples should be allowed to adopt children, and I wanted to see how it was handled. Since the program wouldn't start for another hour, I surfed through the channels until I found *Biography* on A&E, which was profiling Marilyn Monroe. I watched that then turned to the special on gay adoption, where Rosie O'Donnell talked openly about her lesbian relationship and how it impacted the children she was raising. As that program ended, the network aired a thirty-minute program on the Catholic Church and the millions of dollars in damages the church must pay to people—usually men—who have been sexually molested by priests.

After more than three hours of back-to-back programs—and getting very little work done because I'd been so engrossed—I went to bed with a heavy heart.

In that one evening I'd seen so much heartache.

Marilyn's molestation as a child and her immorality, which she considered a potential cause of her two crushing miscarriages.

Rosie's obviously painful and difficult childhood.

The battered, abused, rejected children moved from one foster home to another, often beaten, misused, sexually abused—and now up for adoption.

The young priest who's decided he doesn't believe in God anymore because of the priests who abused their authority over him as a boy and then as a seminarian.

All I could think was, "O Father, Father, how different it would be if we would only listen to You, if we would live by Your book and handle sex Your way."

Then I thought of all the people who are totally ignorant of God's way, and I realized how important the message of this book is, how it can change lives as it brings people face to face with what God says.

We've dealt so much in this book with how sin has tainted God's design, with how sex has become dirty, distorted, and destructive, that you may have thought it impossible for anything beautiful to ever come from it. Remember way back in the first chapter when we talked about God's original plan for sex to serve as a picture of Christ's divine love for His bride? Tragically, as we've seen, humans have twisted and perverted this metaphor until it's barely recognizable.

So in these final pages, whether you are married or single, young or old, we need to explore the beauty of sex within marriage. We'll examine the exquisite oneness and delight of knowing one another within the boundaries of His precepts, so we can capture again the vision God meant for us to have. Let's look together at the Song of Solomon, which from beginning to end shows us what God intended when He created us male and female, when He brought Eve to Adam that they might become one flesh and establish a family.

Here is a love to be rejoiced in, extolled.[1] The woman (she's called "the Shulammite" in 6:13) has found one whom her soul loves. The one she loves is Solomon himself, as we learn from the very first line. The eight chapters of this book consist primarily of a dialogue between these two lovers, the bride and the bridegroom—with interjected choruses from the "daughters of Jerusalem."

In the first two chapters of this "Song of Songs" we observe Solomon and the Shulammite in their courtship. Then in 3:6–5:2 we join the wedding party and read of the consummation of their marriage, when love is first expressed and experienced.[2] From 5:2 to the end of the book, we read of "love tried and triumphant."[3] In this book we find courtship and marriage as it ought to be—a man and a woman enraptured with one another and not ashamed to let it be known.

As you read the verses quoted throughout this chapter, mark every reference to *love* with the color red, including its synonyms and pronouns, or mark it with a heart so it will catch your eye and your heart.

Also, as we move quickly through this love story, watch the progression of the couple's physical relationship before and after marriage. If you're single, you'll find valuable insights in chapters 1–4.

THE BRIDE-TO-BE AND HER BELOVED

As the book opens, we find the Shulammite maiden longing for her lover.

SONG 1

² May he kiss me with the kisses of his mouth! For your love is better than wine.

She wanted to be kissed! How well I remember that longing. When I was a teenager, my kisses were special, not given to just anyone. My reserve wasn't because I knew the Lord or really feared God; it was simply that kisses were special to me! I had a very high regard for marriage, as modeled by my parents. My dad taught me that men dated bad girls, but they didn't marry them—and I wanted to get married.

I remember when my first husband, Tom, an outstanding man and athlete, told me how he felt when I finally let him kiss me. He wanted to run into the fraternity house where he was living as a college student and shout for all to hear, "Guess who I just kissed!" I had dated many of his fraternity brothers, but I'd never kissed one of them.

But once I had experienced the wonder of my lips touching those of my special someone, it was hard for me to think of anything else. I would replay the moment over and over in my mind.

Solomon and his beautiful woman feel the same way about each other. Listen to their conversation, realizing that they are soon to be married. Not only is their love pure, but quite possibly she had never kissed another man. Follow their words closely. Notice how they express their desires, their appreciation of each other.

⁹ To me, my darling, you are like my mare among the chariots of

Pharaoh.

¹⁰ Your cheeks are lovely with ornaments, your neck with strings of beads.

¹¹ We will make for you ornaments of gold with beads of silver.

This is Middle East talk from about three thousand years ago. In those times, men were as attached to their horses as they are to their cars today. Their steeds were decorated with all sorts of ornaments that jingled, jangled, and flashed in the sun. You might compare it to America in the fifties and sixties—revved up cars painted with lightning streaks and decorated with fuzzy dice dangling from the rearview mirror. Men still equip their cars with all sorts of electronic gadgets that cause other guys to go, "Whoa, man! You've got it all!"

Solomon had it all—an outstanding horse and an outstanding woman! Just like the automobile ads on television, his mare showed up the mares of Pharaoh; Solomon's darling was the most beautiful of women.

And what about the thoughts of this young maiden, standing at the well where he watered his flocks? How did she feel about him? Listen to her description of the man who has captured her heart:

13 My beloved is to me a pouch of myrrh which lies all night between my breasts.

14 My beloved is to me a cluster of henna blossoms in the vineyards of Engedi.

Solomon sweetened her life. His presence, the very thought of him, brought a pleasant fragrance like that of myrrh and henna. People love to be around those who make them feel good about themselves. This is what makes them come back.

Watch how Solomon responds.

15 How beautiful you are, my darling, how beautiful you are! Your eyes are like doves.

Did you notice that before Solomon ever talks to her about her body, he talks to her about her eyes? Today a woman so often finds herself solely the object of sex, evaluated by the size of her breasts, the firmness of her "buns."

In our sex-obsessed society, a wave of recent books tells women how to gain the sexual satisfaction they deserve. According to an article in *USA Today*, "several of the authors say Gen X women are having dramatic problems being satisfied with the body they bring into the bedroom." In their attempts to feel sexually desirable, young women "have moved from the need for corsets to the need for abdominal crunches," says Sallie Foley, a sex therapist and coauthor of *Sex Matters for Women*. "Gen X women have internalized this sense of the body perfect, and that is an impossible ideal," she continues. "They think if they have a perfect body, they will have better sex, and that shows a profound misunderstanding about sexuality." It's simply not true, she says, that women who have infomercial bodies "are having better sex."[4]

What makes the Song of Solomon a classic is that it's not about the tawdry ogling of a body—although, as you will see, this man and this woman greatly appreciate one another's physical attributes. Rather it's about love and pleasure as God intended it. This love is not smeared on the streets or in the locker rooms; its purity and sacredness remain untainted by trash talk. And comparison is never made to past lovers or the ideal woman. Solomon treasures the Shulammite for *who* she is, *just* as she is. How important this is to a beautiful sexual relationship.

If you want your physical relationship to soar, then you will hold your beloved in the highest of esteem. Love begets love, and gracious words beget gracious words. Listen to the Shulammite's response:

16 How handsome you are, my beloved, and so pleasant!

Isn't this what we want to hear, need to hear—that we're special in the eyes of our beloved, that we ourselves are beloved? Twenty-seven times she refers to Solomon as "beloved." How many hearts long to be called beloved! Women tell me over and over again what it means to hear me address them that way: "No one ever called me that before." But it's not just women; men, too, need to know they're beloved, special to someone. The word is used throughout the Epistles as men of God write to the people of God. I use the term a lot because that's genuinely the way I feel about people. In fact, as I've written this book I've had to restrain myself for fear that I might turn some of you off, but that name expresses how I feel about each soul lovingly created by our God.

PASSION WITH PURITY

As we continue reading in chapter 2, listen as this confident bride-to-be revels in her uniqueness. Observe as she delights in how special she is to him and he to her. What a difference a healthy self-image makes in a marriage! Mark the *I* and *me* for the woman in one color or with a symbol like this ♀ and the *he* in a different color or with a symbol like this ♂.

SONG 2

1 I am the rose of Sharon, the lily of the valleys.

He agrees and responds:

² Like a lily among the thorns, so is my darling among the maidens.

She has chosen him—he has won the prize! What an ego builder to a man, to believe that the woman he's about to marry is incredibly special— and what a wonder this awareness is to his bride. This is the kind of man a woman wants to cover her, sustain her, hold her.

³ Like an apple tree among the trees of the forest, so is my beloved among the young men. In his shade I took great delight and sat down, and his fruit was sweet to my taste.

⁴ He has brought me to his banquet hall, and his banner over me is love.

⁵ Sustain me with raisin cakes, refresh me with apples, because I am lovesick.

⁶ Let his left hand be under my head and his right hand embrace me.

Do you hear the admiration as she leans on him verbally, expressing her delight in his provision? Yet in all their exuberantly expressed passion for one another, they're aware that they must be cautious. The Shulammite and her husband-to-be know what desires wage war in their flesh. Love is not to be awakened until the right time. Listen to his caution:

⁷ Daughters of Jerusalem, I charge you by the gazelles and by the does of the field: Do not arouse or awaken love until it so desires. (NIV)⁵

We find variations of this phrase repeated in 3:5 and 8:4. Solomon is urging the daughters of Jerusalem to remain pure, to not awaken love when it cannot be fulfilled. He admonishes them—and us—to be vigilant against any compromise that would taint their relationship. Love is to be expressed sexually in only one place and that, as you know by now, is in the marriage bed.

There's a similar warning in the verse I want us to look at next. Note what the foxes want to do to the vineyard.

15 Catch the foxes for us, the little foxes that are ruining the vineyards, while our vineyards are in blossom.

Watch out for the foxes that want to steal your fruit! How I wish I'd heard and heeded this advice in my youth. I wish I'd been warned about the little things that would steal the beauty of innocence. It's so hard for me to believe that I became an immoral woman. Sensuality was in my mind from childhood, but purity was my desire. It would have been so wonderful to have known only one man all my life, to have realized what I longed for in a marriage, what I saved myself for. Being the perfectionist that I am, I constantly have to bring my grief and regret into submission to all I know from the Scriptures: "Forgetting what lies behind *[and which I can never change]* and reaching forward to...the prize of the upward call of God in Christ Jesus" (Philippians 3:13-14).

The Shulammite would never have to deal with such things, and I pray you won't either.

Oh, my friend, if you want to know the pure beauty of being one flesh with your husband or wife, you must do everything you can to protect your mind, your eyes, to guard yourself from sexual experiences that aren't according to God. When you wait, when you guard your mind, when you don't permit your eyes to watch others in immoral acts, then you come to the marriage bed with no expectations, no comparisons. You have known no one else, so all can be discovered together, explored together. No little foxes have spoiled the vines or eaten the fruit you want to save for the one and only lover you'll ever know until death parts you. If you catch the foxes before they eat your innocence, you'll have the high and unique privilege of initiating each other into the wonder of love. Then it will be beautiful, because it's untainted by the world.

BEHOLD, THE BRIDEGROOM COMES

In chapter 3 we come to the marriage as Solomon and his companions—sixty mighty men—go to get his bride on the day of his wedding.

SONG 3

¹¹ Go forth, O daughters of Zion, and gaze on King Solomon with the

crown with which his mother has crowned him on the day of his wedding, and

on the day of his gladness of heart.

No shame. No guilt. No child in the womb. A white dress and purity. There is gladness of heart, for at long last they will know each other in the fullness of the word.

The day is marked forever in their minds and hearts, a day set apart, a day waited for.

This is the day she shall give her bridegroom the gift she can give only once, and he will know that he is the first—and the last.

This is the day they will become one flesh in the literal sense of the word.

Now he talks to her of love, of the allure of her body in words that convey such beauty to her, though they sound strange in our culture and times. This is not smut or filth, not chat-room talk with someone you've never even seen. His words extol who she is, what he knows of her. These are words she'll treasure for a lifetime, erotic but pure. Words chosen to awaken love, for now it is God's time.

The Song of Solomon. One book out of sixty-six, devoted to one thing—the beauty of an undefiled marriage bed. Written for a thousand generations, preserved throughout the millennia, never altered, because its truths are timeless. This is God's textbook for those who would listen to His precepts and keep them, who would experience the beauty of becoming one flesh.

Do you realize that this is the only time God ever takes you behind closed doors into the bridal chamber of another? Listen carefully to what Solomon says to his darling, his bride, as he consummates their covenant of marriage. Mark every reference to his *wife* and learn well. This is sex according to God.

SONG 4

¹ How beautiful you are, my darling, how beautiful you are! Your eyes are like doves behind your veil; your hair is like a flock of goats that have descended from Mount Gilead.

² Your teeth are like a flock of newly shorn ewes which have come up from their washing, all of which bear twins, and not one among them has lost her young.

³ Your lips are like a scarlet thread, and your mouth is lovely. Your temples are like a slice of a pomegranate behind your veil.

⁴ Your neck is like the tower of David, built with rows of stones on which are hung a thousand shields, all the round shields of the mighty men.

⁵ Your two breasts are like two fawns, twins of a gazelle which feed among the lilies.

⁶ Until the cool of the day when the shadows flee away, I will go my way to the mountain of myrrh and to the hill of frankincense.

⁷ You are altogether beautiful, my darling, and there is no blemish in you.

⁸ Come with me from Lebanon, my bride, may you come with me from Lebanon. Journey down from the summit of Amana, from the summit of Senir and Hermon, from the dens of lions, from the mountains of leopards.

⁹ You have made my heart beat faster, my sister, my bride; you have made my heart beat faster with a single glance of your eyes, with a single strand of your necklace.

¹⁰ How beautiful is your love, my sister, my bride! How much better is your love than wine, and the fragrance of your oils than all kinds of spices!

¹¹ Your lips, my bride, drip honey; honey and milk are under your tongue, and the fragrance of your garments is like the fragrance of Lebanon.

¹² A garden locked is my sister, my bride, a rock garden locked, a spring sealed up.

¹³ Your shoots are an orchard of pomegranates with choice fruits, henna with nard plants,

¹⁴ Nard and saffron, calamus and cinnamon, with all the trees of frankincense, myrrh and aloes, along with all the finest spices.

¹⁵ You are a garden spring, a well of fresh water, and streams flowing from Lebanon.

Did you grasp all that he's saying? Read it again. Ponder his words once more. This time mark the word *garden* with a color or a symbol such as an apple, like this: . Mark the phrase *with me* in yet another distinctive way.

And what is the garden, bearing luscious fruits, that has been locked until now? What is this spring of fresh water that has been sealed up? It's the purity of virginity, a holy innocence to be discovered and delighted in.

And what is the bride's response to her beloved? Listen carefully and learn, for his words, his appreciation of her have made her ready to receive him. This is why she responds this way.

16 Awake, O north wind, and come, wind of the south; make my garden

breathe out fragrance, let its spices be wafted abroad. May my beloved come

into his garden and eat its choice fruits!

She is ready. She has not been rushed. He has considered her needs. He has not just desired her; he has admired her, and now she longs for him. "May my beloved come into *his* garden."

She is his. His alone. Just as God intended.

Is sex beautiful? Yes, beautiful beyond description. When it is according to God, it's all He designed it to be. It's not what is portrayed on the movie screen, the television screen. That is man's version, his picture of raw, animal passion. What we see here in the Song of Solomon is sacred love, love that frees one another from performance, from keeping up with the bodies of others, the passion of others, the panting of others. This is for the two of you alone. This is where you discover each other and please each other—and if you're not pleased, sacred love means helping one another, being patient and understanding. This is where you're secure in one another's love and commitment, regardless of what happens or doesn't happen on any particular night.

A single friend told me about another friend who wearied of waiting until marriage for sex. When no one who suited her came along to propose marriage, she decided to experience sex on her next business trip. The whole thing was carefully calculated. She scanned the crowd, picked out a single man, and went to bed with him. That night she surrendered her virginity to a man who meant nothing to her, a man she really didn't even know. And all because she wanted to know what sex was like.

When she got home, she called my friend to tell her about the weekend. Her words of pathos stuck in my friend's memory: "Is this what poets write about, the subject of love songs, the themes of great movies?" Her first sexual experience was disappointing, a disheartening letdown. Why? I believe it's because the encounter didn't take place in God's intended setting of marriage, a commitment for life that promises monogamy until death.

If she'd only waited, she might have enjoyed the beauty of sex according to God, accompanied by the gentle words and caresses of a husband who cherished the gift she had saved, as we see in the opening verse of chapter 5 in the Song of Solomon.

SONG 5

¹ I have come into my garden, my sister, my bride; I have gathered my myrrh along with my balsam. I have eaten my honeycomb and my honey; I have drunk my wine and my milk.

And the two became "one flesh. And the man and his wife were both naked and were not ashamed" (Genesis 2:24-25).

LOVE MEANS SACRIFICE

Will sex always be this good, even as time passes? Will they always want each other? No.

Sex is beautiful, but it isn't always desired. Watch and listen. The wedding is scarcely over when the bride makes a foolish mistake.

² I was asleep, but my heart was awake. A voice! My beloved was knocking: "Open to me, my sister, my darling, my dove, my perfect one! For my head is drenched with dew, my locks with the damp of the night."

³ I have taken off my dress, how can I put it on again? I have washed my feet, how can I dirty them again?

⁴ My beloved extended his hand through the opening, and my feelings were aroused for him.

⁵ I arose to open to my beloved; and my hands dripped with myrrh, and my fingers with liquid myrrh, on the handles of the bolt.

⁶ I opened to my beloved, but my beloved had turned away and had gone! My heart went out to him as he spoke. I searched for him but I did not find him; I called him but he did not answer me.

Sometimes sex is a bother. You're too tired…busy…preoccupied…whatever! But even then love is to be nurtured. Love involves sacrifice, meeting the needs of your mate even when you don't want to. Maybe it's not convenient, it's uncomfortable, it's not on your timetable—but you do it anyway for the sake of love, not passion.

"But it's *my* body," you protest. "Aren't I within my rights to say no?"

In 1 Corinthians, God gives us His general rule of thumb for when married couples should have sex. Read it and mark every reference to the *wife* and to the *husband* as you did when marking Song of Solomon.

1 CORINTHIANS 7:2-5

² But because of immoralities, each man is to have his own wife, and each woman is to have her own husband.

³ The husband must fulfill his duty to his wife, and likewise also the wife to her husband.

⁴ The wife does not have authority over her own body, but the husband does; and likewise also the husband does not have authority over his own body, but the wife does.

⁵ Stop depriving one another, except by agreement for a time, so that you may devote yourselves to prayer, and come together again so that Satan will not tempt you because of your lack of self-control.

What did you learn from marking *husband* and *wife*?

What would you say is the "when" for sex?

It seems to me that the when for sex is when sex is asked for. Men need intercourse more often than their wives do. As we've seen, it's a matter of the eyes for them—and in a culture permeated with sex, they're bombarded with visual images that trigger the switch in their brains. For women it's a matter of touch, and even then we want the circumstances to be just right.

Yet in verse 4 we learn that when we marry, each of us surrenders the authority of our body to our spouse. We've given up our right to say no. Of course there needs to be consideration and understanding on the part of whoever's doing the asking—which most often will be the man. However, I don't think either person will want to deprive the other, when we remember that love serves another and endures all things!

One of our Precept leaders told me how God taught her—in a very scary and graphic way—the importance of meeting her husband's sexual needs. I'm going to change their names as I relate her story, but I want you to see God's awesome, sovereign grace at work in these two people's lives.

I fell so deeply into my role as a mother. God had give me three beautiful children and they became the center of my world. Those early days were so exhausting. By the time Mike would get home from work, I would be so tired. I knew he was drawing away some and seemed quiet, but I was too tired to worry. I'd go to bed early and he would stay up late, working upstairs on the computer.

He knew I was tired and he didn't want to push me for attention. As the days went on, he began to feel I no longer liked him. He began to be drawn to pornography and I was not meeting his sexual desires. He decided not to have an affair, since all he really wanted was sexual attention and he knew an affair was wrong.

He became interested in the Internet sites. One night he decided to send out a homosexual request so he could meet someone on his next business trip. He still loved me; he just wanted the attention, so this seemed reasonable to him, and I'd never know. Satan had brainwashed him into believing some strange logic....

So he types the request in, and as he does, he copies it into the
"buffer" space with a CTRL-C. The next day, I am editing something
on the computer and by accident I hit the CTRL-V, which copies
what he put into the buffer into my document. (Have you got chill
bumps, yet?) So here in my document is MWM, 5_11, seeks homosexual experience. It takes me a minute. I thought it was a computer
virus, but then it hits home what this really is. I was cut to the core. I
couldn't believe this of him. I called him at work to come home early.
And we began to talk.

As truly awful as these days were, we both knew immediately
that we had been touched by God. By these unusual circumstances
we knew God had given us a huge wake-up call. He had intervened at
just the moment where an awful mistake might have been made and
serious damage would have been done. Not to deny we still had big
problems, but they could have been so much worse if other people
had become involved.

Their story goes on to tell of great triumph as both of them did what was
necessary to correct their problem. My friend learned a great lesson about the
importance of meeting her husband's sexual needs and making him feel like
the most important person in her life, next to Jesus Christ. And speaking of
Jesus, they both teach about Him week after week as they take people
through the Bible precept upon precept.

And how is their marriage now, several years later? I'll let her tell you:

Our marriage is better and stronger than ever before. We are so happy.
I know that all those "old fashioned" marriage ideas my Mom used to
tell me are so important. I just wish she had told me why and pointed
me to the Word of God for biblical reasons. We must love our husbands and make them feel loved and special.

To be honest, we're scared to mess up, we are afraid of what God
might do this time. <grin>. But [ours] is more than a good marriage;
through our experience and through Precepts, we are stronger Christians. Our lives have been changed and God is part of our daily lives
and we are living for Him now.

It's wonderful to read stories of victory like this, isn't it? But what do you do when your husband or wife won't—or can't—meet your sexual needs? This can be an incredibly difficult and painful situation, a state of literal agony or torment if you have a strong sex drive. When your mate simply turns his or her back to you night after night, you have to deal with all sorts of thoughts and feelings—rejection, inadequacy, recrimination, doubt about your spouse's sexuality, your sexuality—and, of course, you ache with the physical longing for satisfaction. It makes it very hard to get to sleep. You feel like an amputee. A vital part of you has been cut off, yet there's the residual phantom pain. I've agonized with so many who've written me about their loss.

Marriage is a covenant, a solemn binding agreement, and there's no divorce or escape clause for this problem. So what do you do?

First, find out why your mate has lost interest. The problem may be as simple as a loss of sleep, as we saw in the letter I just shared. When the average person gets fewer than six hours of sleep a night for several nights in a row, their hormone levels drop. Other physical reasons may be at the core of the problem, or it may be an emotional issue, a sense of low personal worth. Though any number of issues could be the source of the physical distance, you need to pursue an answer, because it's good for a couple to have sex. It's good for your relationship as well as for your body.

What if you discover the root of the problem, but your spouse is unwilling to resolve it? What do you do if one partner simply cannot or will not fulfill his or her duty in this area? Then, beloved, you have to endure it, just as a single person has to live without sex. God's grace is sufficient; it has to be, because there's no other legitimate way to satisfy your desire. So ask Him for His power in your weakness and move on, avoiding those things that arouse and awaken your desires, guarding your heart, keeping your thoughts under His control. Remember, sex is important to marriage, but it's only one aspect of the relationship.

For a while now I've kept a note someone scribbled for me on the back of an advertisement, saving it because it touched my heart. A dear sister in Christ wrote, "I'm not sure you remember my letter I wrote to you about two years ago. It was about the lack of intimacy in my relationship with my husband. Well, it's been six years now, in April, and needless to say, it's still lacking. But it seems that I am at peace with this because I do feel the love he has for me, regardless of the sexual part of it. Thanks for the wonderful study material. It has helped me greatly!"

I believe the last two sentences explain where her strength and perspective come from—studying God's Word inductively, discovering truth for herself so that she knows that she knows. If you'll do the same, you'll find His Word can get you through any situation, beloved.

KEEPING THE FIRE ALIVE

And what sustains the beauty of sex? Valuing it. Giving sex the time and attention it needs. In chapter 5, when the Shulammite didn't meet her husband's needs, it seemed she was too tired to get out of bed and put on something and come to the door. She had washed her feet and would have to wash them again. It was wearying. Even when she saw him trying to reach the bolt through the window and open the door himself, she didn't move until it was too late.

I believe one of the greatest hindrances to a wonderful and beautiful sex life is the wife's working outside the home, especially when the couple has children. Our schedules are so jammed that, as I just mentioned, many of us are too exhausted for sex—and it is sex that nurtures a marriage. Good sex takes time if both are to be satisfied.[6]

The Shulammite soon recognizes her mistake in not rousing herself for her husband. She yearns to be with him, with the same longing she felt before their wedding. "I must seek him whom my soul loves.... I sought him" (Song 3:2). A woman's desire to be with her husband—in ways that are healthy, not smothering—is one of the cords that ties a man to home and keeps him from wandering the neighborhood.

As she eagerly anticipates his return, she begins to list all the things she loves about him—his hair, his eyes, his cheeks, his hands, and more.

Here, as throughout the Song of Solomon, you see the Shulammite's admiration of her husband and her expressed desire to be with him. This is what keeps a man at home, not just sex. Sex can be very mechanical, and if it's merely to find release for one's passions, then basically anyone will do. Simply close your eyes, put your mind somewhere else, and do it! But God intended the uniting of the two into one flesh to be much more than that. It's an expression of gratitude, of delight in the oneness of heart, mind, soul, and body. It is knowing, *This is bone of my bone, flesh of my flesh.* It is sealing the other upon your heart, possessing your possession, being able to delight the one who delights you, needs you, wants you. It's the expression not just of love but of friendship on the highest level. Marriage is an exclusive relationship, for this is where you'll give yourself to one another in a way no one else will ever share.

Listen to what the Shulammite says of her husband to others:

SONG 5:16

¹⁶ His mouth is full of sweetness. And he is wholly desirable. This is my

beloved and this is my friend, O daughters of Jerusalem.

"His mouth is full of sweetness." Given how women are made, this comment may have more to do with how he talks to her than how he kisses her!

The man is commanded to love his wife with *agape* love, a selfless love that desires another's highest good. But this love is commanded, something to be done regardless of how one feels. What all of us really long for is the love that brings delight to a marriage, the handholding, the winking, the "I'm looking forward to tonight" signals, the things that convey, "I am my beloved's, and he is mine." This is the *phileo* love that makes marriage rich—the love of friendship, admiration, appreciation, and delight because of what you see in the other person or what he (or she) evokes in you because of who he is and how he treats you. The kindnesses, the compliments during the day make a woman want to say yes, to roll into her husband's arms rather than teetering on the edge of the bed for fear he'll get ideas.

My desire to draw closer to my husband is never stronger than when he prays for me, when I hear him thank God for the things he sees, he admires, he appreciates. And when I admire Jack, when he feels good about himself, the whole mood around the house can change. The sun comes out, the black clouds blown away by the sweetness of my speech.

Phileo is the love we long for—and this is the love and friendship you see in the Song of Solomon; this is why she calls her husband "my friend." Put it into practice and watch what happens. See what it does to your sex life. Just remember, if you haven't expressed this kind of love in a while, it might take your mate some time to believe you're really sincere. But when he or she is finally convinced, you'll see things change in the living room as well as in the bedroom.

There's more to be learned in this regard. As we look at the text, notice how Solomon affirms his wife. Mark every reference to *her*.

SONG 6:1-9

¹ Where has your beloved gone, O most beautiful among women? Where has your beloved turned, that we may seek him with you?

² My beloved has gone down to his garden, to the beds of balsam, to pasture his flock in the gardens and gather lilies.

³ I am my beloved's and my beloved is mine, he who pastures his flock among the lilies.

⁴ You are as beautiful as Tirzah, my darling, as lovely as Jerusalem, as awesome as an army with banners.

⁵ Turn your eyes away from me, for they have confused me; your hair is like a flock of goats that have descended from Gilead.

⁶ Your teeth are like a flock of ewes which have come up from their washing, all of which bear twins, and not one among them has lost her young.

⁷ Your temples are like a slice of a pomegranate behind your veil.

⁸ There are sixty queens and eighty concubines, and maidens without number;

⁹ But my dove, my perfect one, is unique…

In this day and age when the competition is so great—when so much is revealed and flaunted—it's important for a woman to keep herself attractive for her husband, to know his likes and dislikes. When he comes home, she needs to make him feel welcome, to look attractive, to smell good. Remember, he's probably spent his workday with women dressed for success. What a man sees affects him.

However, at the same time it's important for the man to let his wife know that it's not other women's bodies he longs for or lusts after. If he'll make it a habit to turn away from attractive women instead of being fascinated with their every move, and if he'll learn to constantly remind his wife of her uniqueness, her beauty in his eyes, it will make what happens in the bedroom so much more special. Then both will know they're special to one another.

Let's read on, for there's more to learn.

SONG 7

¹ How beautiful are your feet in sandals, O prince's daughter! The curves of your hips are like jewels, the work of the hands of an artist.

² Your navel is like a round goblet which never lacks mixed wine; your belly is like a heap of wheat fenced about with lilies.

³ Your two breasts are like two fawns, twins of a gazelle.

⁴ Your neck is like a tower of ivory, your eyes like the pools in Heshbon by the gate of Bath-rabbim; your nose is like the tower of Lebanon, which faces toward Damascus.

⁵ Your head crowns you like Carmel, and the flowing locks of your head are like purple threads; the king is captivated by your tresses.

⁶ How beautiful and how delightful you are, my love, with all your charms!

⁷ Your stature is like a palm tree, and your breasts are like its clusters.

⁸ I said, "I will climb the palm tree, I will take hold of its fruit stalks." Oh,

may your breasts be like clusters of the vine, and the fragrance of your breath like apples,

⁹ And your mouth like the best wine! It goes down smoothly for my beloved, flowing gently through the lips of those who fall asleep.

And we thought the wedding night was wonderful! (You did notice, didn't you, that she wasn't bundled up in flannel pajamas?)

What you just read is the experience of love, of learning to know, appreciate, and delight one another. In verse 6 we see that his wife is not only beautiful in his eyes, she is delightful. He loves her personality.

How I want to be delightful! Fun, interesting to be with.

Joyful, not morbid.

Positive, not negative.

Building up, not tearing down.

Encouraging, not haranguing.

And what does this dear woman know without a shadow of a doubt?

¹⁰ I am my beloved's, and his desire is for me.

That's what every woman needs to be assured of: "His desire is for *me.*" Do you remember what Solomon said on their wedding night? Twice he talked of her being "with me...come with me." This is the beauty of sex according to God. Sex creates a oneness that goes far beyond the bedroom. This is a companionship we all need—but especially the man. Remember, woman was made because it was not good for man to be alone.

And how does Solomon's wife respond to such love and passion? She plans an outing for them, a time to get away, to make love.

¹¹ Come, my beloved, let us go out into the country, let us spend the night in the villages.

¹² Let us rise early and go to the vineyards; let us see whether the vine has

budded and its blossoms have opened, and whether the pomegranates have bloomed. There I will give you my love.

13 The mandrakes have given forth fragrance; and over our doors are all choice fruits, both new and old, which I have saved up for you, my beloved.

Mandrakes were believed to be an aphrodisiac. This wife has some delights in mind for her husband. What are they? It doesn't matter; they're for the two of them alone—beautiful and pleasing.

And what message does she send to her husband through her careful arrangements? She affirms his manhood; her actions and words nurture him, build his confidence. When a man is down on himself—when it's rough at work and he's not appreciated, when he's laid off or loses his job—that's when he most needs you *with* him in the bedroom. He longs to be assured that you need him, want him, believe in him, and delight in him. This is part of Ephesians 5:33, reverencing your husband.

When a friend's husband lost his job and it took ages for him to find another, she made a point of making sure they made love frequently. It was her way of letting him know how special he was to her, how much she needed him. It sustained him well. He later confided that her delight in him sexually kept him from feeling like a failure as a man.

A LIFETIME OF INTIMACY

And what about those who hop from one person's bed to another in search of the sexual pleasure described in the Song of Solomon? You know they will never be satisfied, for sex according to God is so much more. What makes sex so beautiful is more than the act itself, the release of sexual tension. Rather, it's the whole giving of oneself to another. It is serving each other, ministering life and encouragement—and that's why a woman or a man doesn't want just another bed partner. It's not just the climax, the orgasm; it's the oneness that goes beyond the physical and touches spirit and soul.

The couple we meet in the Song of Solomon shares a love that will never be violated, a covenant never to be broken. This is the assurance he gives her.

SONG 8:6-7

⁶ Put me like a seal over your heart, like a seal on your arm. For love is as

strong as death, jealousy is as severe as Sheol; its flashes are flashes of fire, the

very flame of the LORD.

⁷ Many waters cannot quench love, nor will rivers overflow it; if a man

were to give all the riches of his house for love, it would be utterly despised.

This is what every bride longs to hear,
    the assurance we each seek,
            the knowledge that on earth, as in heaven, there is One
            who will never leave us, never forsake us.
The seal was a mark of ownership. When two become one flesh, they are
owned by each other for life, "until death do us part."
    There's a divine jealousy even as God was jealous over Israel,[7] a godly jeal-
ousy for those betrothed to Jesus Christ.[8]
    And because this couple's relationship is so very beautiful, they want their
little sister—who hasn't yet come to sexual maturity—to enjoy the same
experience, the same intimacy when she finds the one who will love her
above all else.
    Listen once again, dear single ones.

SONG 8:8-10

⁸ We have a little sister, and she has no breasts; what shall we do for our sis-

ter on the day when she is spoken for?

⁹ If she is a wall, we will build on her a battlement of silver; but if she is a

door, we will barricade her with planks of cedar.

They're going to protect this girl's virginity at all costs—with walls and
barricades, if necessary—so that if the time and opportunity ever come for
her to marry, she, too, will experience the beauty of sex as God intended it.

They want her to know sex according to God, to discover for herself the unparalleled joy that comes with it.

¹⁰ I was a wall, and my breasts were like towers; then I became in his eyes as one who finds peace.

Oh, the peace that comes when sex is according to God, not man.

THE PROMISE OF ETERNITY

As you read this you may be saddened, grieved because you believe you'll never experience the beauty of sex. You may be thinking, *Why should I care whether sex is beautiful or not? I know I'll never marry.*

My friend, Jesus knows exactly what you're facing. Jesus was the virgin of virgins when it came to sexual purity. He lived thirty years and never knew what it was to touch a woman. Yet He was cut off in the prime of life for everyone who had been immoral. He was "cut off and [had] nothing" (Daniel 9:26).

However, in His selflessness, in His sacrifice He gained a bride—and soon He will come for her and take her home. Then each of us who is part of the body of Jesus Christ, the church, will know the beauty of oneness, a union of unions hitherto unimaginable.

Single or married, widowed or divorced, pure or living with regret—a day of inexplicable beauty, wordless joy, and absolute fulfillment is coming for each and every one of God's children. It's called the marriage supper of the Lamb. You may have lost out on your heart's desire on earth, but you won't in heaven! We're on earth for only about three score years and ten—seventy years or so. But heaven is for eternity. No wonder they shout Hallelujah!

Then I heard something like the voice of a great multitude and like the sound of many waters and like the sound of mighty peals of thunder, saying,

"Hallelujah! For the Lord our God, the Almighty, reigns.

"Let us rejoice and be glad and give the glory to Him, for the marriage of the Lamb has come and His bride has made herself ready." It was given to her to clothe herself in fine linen, bright and clean; for the fine linen is the righteous acts of the saints.

Then he said to me, "Write, 'Blessed are those who are invited to the marriage supper of the Lamb.'" And he said to me, "These are true words of God." (Revelation 19:6-9)

Notes

INTRODUCTION

1. National Coalition for the Protection of Children and Families, 800 Compton Road, Suite 9224, Cincinnati, OH 45231; 513-521-6227.
2. "William Wilberforce and the Abolition of the Slave Trade," *Christian History,* no. 53 (1997): 17.
3. John Pollock, *Wilberforce* (London: Constable, 1977).

CHAPTER I

1. Dr. James Dobson, *Bringing Up Boys: Practical Advice and Encouragement for Those Shaping the Next Generation of Men* (Wheaton, Ill.: Tyndale, 2001), 19-28.
2. Malachi 2:14-16.
3. Ezekiel 16.

CHAPTER 2

1. This is what we see in the story of Mary and Joseph. Mary, a virgin, was engaged to Joseph when the angel informed her she would conceive in her womb and give birth to the Son of God. When Joseph found out she was with child, he decided to put Mary away privately, to divorce her. The divorce would absolve him from the covenant agreement.
2. Ephraim Katz, "Production Code," *The Film Encyclopedia* (New York: HarperCollins, 1994).
3. Katz, "Production Code."
4. Psalm 139:13,15-16.

Chapter 3

1. Senator Bill Frist, M.D., letter dated 5 February 2002.
2. Barna Research Group, "Christians Are More Likely to Experience Divorce Than Are Non-Christians," 21 December 1999. Found at www.barna.org.
3. Alvin J. Schmidt, *Under the Influence: How Christianity Transformed Civilization* (Grand Rapids: Zondervan, 2001), 79-80.
4. John R. Clarke, *Looking at Lovemaking: Construction of Sexuality in Roman Art, 100 B.C.–A.D. 250* (Berkeley, Calif.: University of California Press, 1998).
5. Schmidt, *Under the Influence,* 82.
6. Charles Leerhsen, "Magic's Message," *Newsweek,* 18 November 1991, 58.

Chapter 4

1. Matthew 25:41; Revelation 20.
2. Romans 5:12.
3. Genesis 1:26-27.
4. Genesis 5:3.
5. Psalm 51:5.
6. R. Laird Harris, Gleason L. Archer Jr., and Bruce K. Waltke, eds., *Theological Wordbook of the Old Testament,* 2 vols. (Chicago: Moody, 1980), 2:542.
7. *Focus on the Family* magazine, February 2002, 10-11. The pastor's identity is withheld.
8. Judith A. Reisman, *Kinsey: Crimes and Consequences,* 2nd ed. (Crestwood, Ky.: Institute for Media Education, Inc., 1998). This book can be purchased by writing to the Institute for Media Education, Inc., Box 1136, Crestwood, KY 40014-9523. It's extremely valuable for those concerned about the moral fiber of our nation and how we can reverse the tide.
9. Reisman, *Kinsey.*
10. Tom Bethell, "Mortal Sins," *National Review,* 19 May 1997, 37.
11. Reisman, *Kinsey,* 210.

12. Reisman, *Kinsey*, 210.

13. *Focus on the Family*, February 2002, 10-11. The pastor's identity is withheld.

CHAPTER 5

1. *Gods and Heroes in Greek Mythology* (Florence, Italy: Casa Editrice Bonechi, 1998), 109-13.

2. Proverbs 1:1-2; 6:24.

3. Laird Harris, Gleason L. Archer Jr., and Bruce K. Waltke, eds., *Theological Wordbook of the Old Testament*, 2 vols. (Chicago: Moody, 1980), 2:551.

4. "Rise in Herpes Simplex Keratitis Seen Due to Oral-Genital Contact," *Ophthalmology Times*, 1 July 1982, cover.

5. *Ophthalmology Times*, 32.

6. Dr. Tom Coburn, an obstetrician and a former Republican congressman from Oklahoma, has been named by President George W. Bush Jr. to cochair the Presidential Advisory Council on HIV/AIDS. In an interview with *Newsweek*, he made the following observations: "I would not ever recommend to one of my patients to have sex with someone with HIV with a condom. Because I know the statistics. They break. They slip. What we've done is not told the whole truth about condoms.... I believe that monogamy is the answer to HIV infection. I understand that people think I'm not a realist in this area. But I'm monogamous, and there are hundreds and hundreds of millions of people out there that are monogamous." David France, "'I'm Not Ashamed of My Opinions,'" *Newsweek*, 5 February 2002. See also www.msnbc.com/news.

7. Psalm 139:11-12.

8. Stephen Arterburn and Fred Stoeker, *Every Man's Battle* (Colorado Springs: WaterBrook, 2000), 13-4.

9. Arterburn and Stoeker, *Every Man's Battle*, 13-4.

10. Robert E. Reccord, *Beneath the Surface* (Nashville: Broadman & Holman, 2002), 73-5.

11. Reccord, *Beneath the Surface*, 30.

12. Jeremiah 6:15.

13. Hebrews 10:31.

14. Diane Passno, *Feminism: Mystique or Mistake?* (Wheaton, Ill.: Tyndale, 2000), 35.

15. *Gods and Heroes in Greek Mythology,* 67; Sam Storms, *Pleasures Evermore* (Colorado Springs: NavPress, 2001).

Chapter 6

1. Romans 5:20.

2. Hebrews 9:27.

Chapter 7

1. Dorie Van Stone is the coauthor with Dr. Erwin Lutzer of *Dorie: The Girl Nobody Loved* and *No Place to Cry,* both published by Moody Press, Chicago. Dorie is a staff member of Precept Ministries International.

2. Titus 3:5.

3. Isaiah 66:24.

4. Revelation 10:7 is interesting to ponder in light of this!

5. Hebrews 10:30.

Chapter 8

1. Nimrod is mentioned in Genesis as the mighty hunter against God (literally, "in the face of God," Genesis 10:9). The beginning of Nimrod's kingdom was Babel (10:10), which has continually rebelled against God.

2. Proverbs 28:13.

3. Matthew 6:12-15; 18:21-35.

4. Matthew 18:23-35.

Chapter 9

1. John Leland, "Bisexuality Emerges as a New Sexual Identity," *Newsweek,* 17 July 1995, 48.

2. 2 Timothy 2:22; 1 Thessalonians 5:22, KJV.

3. Mary Howitt (1799–1888), "The Spider and the Fly."

4. 1 Corinthians 6:9-10.

5. Hebrews 12:14.

6. Genesis 25:27-34; Hebrews 12:16-17.

7. Romans 6:12-13.

CHAPTER 10

1. Numbers 25:1-3; Revelation 2:14.

2. You see this in Romans 1.

3. Proverbs 23:7.

4. Proverbs 4:23, KJV.

5. John 8:7, author's paraphrase.

6. J. L. McGaugh, "Preserving the Presence of the Past," *American Psychologist,* February 1983, 161. Found at www.enoughisenough.org.

7. Dr. Victor B. Cline, *Pornography's Effects on Adults and Children* (New York: Morality in Media, 1996). Morality in Media can be contacted at 475 Riverside Drive, New York, NY 10115; 212-870-3222.

8. Eric Schlosser, "The Business of Pornography," *U.S. News and World Report,* 10 February 1997.

9. Cline, *Pornography's Effects on Adults and Children.*

10. Found at http://www.family.org/pastor/resources/sos/a0006443.html, 30 November 2000.

11. W. Marshall, "Use of Sexually Explicit Stimuli by Rapists, Child Molesters and Non-Offenders," *Journal of Sex Research,* no. 25 (1988): 267. Found at http://www.family.org/pastor/resources/sos/ a0006443.html, 30 November 2000.

12. Cline, *Pornography's Effects on Adults and Children.*

13. There is a Covenant Eyes Internet Accountability software that removes the secrecy of using the Internet. You choose accountability partners who are programmed in to every Web site you visit. This is not a filter. Rather, it provides direct accountability, cannot be erased or bypassed, and is dependable, inexpensive, and easy to use. You can sign up and download this unique Internet service program via e-mail. For more information visit www.covenanteyes.com or call toll free 877-479-1119.

14. Read *The Silent War* by Henry J. Rogers (Green Forest, Ark.: New Leaf Press, 2001) and *Every Man's Battle* by Stephen Arterburn and Fred Stoeker (Colorado Springs: WaterBrook, 2000).
15. 1 Corinthians 11:31.
16. All this is explained thoroughly in my book *Our Covenant God: Learning to Trust Him* (Colorado Springs: WaterBrook, 1999).
17. For a study on this topic, see my book *Lord, Is It Warfare? Teach Me to Stand* (Colorado Springs: WaterBrook, 2000). This study covers the whole topic and has helped so many, including me.
18. 2 Corinthians 2:14.

CHAPTER 11

1. Song of Solomon 1:4.
2. Irving Jensen, *Survey of the Old Testament* (Chicago: Moody Press, 1978), 314.
3. Jensen, *Survey of the Old Testament,* 314.
4. Karen S. Peterson, "Sex Books Sell Satisfaction," *USA Today,* 13 March 2002, 6D.
5. I chose to quote this verse from the *New International Version* because it translates *love* as a neutral pronoun, whereas some other translations refer to it as *he* or *she.*
6. You can find some very helpful insights in two books I would recommend highly if you are married or engaged to be married: *Intimate Issues* by Linda Dillow and Lorraine Pintus and *Sacred Sex* by Tim Gardner, both published by WaterBrook Press. And if you want a quick read, I have a chapter on it in my book *A Marriage Without Regrets.*
7. Exodus 34:14.
8. 2 Corinthians 11:2.

Recommended Resources

Arterburn, Stephen and Fred Stoeker with Mike Yorkey. *Every Man's Battle.* Colorado Springs: WaterBrook, 2000.

Arthur, Kay. *A Marriage Without Regrets.* Eugene, Oreg.: Harvest House, 2000.

————. *Lord, Heal My Hurts.* Colorado Springs: WaterBrook, 2000.

————. *Lord, I Need Grace to Make It Today.* Colorado Springs: Water-Brook, 2000.

————. *Lord, Is It Warfare? Teach Me to Stand.* Colorado Springs: WaterBrook, 2000.

————. *Our Covenant God: Learning to Trust Him.* Colorado Springs: WaterBrook, 1999.

Bennett, William J. *The Broken Hearth: Reversing the Moral Collapse of the American Family.* Colorado Springs: WaterBrook, 2001.

Covenant Eyes Internet Accountability offers software that enables Internet users to be held accountable in their Internet use. Contact Mr. Lynn McClurg at 321 N. Shiawassee, Suite B, Corunna, MI 48817. Phone: 989-743-1100; toll-free phone: 877-479-1119; fax: 989-743-1103. Web site: www.covenanteyes.com; e-mail: office@covenanteyes.com.

Dillow, Linda, and Lorraine Pintus. *Intimate Issues: 21 Questions Christian Women Ask About Sex.* Colorado Springs: WaterBrook, 1999.

Dobson, Dr. James. *Bringing Up Boys: Practical Advice and Encouragement for Those Shaping the Next Generation of Men.* Wheaton, Ill.: Tyndale, 2001.

Gardner, Tim. *Sacred Sex: A Spiritual Celebration of Oneness in Marriage.* Colorado Springs: WaterBrook, 2002.

The National Coalition for the Protection of Children and Families offers an interactive video series titled *Sex and Young America: The Real Deal.* Contact Jerry Kirk at 800 Compton Rd., Suite 9224, Cincinnati, OH 45231. Phone: 513-521-6227. Web site: www.sexandyoungamerica.com.

Passno, Diane. *Feminism: Mystique or Mistake?* Wheaton, Ill.: Tyndale, 2000.

Reccord, Bob. *Beneath the Surface: Steering Clear of the Dangers That Could Leave You Shipwrecked.* Nashville: Broadman & Holman, 2002.

Reisman, Judith A. *Kinsey: Crimes and Consequences.* Crestwood, Ky.: Institute for Media Education, Inc.; Second Edition, 1998.

Rogers, Henry J. *The Silent War: Ministering to Those Trapped in the Deception of Pornography.* Green Forest, Ark.: New Leaf Press, 2001.

RSVP America (Restoring Social Virtue and Purity to America). P.O. Box 1136, Crestwood, KY 40014. Phone: 1-800-837-0544.

Van Stone, Doris and Erwin W. Lutzer. *Dorie: The Girl Nobody Loved.* Chicago: Moody, 1981.

Van Stone, Doris and Erwin W. Lutzer. *No Place to Cry: The Hurt and Healing of Sexual Abuse.* Chicago: Moody, 1990.

Acknowledgments

When God saved us, He didn't set us aside as "one" to accomplish His work. Rather, He graciously placed us in His body, the church—a body with many members, all gifted in different ways. No book I write would ever be as good as it could be without my talented and gifted brothers and sisters in Christ.

When God gave me the privilege of publishing with WaterBrook, He put me into a wonderful, talented, and godly family. How I thank Him for Dan, Steve, and Don who urged me on and prayed for me along the way, and for Laura, Thomas, and my dear Rebecca, who worked so diligently with me on this manuscript with the prayer that it would meet a great need in the church and, through the church, in the world.

My thanks also goes to Bunny for diligently sorting through piles of letters to help me find the right illustrations so that our hearts would be touched by the hearts of the precious people who trusted me with their pain and shared their victories.

And, Sweetheart, where would I be if you did not so graciously allow me all the hours it takes to write a book like this and help me along the way by clearing the table and cleaning up the kitchen evening after evening so I could keep writing. Your love and prayers mean so much to me, my husband.

How I pray, my Father, that You will take your truths in this book and share them through your people to bring about another sexual revolution before we self-destruct on the altar of our unbridled lust. God forgive us.

About Kay Arthur and Precept
Ministries International

Kay Arthur, executive vice president and cofounder of Precept Ministries International, is known around the world as a Bible teacher, author, conference speaker, and host of national radio and television programs.

Kay and her husband, Jack, founded Precept Ministries in 1970 in Chattanooga, Tennessee. Started as a fledgling ministry for teens, Precept today is a worldwide outreach that establishes children, teens, and adults in God's Word so that they can discover the Bible's truths for themselves. Precept inductive Bible studies are taught in all 50 states. The studies have been translated into 66 languages, reaching 120 countries.

Kay is the author of more than 120 books and inductive Bible study courses, with a total of more than 5 million books in print. Four of her books have received the ECPA Gold Medallion Book Award. She is sought after by groups throughout the world as an inspiring Bible teacher and conference speaker. Kay is also well known globally through her daily and weekly television programs.

Contact Precept Ministries for more information about inductive Bible studies in your area.

Precept Ministries International
P.O. Box 182218
Chattanooga, TN 37422-7218
800-763-8280
www.precept.org